CW00434428

PEASANTS
and
WORKERS
in
NEPAL

Peasants and Workers in Nepal

Edited by
D. SEDDON, P. BLAIKIE and J. CAMERON

ADROIT PUBLISHERS
Delhi-110 053

Published by
ADROIT PUBLISHERS
C-8/2, Yamuna Vihar, Delhi-110 053
Phone: 3266030, 3242552

Distributors
AKHIL BOOK DISTRIBUTORS
4675/21, Ganpati Bhawan, Ansari Road,
Darya Ganj, New Delhi-110 002
e-mail: akhilbooks@yahoo.com
Phones : 3266030, 3242552

ISBN : 81-87392-31-2

Layout by
Sudhir Kumar Vatsa

Laser Typeset by
Nidhi Laser Point
e-mail: nidhi_vatsa@hotmail.com

Printed in India on behalf of M/s Adroit Publishers by
Arpit Printographer, B-7, Saraswati Complex,
Subhash Chowk, Laxmi Nagar, Delhi-110 092

PREFACE TO THE SECOND EDITION

The fieldwork on which this collection of essays on 'peasants and workers in Nepal' is based was undertaken in the mid-1970s, by an international team associated with the Overseas Development Group at the University of East Anglia. The fieldwork also gave rise to several other publications, including 'Nepal in Crisis' and 'The Struggle for Basic Needs in Nepal' (both now re-published by Adroit Publishers), by the same authors. In this collection, however, an attempt was made to look in more detail at specific social groups, their position within the broader political economy of Nepal and their characteristics. Although the fieldwork and the original collection of essays may seem at first sight to relate to the realities of a world of the past—after all, it is now nearly 30 years since the original fieldwork was carried out, and 20 years since the first Indian edition was published—it is our view that the realities described and analysed in the chapters of this book remain largely valid and pertinent even today. There is no doubt that there have been important economic, social and political changes in Nepal since the mid-1970s—notably, in the political sphere the Jana Andolan or Peoples' Movement and, since 1996, the Peoples' War, and in the economic sphere the ever-greater integration of the economy of Nepal (through flows of capital, commodities and labour) into the wider regional and global economy—the significance of which should not be underestimated. But it is arguable that despite these important changes, certain fundamental structures remain in place, which constrain the broad-based social, economic and political development that many of us had hoped might be unleashed by the political events of 1990. Given the durability and the continuing reproduction of these structures (and the associated constraints on the progressive evolution of the political economy of Nepal), some have concluded—understandably—that only revolutionary change through an armed struggle will 'break the chains' and release the creative energy and potential of the Nepali people. Whatever one's views of the contemporary political crisis, and its relationship to the deeper long-term social and economic crisis, it is more important than ever that the realities of the lives of the mass of the Nepali people—in the rural and, increasingly, in the urban areas—be examined carefully and sympathetically, and understood, in order that they may provide the secure foundations for a progressive transformation of Nepali economy and society as a whole. Imported ideologies, whether from the 'right' or the 'left', and 'new policy prescriptions', must be subjected to the litmus test of their applicability to the realities of the lives of peasants and workers, and scrutinised critically to see what role, if any, they may play in improving the quality of life for the majority of the Nepali people. Today, among the lending and 'development' agencies there is a rhetoric of support for 'poverty alleviation' and livelihoods analysis—which claims to be centrally concerned with exploring real lives at the 'grass-roots'. If such a rhetoric is ever to be more than simply window-dressing for an imperialist agenda in Nepal, serious attention must be paid to the real lives of ordinary people, their needs and their demands, and to ways in which those needs and demands could be fulfilled, as well as to the effects of the prevailing structures of oppression, discrimination and exploitation on their lives, and to ways in which those structures might be eliminated or transformed. Strategic and selective pressure will be needed to reduce the power and influence of those who continue to resist progressive change. Within the government, the administration and the bureaucracy, there is a need for those committed to 'good governance' and to effective policy formulation and implementation join together to create a new force against inertia and corruption and for dynamism, transparency and efficiency. Decentralisation must be a part of that agenda, giving greater powers to local government at district and village development committee level, and by implication providing more open and accessible policy-making procedures and better service to the ordinary peasants and workers who constitute the majority of those supposedly 'served' by the state. Political parties and movements within Nepal, whether those operating within the framework of the parliamentary process or outside it, need also to examine and understand the real lives of their constituency in the broadest sense, and to take very seriously the real needs and demands of peasants and workers, and make the necessary commitment to translate those into effective policies and practices. Trades unions need to extend their commitment to supporting their members more widely, to include the majority of working people in Nepal, and not just the few who work in the formal sector, and to increase their activities on behalf of this broader membership. National NGOs must also, to be credible, work closely with—and not simply try to speak 'on behalf of'—peasants and workers, and find ways of strengthening their individual and collective capacities. Finally, intellectuals and academics, whose role it is to 'seek the truth' and to 'speak truth to power' must become more familiar with the realities of life at the 'grassroots', in both town and country, and learn how to speak with as well as on behalf of the peasants and workers. This collection provides an introduction to certain aspects of the lives and circumstances of peasants and workers, based on the realities as we found them in the mid-1970s in west central Nepal (today the Western Development Region). It tries to emphasise not only the constraints and conditions under which these groups struggle to survive and gain a little room for manoeuvre, but also their 'agency'—their initiatives and efforts. It recognises, not only the specific circumstances and struggles of poor peasants and agricultural labourers, but considers special groups within the secategories—rural artisans (the so-called 'occupational castes' for the most part), porters, and highway construction workers. It also examines in some detail—in a way surprisingly few studies have done over the last 30 years—the characteristics of the urban labour force, including thoseworking at the lower levels of the public sector; and includes a consideration of small scale business in the informal sector. The author shope that this new edition will stimulate further research and renewed interest in the conditions, circumstances and lives of 'peasants and workers in Nepal'—and will contribute to recognition of the fact that only policies and programmes based on the real circumstances, needs, demands and potential of these people will prove successful in transforming Nepal and promoting real development.

David Seddon
November, 2001

CONTENTS

MAP 1

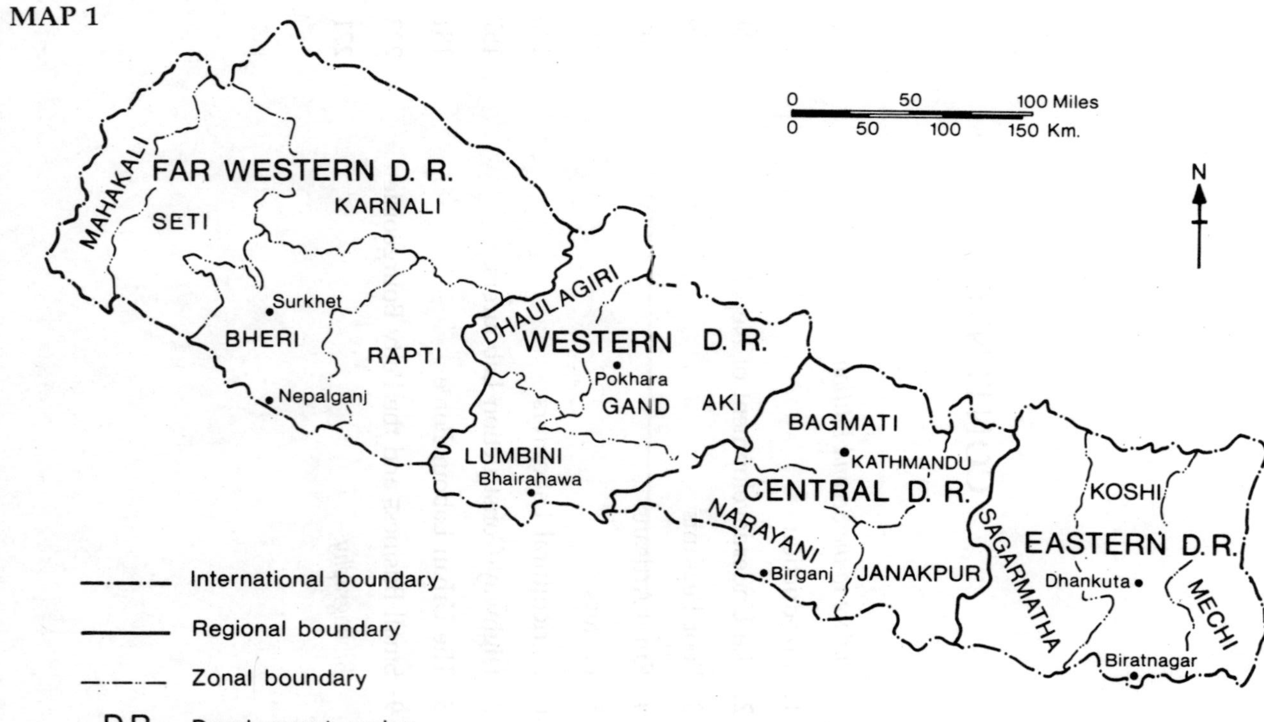
0 50 100 Miles
0 50 100 150 Km.
N
MAHAKALI
FAR WESTERN D. R.
SETI
KARNALI
Surkhet
BHERI
RAPTI
Nepalganj
DHAULAGIRI
WESTERN D. R.
Pokhara
GAND AKI
LUMBINI
Bhairahawa
BAGMATI
KATHMANDU
CENTRAL D. R.
NARAYANI
Birganj
JANAKPUR
SAGARMATHA
KOSHI
EASTERN D. R.
Dhankuta
MECHI
Biratnagar
International boundary
Regional boundary
Zonal boundary
D.R. Development region

CHAPTER 1

INTRODUCTION

The Context of the Present Work

During 1974 and 1975 the three contributors to this collection of essays were engaged, with two others, in a research project (The Overseas Development Group Nepal Roads Research Project) to investigate the economic and social effects of building three motorable roads through the hills (Siddartha Rajmarga and Prithivi Rajmarga) and plains (Mahendra Rajmarga) of west central Nepal (*see* Map 2). Conceived more broadly than most such 'evaluations', this project (which was carried out under the auspices of the British Ministry of Overseas Development who also funded the work) provided a unique opportunity for five individuals from different branches of the social sciences—agricultural economics, anthropology, geography, economics and sociology—to confront the theoretical and practical problems of interdisciplinary research through an analysis of the determinants of economic and social change in Nepal; it also obliged us to confront not only the theoretical issues of underdevelopment but also its social and political implications in one of the world's poorest and most precarious states. This book, in its approach and its focus, is a product of this double confrontation with what we have referred to elsewhere as 'the crisis in Nepal' (cf Blaikie, Cameron and Seddon 1978), and should therefore be read as a contribution to the analysis and underdevelopment and the role of the lower classes in general as well as to the study of Nepal as a specific case.

The original fieldwork resulted in a major report on the effects of roads in west central Nepal (cf Blaikie, Cameron, Feldman, Fournier and Seddon 1976; Blaikie, Cameron and Seddon 1977), but the approach developed there for the analysis of the Nepalese political economy and its historical evolution led naturally to a more detailed consideration of the nature of underdevelopment in Nepal, and in particular of the spatial and social aspects of inequality (cf Blaikie, Cameron, Seddon and Fleming 1977). Exploration of the significance of such concepts as 'centre' and periphery' in the context of dependency and underdevelopment allowed us to identify Nepal as a periphery of India and to begin to explain the crisis in Nepal in terms of a history of dependency from the mid-19th century onwards (cf Blaikie, Cameron and Seddon 1978). At the same time we recognised that:

> "as in the case of relations between 'centre' and 'periphery' at the international level, so within a given country we are dealing not merely with flows between spatially defined regions but also with complex economic and political structures involving relations between different sections of society with differing and often conflicting interests" (Blaikie, Cameron, Seddon and Fleming 1977: 61).

Underlying spatial patterns of inequality are structural relations of economic and political inequality associated with the production, appropriation and realisation of surplus; in other words, class relations. Subsequently, we have focused our attention more sharply on the internal evolution of the Nepalese political economy, conceived essentially in terms of relations between classes and the dynamic of those relations, and have concentrated in particular on the lower classes—peasants, workers and the petty bourgeoisie and their position and role within the political economy. Our concern, as expressed in the essays that make up this book, has been two-fold: first, to place the lower classes within the wider set of economic and political relationships which we have argued constitute the underlying determinants of the crisis in Nepal

MAP 2

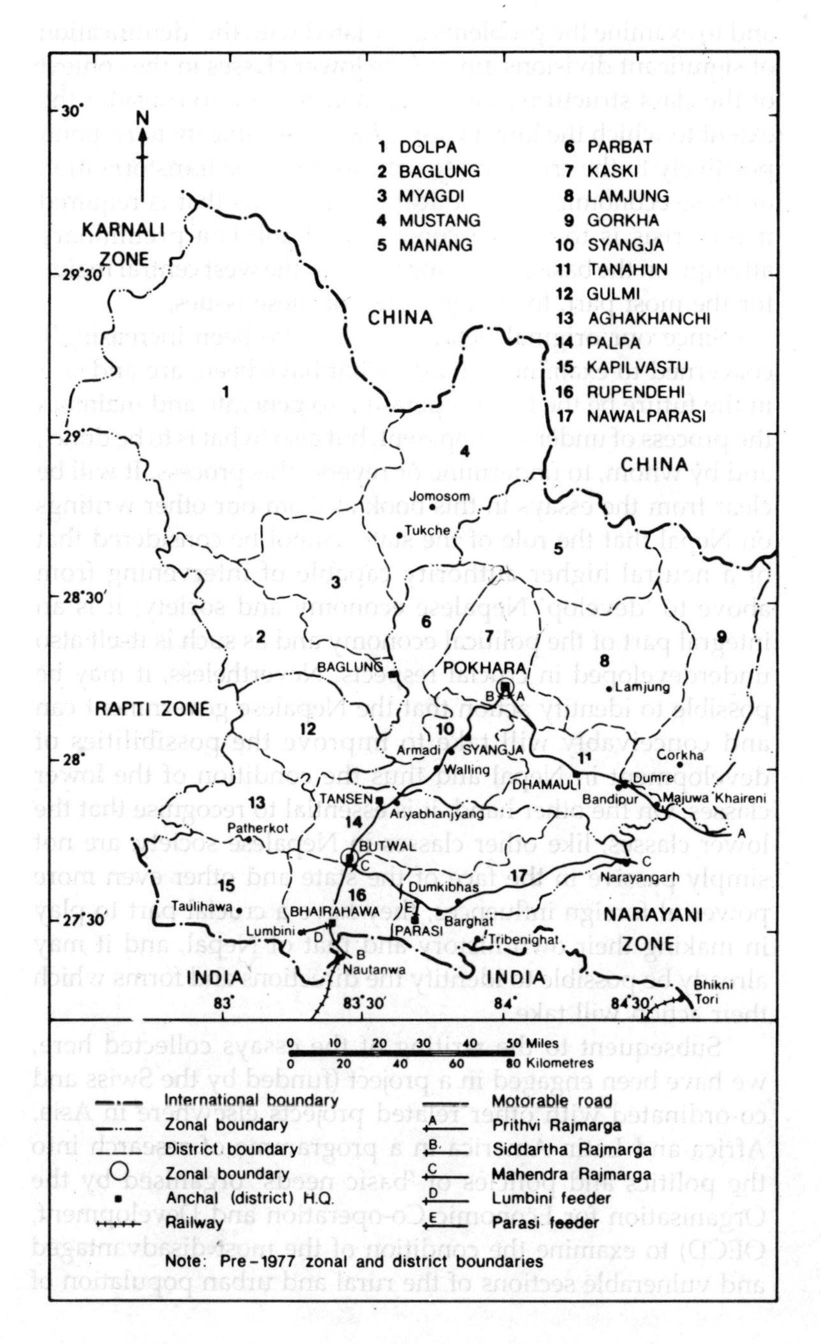
1 DOLPA
2 BAGLUNG
3 MYAGDI
4 MUSTANG
5 MANANG
6 PARBAT
7 KASKI
8 LAMJUNG
9 GORKHA
10 SYANGJA
11 TANAHUN
12 GULMI
13 AGHAKHANCHI
14 PALPA
15 KAPILVASTU
16 RUPENDEHI
17 NAWALPARASI
N
30°
29°30′
29°
28°30′
28°
27°30′
83°
83°30′
84°
84°30′
KARNALI ZONE
CHINA
CHINA
RAPTI ZONE
NARAYANI ZONE
INDIA
INDIA
Jomosom
Tukche
BAGLUNG
POKHARA
Lamjung
Armadi
SYANGJA
Walling
Gorkha
DHAMAULI
Dumre
Bandipur
Majuwa Khaireni
TANSEN
Aryabhanjyang
Patherkot
BUTWAL
Narayangarh
Dumkibhas
Taulihawa
BHAIRAHAWA
PARASI
Barghat
Lumbini
Tribenighat
Nautanwa
Bhikni Tori
0 10 20 30 40 50 Miles
0 20 40 60 80 Kilometres
International boundary
Zonal boundary
District boundary
Zonal boundary
Anchal (district) H.Q.
Railway
Motorable road
Prithvi Rajmarga
Siddartha Rajmarga
Mahendra Rajmarga
Lumbini feeder
Parasi feeder
Note: Pre-1977 zonal and district boundaries

and to examine the problems associated with the identification of significant divisions among the lower classes in the context of the class structure as a whole; and second, to consider the extent to which the lower classes have the capacity to respond positively to the crisis and to contribute to the transformation of those economic and political relationships that is required if the crisis is to be overcome. This book is a preliminary attempt, on the basis of investigations in the west central region for the most part, to explore some of these issues.

Since our original fieldwork we have been increasingly concerned to examine not only what have been, are and will in the future be the forces operating to generate and maintain the process of underdevelopment, but also 'what is to be done', and by whom, to undermine or reverse this process. It will be clear from the essays in this book as from our other writings on Nepal that the role of the state cannot be considered that of a neutral higher authority capable of intervening from above to 'develop' Nepalese economy and society; it is an integral part of the political economy and as such is itself also underdeveloped in crucial respects. Nevertheless, it may be possible to identify action that the Nepalese government can and conceivably will take to improve the possibilities of development in Nepal and thus the condition of the lower classes. On the other hand, it is essential to recognise that the lower classes, like other classes in Nepalese society, are not simply passive in the face of the state and other even more powerful foreign influences; they have a crucial part to play in making their own history and that of Nepal, and it may already be possible to identify the directions and forms which their action will take.

Subsequent to the writing of the essays collected here, we have been engaged in a project (funded by the Swiss and co-ordinated with other related projects elsewhere in Asia, Africa and Latin America in a programme of research into the politics and policies of 'basic needs' organised by the Organisation for Economic Co-operation and Development, OECD) to examine the condition of the most disadvantaged and vulnerable sections of the rural and urban population of

Nepal and consider what, if any, policy recommendations might serve the interests of 'the poorest of the poor'. It is our belief that a prerequisite for any such work, and certainly for any valid policy recommendations, must be an adequate theoretical basis both for an understanding of how 'poverty' is created and reproduced over time and also for an appreciation of the role of the state in this process; only then will it be possible to identify the means whereby 'poverty' may be reduced, or more precisely the ways in which changes might be encouraged which increase the chances that 'poverty' might be reduced, for 'poverty' is merely a reflection of underlying processes and relationships within the political economy as a whole.

Clearly, it is not adequate, in order to provide readers with an introduction to our approach and to the theoretical perspective with which it is linked, merely to situate the present work in time or in general terms. Although there is no doubt that our approach and theoretical perspective is, in an important sense, the product of a double confrontation—theoretical and political - with underdevelopment in Nepal, further explanation is required, for its roots are in fact deep and diverse. First, all five members of the original research team had experienced, in the different branches of the social sciences in which they were trained, the upsurge of doubt and uncertainty regarding the adequacy of Western social science that took place in the late 1960's and early 1970's; secondly, four out of the five had already experienced elsewhere than Nepal the problems of fieldwork in an underdeveloped country and the theoretical and personal introspection needed to come to terms with economic and social issues in such a situation; and finally all five would have regarded themselves as more or less politically 'radical' even prior to undertaking research in Nepal. While the last two factors undoubtedly contributed to the development of a distinctive approach to the analysis of Nepalese economy and society it is the first that we feel requires further explanation here.

The Social Sciences, Marxist Theory and Underdevelopment

It is now clear that the late 1960's and early 1970's constituted a period of major upheaval and change, involving unprecedented self-criticism and radical re-thinking, in the various established disciplines of Western social and human science (cf Copans and Seddon 1978). Recognition of the inadequacy of previous approaches to the study of society within the distinct fields of anthropology, economics, sociology, geography and history has led many to identify a general 'crisis in the social sciences' (see, for example, the opening editorial of the journal Economy and Society in 1972), and certainly the term 'crisis' has been widely used with respect to the various individual disciplines.

It appears to be generally agreed that the crisis in the social sciences is in some way 'moral' (that is, it has to do with values) and even political, as well as theoretical and practical, and that it is intimately related to the fundamental economic and political changes that have taken place in the world since the 1950's. For most, the crisis developed as a result of the inability of the social sciences to provide even a sufficiently sharp and coherent account of the major changes taking place, let alone to explain them. The implications of the crisis for the future of social science and the alternative approaches that might be adopted have been very differently regarded, however, according to the intellectual and ideological perspective of the social scientist concerned. For most, the crisis was predominantly, if not entirely, an intellectual crisis; for some, however, it was an aspect of a more general economic and political crisis of the West.

Thus, one important aspect of the crisis has been a growing disillusionment and dissatisfaction with what might be termed the tradition of liberal scholarship, including in this epistemology, theory, method and implicit political stance. It is significant that the most far-reaching criticism and probably the most effective critique of the social sciences as they are presently constituted has come from Marxists or from those who, whatever their political practice, have adopted Marxist theory as a basis for the analysis of economy and society. Furthermore,

> "it is the Marxists, more than any other group of scholars, who offer not only a critique of, but also a powerful alternative to, the present fragmented and admittedly unsatisfactory approaches through the established disciplines and traditions of 'liberal' scholarship to the study of society. The full meaning of the suggestion that the crisis in the social sciences is a political as well as theoretical and practical crisis, only becomes in the Marxist critique" (Copans and Seddon 1978: 1-2).

As has been suggested above, the crisis in the social sciences was closely linked to fundamental economic and political changes over the last twenty-five years. Indeed, as Booth has observed,

> "in retrospect it is clear that in the decade or so following the Second World War bourgeois social science in the metropolitan countries was presented with an intellectual challenge of unprecedented human significance. The events which filled these years—the foundation of the United Nations, the Chinese Revolution, the Cold War, and the rise of nationalist movements throughout the colonial world—combined to produce the recognition of a new problem at the level of world consciousness: the problem of *underdevelopment*. In retrospect it is also plain that, straightforward ideological barriers aside, these years found the various social science disciplines singularly ill-equipped to meet the challenge of providing a factually exact and theoretically adequate account of the sources of underdevelopment and the conditions for its definitive suppression" (Booth 1975: 53).

Thus it is of considerable significance that the most perspective, original and powerful contributions to the analysis of the process of underdevelopment should have come over the last decade or so from social scientists working in the Marxist tradition. Their work has in fact been two-fold: in the first place to provide a critique of the social sciences and their partial and inadequate analyses of underdevelopment (*e.g.* Baran and Hobsbawm 1961; Frank 1971) and, secondly, to provide a general framework for an alternative mode of analysis, founded on basic principles of Marxist theory but attempting to construct new approaches appropriate for explaining the particular economic and political conditions of the post-colonial world yet establishing their historical roots (e.g. Amin 1974; Baran and Sweezy 1968; Dos Santos 1973; Emmanuel 1972; Frank 1969; Kay 1975; Kemp 1967). The widespread concern of Marxists with problems of *underdevelopment* is itself a relatively recent phenomenon (although Marx, Engels and Lenin established important bases for future work in this area) and more recent studies are as concerned with identifying weaknesses and inadequacies in such pioneering Marxist work of underdevelopment and imperialism as they are with a critique of more conventional analyses. Much of the criticism has been directed at the 'economistic' tendencies of many global Marxist analyses and at the corresponding relative neglect of the changing structure of class relations both within underdeveloped economies and societies and on an international scale. Even within the new tradition of Marxist approaches to underdevelopment, therefore, there is debate and disagreement; but much of this appears to be constructive and progressive in its concern to develop rather than to destroy a distinctive mode of analysis (cf for example Foster-Carter 1974; Leys 1975; Oxaal, Barnett and Booth 1975).

The crisis in the social sciences and the emergence of Marxist approaches to the study of underdevelopment provided the intellectual background, as it were, of all five members of the research team in Nepal when they started fieldwork in 1974; furthermore, some of the new work within the Marxist tradition appeared highly relevant to the particular circumstances of Nepal. At the same time, each member of the original research team had been trained in a specific branch of the social sciences and saw benefits to be gained from making use of distinctive 'disciplinary' skills and techniques and from drawing on personal knowledge of related work carried out elsewhere by colleagues in the same discipline. Consequently, a general approach was adopted which drew heavily on recent writings in the Marxist tradition and which attempted to overcome the fragmentation of the disciplines in order to contract a history of the political economy of Nepal and to analyse its contemporary dynamic; but at the same time this general approach was conditioned, often in crucial respects, by the 'disciplinary' bias of each member of the team. The contradictions associated with this situation have not yet been finally resolved, as may be apparent in some of our writings (e.g. in particular Blaikie, Cameron, Feldman, Fournier and Seddon 1976), although a major effort has been made in our most recent work to develop a consistent, coherent mode of analysis in which the distinctive bias of anthropology, sociology, economics and geography, for example, assists rather than hinders the explanation of social processes.

In so far as our approach in general recognises that underdevelopment is a process rather than a 'state of backwardness' it is necessary to analyse the complex historical development of underdevelopment in Nepal (see Chapter 2). Yet economics, geography, anthropology and sociology have all been overwhelmingly concerned with functionalist explanations of economic and social relations and have generally failed to incorporate within their theories and models the problems of the transformation of social and economic systems. Even in the analysis of development and underdevelopment it is common to find conventional social scientists writing of 'traditional' and 'modern' forms of economy and society with no recognition of the complex historical processes that have linked the underdeveloped and the so-called developed countries together for over two centuries in most cases, and often for longer. As Frank has argued in criticism of Rostow's study of the *Stages of Economic Growth*:

> "Rostow's stages and thesis are incorrect primarily because they do not correspond at all to the past or present reality of the underdeveloped countries whose development they are supposed to guide. It is explicit in Rostow...that underdevelopment is the original stage of what are supposedly traditional societies—that there were no stages prior to the present stage of underdevelopment. It is further explicit in Rostow that the now developed societies were once underdeveloped. But all this is quite contrary to fact. This entire approach to economic development and cultural change

> attributes a history to the developed countries but denies all history to the underdeveloped ones. The countries that are today underdeveloped evidently have had a history no less than have the developed ones. None of them, for example India, is today the way it was centuries or even decades ago. Moreover, reference to even any schoolboy world history confirms that the history of the now underdeveloped countries has been most intimately related to the history of the now developed ones for at least several centuries" (Frank 1971: 18).

Even anthropology, the discipline primarily concerned with forms of economy and society that other conventional social Scientists might regard as 'traditional', has generally failed to incorporate within its theoretical perspective any analysis of the economic and social conditions for the transformation of these forms, and has struggled unsuccessfully with the problem of how to analyse social change. Consequently, it was necessary to draw on recent work in the Marxist tradition on non-capitalist social formations in order to be able to construct a history of Nepal; for Nepal, although affected in important ways by its incorporation into the world economy over the past two centuries nevertheless remains a predominantly non-capitalist agrarian economy and society with a distinctive internal dynamic (see sections 3 and 4 below).

But the historical evolution of the Nepalese political economy cannot be understood without recognising the fact of its progressive integration into a wider system dominated by international capitalism. Anthropology has always claimed distinction as the only social science discipline which considers social systems in their totality; and yet it can be shown that, despite this claim, anthropology has failed to analyse the significant totality within which local villages, tribes and even states have been incorporated, in most cases for centuries. Anthropology, as Kathleen Gough has pointed out, has been weak in two major respects: firstly, anthropologists have failed to analyse the structure of Western imperialism as an international system and an interconnected political economy, or to investigate the general and particular features of its impact on the non-Western world; secondly, anthropologists, when studying social change have tended to produce essentially factual accounts and to remain at a very low level of theoretical elaboration, producing only limited hypotheses regarding the impact of 'the outside world' on local communities. She suggests that the excessively empiricist approach of anthropology is related to its failure to consider the total system of which its traditional object - primitive society —was an integral part when anthropologists first studied it (cf Copans and Seddon 1978: 14-16; Gough 1968). Thus given its functionalist perspective, its inability to identify the endogenous determinants of change in non-Western societies, and its failure to recognise the existence let alone the nature of the totality within which 'local communities' have been incorporated, conventional anthropology has no means of analysing change at local level, except in the most partial fashion in terms of 'local responses to outside forces', and certainly no means of identifying the contribution 'local communities' may make to change on a wider scale.

If anthropology, which is primarily concerned with the description and analysis of non-Western, non-capitalist societies appears unable to provide an adequate theoretical framework for the explanation of underdevelopment and can only describe its local 'effects', what of the other social sciences? As we have already seen, much of the conventional thinking in economics regarding the nature of development and underdevelopment is rendered totally inadequate by its gross ignorance of world history and its construction of inappropriate models for 'traditional' society. In so far as economics is constructed essentially as a mode of analysis of contemporary capitalism, however, and in so far as underdevelopment is related to the expansion of capitalism throughout the world and the sub-ordination of non-capitalist modes of production to its 'laws of motion', it might appear that economics could provide the basis of an approach to underdevelopment. The most prevalent school of thought in the field of development economics can crudely be characterised as diffusionist, for it envisages development essentially as a process whereby capital, technology, institutions and ultimately an 'outlook on life' are diffused, spreading outwards from the metropolitan developed countries to the national capitals of the underdeveloped ones and from these in turn to their provincial capitals and finally to the peripheral hinterland. This approach, like that of 'the stages of growth', is founded on a notion of dualism: that there can be identified a 'modern' and a 'traditional' system and that the expansion of the 'modern' (or the diffusion of those crucial elements that constitute its economic base capital, technology and institutions) reduces the size and significance of the 'traditional', whose only contribution to the process of economic development is seen as that of providing 'surplus' labour for the expanding 'modern' sector (or capitalist mode of production, for modern = capitalist in this model). Such an approach, like that of the stages of growth 'theory', runs counter to the evidence of history, which suggests that what might at first sight appear to be 'traditional' and unchanging has in fact already been transformed and changed in crucial respects, while retaining certain previous forms, by virtue of its incorporation into the wider economic and political system dominated by international capitalism (cf Frank 1971 for a more detailed critique). It also ignores entirely any possibility of a complex dynamic existing within an underdeveloped country (which in its own terms is non-capitalist, or 'traditional', for the most part) which cannot adequately be comprehended through conventional economic analysis founded on assumptions derived solely from a particular interpretation of Western industrial capitalism.

Economics, therefore, appears doubly handicapped; first by its failure to recognise the relevance of world history over the last centuries for the analysis of underdevelopment as a complex process; and secondly, by its central theoretical postulates which in fact derive from one particular form of economy and society (and then in a highly idealised form such that many would argue it is unable to describe or explain adequately changes even within that particular form), and which apply only uncomfortably, if at all, to economies based on non-capitalist modes of production. But there is a third, and equally serious weakness in the approach of conventional economics: it takes as the starting point for its analysis the postulated 'individual', conceiving of the economy as the sum total of decisions and actions taken by 'individuals'. But,

> "to start from the constructed 'individual' is to make a false start, for the model built upon the concept of economic man immediately, albeit surreptitiously, places these 'individuals' in a world which although abstract poses the ideological form of capitalism." (Seddon 1977a: 10).

Such an approach not only denies the historical specificity of different economic systems and modes of production but also tends to obscure the crucial significance of the real structural relations which constrain the decisions and actions of real men in particular societies by presenting the 'individual' as an atomic 'decision-maker' separated from any historical or social context. Such an 'individual' can never, by definition, change the system.

Like economics, geography has tended to analyse change as movement between two equilibrium states in which the causes of the movement are treated as exogenous to the model or in terms of the aggregate of 'decisions' taken by numbers of 'individuals'. Like both economics and anthropology, geography recognises only change that occurs within the system and is unable to deal with changes of that system. Furthermore, like economics, from which it derives all of its theoretical assumptions, geography is based upon the fundamentally erroneous notion that all economies and societies function as does Western industrial economy and society. Geography suffers from an additional weakness in that it concentrates upon an exceptionally exiguous fraction of social reality: the spatial dimension. It is significant, in view of the remarks made above regarding the inadequacies of the diffusionist view of economic change and development predominant in development economics, that most studies in geography that relate to problems of development and underdevelopment have been couched in terms of the spatial diffusion of innovations, often with special reference to the diffusion of information. A recent review of the inherent inadequacies of the inherent inadequacies of conventional geography and studies of the spatial diffusion of innovations in particular argues that:

> "the major problems of diffusion research derive from its own history and that of parts of bourgeois social science as a whole, namely an emphasis being placed on the implicitly ideological adopter, who makes decisions about single technical innovations, as the universal and desired model; the treatment of communication as an exogenous, independent variable inducing change; the enlargement of the role of communication at the expense of resource inequalities in explaining innovation adoption; the division of syntactics, semantics and pragmatics in the treatment of the communication process; an obsession with quantitative model-building which is at present ill-founded in the socio-economic branch of spatial diffusion theory; and the failure of the theory to be of use in developed countries; and to be fundamentally vulnerable in the context of developing countries in the light of current theories of development and underdevelopment" (Blaikie 1978: 26-27).

It is argued, in this review, that diffusion theory fails because it is not derived from any adequate conception of the nature of social change; 'diffusion' is conceived to be the agent of change, or even itself to be change. (cf Blaikie 1978: 29).

Despite these weaknesses inherent in the approaches of the various social science disciplines, which render them inadequate as the basis for an analysis of underdevelopment as a process, all of them are conventionally associated with specific techniques and methodologies which, it was felt, might contribute usefully to the general theoretical approach and methodology of the Nepal project.

Thus, for example, anthropology has conventionally emphasised the importance of long-term participant observation in the analysis of the underlying structures of non-capitalist societies and the value of intensive interviewing of selected informants, while geography, sociology and economics have all been more concerned with questions of representativeness and sampling in order to construct valid quantitative models. In our work we have tried to make use of a variety of methods and techniques of data collection and processing drawn from the conventional practice of anthropology, sociology, economics and geography. The fact remains, however, that whatever methods and techniques are used to collect, process and analyse the data, the terms in which the data are identified and classified ultimately depends on the way in which social data in general is conceptualised; and this depends upon the theoretical perspective and epistemology of the social science adopted. The social science adopted by the Nepal project was not one of the branches of the social sciences identified and discussed above, but one derived largely from the Marxist tradition and from recent development in Marxist theory. The adoption of such an approach was clearly not a simple matter of 'choice' but was pre-conditioned by a variety of prior circumstances, some of which have already been examined; the particular characteristics of this approach and its implications for the analysis of underdevelopment and the condition of the lower classes in Nepal remain to be elaborated, the former in the next two sections of this chapter and the latter in the essays that constitute the remainder of this book.

Elements of an Approach: The Conception of History

Although it is helpful to distinguish initially between history as the product of men's action and History as a product of men's intellect and as a representation of men's action seeing the perception (and writing) of History as distinct from the making of history; it is nevertheless the case, we believe that:

> "History is not a given object, the hitherto existing is nowhere given since (by definition) it does not exist. History is a coherent and unified field only within definite conceptions of that unity; its unity rests on concepts and categories, and just as it is created by them so it can be destroyed by them, and the world will not fall apart. There is no history per se, history given outside the concepts of history. There are only practices of writing and constituting definite *histories*. These practices define the past and transform artefacts (documents, bones, palaces, kitchen middens, etc.) into *representations* of the hitherto existing. The character and status of these representations depend on the

> history in which they are written; in different histories the same artefacts represent different conditions. The different practices of writing history, of constituting representations as the real are the field of action of definite social and political ideologies. For example, 'Marxist' history, Marxism within the limits of the historian's practice, is committed to a definite practice of writing history, history as the history of production, the struggle of the masses, etc." (Hindess and Hirst 1975: 238).

Thus, the conception of Nepalese history, as presented in this book (and elsewhere, cf Blaikie, Cameron and Seddon 1978), is a particular History of Nepal; it is one in which the central dynamic is the changing structure of relations between classes —relations of production, surplus appropriation and domination, economic and political struggle.

In such a conception of history, neither history nor History can be neutral; if history is seen as the history of the class struggle, then it follows that History must always be the History of that class struggle viewed from a partial and ideological standpoint. If it is accepted that "the ideas of the ruling class are in every epoch the ruling ideas" (Marx and Engels 1970: 64) then it comes as no great surprise to find, for example, the History of the Ranas in Nepal (see Chapter 2) to be a History of palace intrigue and internecine struggles between contending fractions of the aristocracy—a 'political' History in the most limited sense. Contemporary Histories do often significantly constrain the possibilities of constructing an alternative History of the period by their selection and restriction of the material for any History; the paucity of materials available on the period of Rana rule for example that relate to the details of economic and social structure limits our ability to reconstruct a History of the Ranas, in our own terms, except in general outline. Only a pioneering work of fundamental 'reconstruction'—such as, for example, Regmi has done for the earlier period of the expanded Gorkha state in his brilliant *Study in Nepali Economic History* (Regmi 1971)—can make available the necessary data for a detailed History of the Ranas in terms other than those provided by the contemporary History, itself a reflection of the ruling ideas of the epoch.

The total inadequacy of accepting contemporary History as the equivalent of history was recognised by Marx and Engels; as they observe,

> "the exponents of this conception of history have... only been able to see in history the political actions of princes and States, religious and all sorts of theoretical struggles, and in each particular epoch have had *to share the illusion of the epoch*. For instance, if an epoch imagines itself to be actuated by purely 'political' or 'religious' motives, although 'religion' and 'politics' are only forms of its true motives, the historian accepts this opinion. The 'idea', the 'conception' of the people in question about their real practices is transformed into the sole determining active force, which controls and determines their practice. When the crude form in which the division of labour appears with the Indians and Egyptians calls forth the caste-system in their State and religion, the historian believes that the caste-system is the power which has produced this crude social form" (Marx and Engels 1970: 60).

The historian is thus trapped, unable to construct his own History and obliged to accept the History of each epoch as history. Without his own theoretical basis for the construction of an 'alternative' History through the re-reading of the materials available and their reproduction in terms of his own concepts and categories, the historian is forced to accept one ideological version of reality as the valid conception of reality. But as Hindess and Hirst have emphasised, "history is a coherent and unified field only within definite conceptions of that unity; its unity rests on concepts and categories. " (Hindess and Hirst 1975: 238). The development of a coherent theoretical apparatus associated with distinctive concepts and categories is thus a prerequisite for the production of any 'alternative' History, and indeed for any analysis of economy and society past or present, for in our conception there is no distinction between the production of History and the activities of social science, for social science must be historical and the foundations for the construction of a scientific History must be those of an integrated social science.

The analysis of 'the caste system', for example, is only possible, we would argue, in terms of an approach which can identify the underlying structures of economic and political relations which, as they developed over time, gave rise to a continually revised religious ideology providing part explanation and part justification of both change and continuity in terms of a complex notion of formal and ritualised relationships between categories defined in terms of 'ritual purity or pollution' (cf Meillassoux 1973). Only with such an approach, based on the construction of an 'independent' theoretical apparatus, is it possible to avoid simply re-presenting the economy and society in which ideas of caste predominate in terms of its own religious ideology and representations; only with such an approach is it possible to explain both underlying economic and political relations and religious ideology, and to reveal the specific .features of the former which generate and reproduce the apparent dominance of the latter.

An initial perspective is provided by such general conceptions as 'the history of all hitherto existing societies is the history of class struggles', but the elaboration of an adequate theoretical apparatus for the analysis of, for example, the historical development of the Nepalese political economy and of the relations between classes within that political economy requires a more refined and sophisticated set of concepts and categories. The materialist conception of history

> "depends on our ability to expound the real process of production starting out from the material production of life itself, and to comprehend the form of intercourse connected with this and created by this mode of production (i.e. civil society in its various stages), as the basis of all history; and to show it in its action as State, to explain all the different theoretical products and forms of consciousness, religion, philosophy, ethics, etc., and trace their origins and growth from that basis; by which means, of course, the whole thing can be depicted in its totality..." (Marx and Engels 1970: 58).

The starting point, therefore, is the conceptualisation and identification of the 'mode of production' upon which are based what Marx and Engels term civil society, the State and various forms of social consciousness. In so far as this is conceived in our approach to the analysis of economy and society predominantly as a matter of theorisation, in terms of which the materials for the construction of a History of the political ecomomy of Nepal are structured, the work of other historians and social scientists embarked on related enterprises, from broadly similar general perspectives must be considered.

We do not intend to develop here an extended discussion of the debate regarding the logical viability and theoretical applicability of the recently revived conception of an 'Asiatic' mode of production (cf Anderson 1975; Hindess and Hirst 1975b) nor shall we attempt to review the rapidly growing literature which is concerned with elaborating the conception to describe and analyse a variety of non-capitalist societies in Africa, the Middle East and Asia (e.g. Antoniadis-Bibicou 1977; Godelier 1978; Coquery 1978; Gallissot 1975; Lacoste 1974; Seddon 1977b; Keyder 1976; Terray 1974; Murray 1975). Suffice it to say here that our approach to the analysis of Nepalese history is much conditioned by this literature and by the adoption of a conception of Nepalese economy and society which identifies a mode of production fundamentally similar to that which characterises a variety of pre-capitalist societies elsewhere. The precise nature of the relations of production and appropriation of surplus, the crucial importance of control over long-distance trade, the particular form of political and legal domination and the nature of the State in Nepal during the 18th and early 19th century, closely approximate to the situation identified in the other societies referred to.

The internal dynamic and evolution of Nepalese economy and society (analysed in Chapter 2) cannot be explained, however, particularly from the second-half of the 19th century onwards, without reference to the significance of Nepal's relative political autonomy combined with its economic subordination to India. The conceptualisation of Nepalese history must, therefore, also derive from theories of underdevelopment and dependency which comprehend the rather specific form of Nepal's incorporation into the world system dominated by international capitalism over the past hundred years. No simple model based on internal dynamics of, for example, the 'Asiatic' mode of production alone could account for the recent history of Nepal in all its complexity.

Much recent discussion has centred around the most adequate conceptualisation of the process of underdevelopment whereby a pre-capitalist society with its own internal dynamic and distinctive history is incorporated within a economic and political system dominated by the capitalist mode of production and its political and ideological superstructures and yet remain itself predominantly non-capitalist in terms of its indigenous modes of production. For all, the most crucial aspect of the process is the subordination of the 'periphery' to the laws of motion of the capitalist mode of production characteristic of the 'centre' (the metropolitan countries of the 'developed' world); and yet the maintenance of non-capitalist forms of production at the periphery is in itself significant and conditions the dynamic of class relations at the periphery. The incorporation, combined with the enforced preservation, of non-capitalist modes of production within a global system dominated by capitalism generates distinctive forms of class structure and distinctive patterns of class struggle in the societies and states whose partial autonomy is thus maintained at the same time as it is continually undermined.

Elements of an Approach: Class and Class Struggle

Hence our approach assumes that history is the history of class struggle, and the category of class becomes the starting point in the analysis of social change in Nepal. This is very different from other studies where caste (in the 'sociological' literature) or region (in the 'geographical') have formed the basic analytical categories, and their implied ideologies. We fully recognise the importance of caste, and of regional heterogeneity in any but the crudest materialist analysis of Nepal, but take as part of our ideological position, the assumption that they are not the determining categories upon which an analysis of social change in Nepal can be based.

The advantages of an analysis based upon class must lie, not in the elegance of the classification procedure, but in the analytical 'work' which it brings to defining (and assisting in a correct analysis of) the class struggle. Hence classification in this instance is not only for the purpose of 'bringing order' to a seemingly chaotic statistical population so that generalisation and hypothesis-testing can be carried out, but because the categorisation of a population into classes itself implies a process of class struggle and social change. One of the most problematic features of the analysis of Nepalese society is that a single individual can take a number of different class positions as he/she can be involved in a number of different production situations. Therefore, while class is an abstract analytical category, which at the same time identifies its contradictions and 'laws of motion' vis-a-vis its own development and relation to other classes, it requires additional but subordinate analytical categories to analyse the conjuncture of a number of class positions in an individual. It is clear that a class position will be modified by another held at a different time and place by the same person. Nepal is a labour exporting economy, and labour is involved both in factories in India, in the service of foreign armies and in the cultivation of a peasant farm at home. Such an individual's class position, and his role in class struggle will not be the same as three separate individuals' class position and role in class struggle, who are each solely involved in each of these activities. Thus, in addition to a class analysis, the other categories are required to grasp the totality of individuals' place in the political economy. For example an individual can be at the same time a woman, a member of an untouchable caste, a farmer, a migrant labourer and a mother, and each category at different points affects how and when other categories apply at a particular conjuncture.

One of the most important effects of the existence of multi class individuals and households in Nepal is the modification of their role in the class struggle. Multiple class positions generally reduce the level, coherence and intensity of class struggle for a number of reasons. First of all, workers who do not *wholly* rely upon payments incurred under a particular set of relations of production are less likely to press as strongly for an improvement in their position than those whose livelihood is entirely derived from them. Even a willingness to 'subsidise' the costs of the reproduction of their labour in a given set of production relations by labour in another (e.g. the family farm) is quite common. Secondly, within one particular set of production relations, there will be a heterogeneity of *overall* interests of each individual involved, which tends to reduce solidarity of a workforce. For example a sub-marginal peasant who is working for a few months in a brick factory will be more militant in his demands for better working conditions than a more advantaged peasant working under identical conditions of work in the brick-factory. Thirdly, the seasonal nature of much of employment of casual labour tends to increase turnover of workers and reduce the time available for a concentration of workers to realise their common position and to organise themselves for concerted action. Nepal is overwhelmingly a peasant society (Chapter 3) and the vast proportion of individuals are involved in attempting to produce sufficient food on the family farm using family, (unpaid) kin or reciprocal labour. Thus, if the most important set of production relations involving the vast majority of the population produces a notoriously conservative and individualistic type of social economic and political behaviour, its effect upon other production relations (e.g. capitalistic ones in Indian factories) will be felt. In this way both the multiple class position and the massive involvement of most of the population in peasant or domestic production causes a two-way reduction in active and progressive class struggle—both at the centres of capitalist production themselves (with all the classic problems of a migrant labour force), as well as in the countryside at home.

However, this explanation must not be misconstrued as to imply a passive peasantry which has willingly provided surplus in the form of tribute, taxes and corvee labour to support a ruling class. Struggle has, it is true, often taken the form of evasion—simply running away and putting as much distance between local lord and the escaping peasant as possible —which in turn encouraged the organisation of slavery by the ruling class to counter this action. However, there are instances mentioned in this book of a more significant struggle, although even these tend to be ephemeral and relate to incidents of local interest, which are not seen as ones uniting a class with a specific objective condition. Riots in Kapilvastu District following the introduction of the scandalous compulsory Savings Scheme involving forcible collections of money and irregularities in the allocation of funds, in which a number of people were killed, were reported in the Nepalese press. On another occasion, members of the untouchable castes rioted and killed two Brahmin priests in a (legally successful) struggle to be allowed to read the scriptures at certain ceremonies (hitherto reserved for the Brahmin priest). Hunger marches by peasants upon the capital during 1973 following two years of widespread crop failures are further examples of concerted action, but not characterised by a clear and committed class consciousness. What class struggle there is in Nepal is largely concentrated in the terai and in the towns, and in the rare cases where a labour force is temporarily concentrated for a specific project (e.g. for the construction of motorable roads as discussed in Chapter 7). In the terai, where over ninety per cent of industrial production is located, the industrial work force is concentrated under capitalist relations of production, and the workers, although forbidden to join trade unions, have managed a greater degree of organisation. Even in other locations at some distance from manufacturing establishments, the spatial concentration of workers itself tends to facilitate such organisation, even if its constituent parts are highly heterogeneous. The organisation for low caste persons (Chapter 9), between rickshaw pullers and between bus drivers (Chapter 8) all derive from the ability albeit limited of workers to overcome the separation of space and time inherent in typical peasant production.

CHAPTER 2

THE UNDERDEVELOPMENT OF NEPAL

The Political Economy of a Tributary State

During the 17th and 18th centuries the area that is now Nepal was divided between numerous petty states. The size and power of any petty state depended on the ability of the ruling class to appropriate in the form of taxation surpluses produced by farmers and others, on their ability to maintain an effective army to defend the borders and encroach upon the territory of other rival states, and on their capacity to control and exploit strategic resources, such as mineral deposits or trade routes. In the hills, the majority of producers were involved in pastoral activities or in shifting cultivation, but the valleys and parts of the terai (the strip of plain stretching between the foothills and the Indian border to the south) were rich in such resources as timber, ivory, etc., and amenable to rice cultivation. For this reason, control over areas of terai was important as a means of deriving revenue for the state coffers. But if the productivity of the hills and their capacity to provide revenue for the state were low, it was from there that the majority of soldiers were recruited and there that martial attributes were encouraged. The nobility, as well as the courtiers, clients, officials and generals of these petty states tended to be 'high caste' (Hindus, of Indo-Aryan extraction Brahmins and Chetris, many of whom claimed descent from ancient Rajput families who ruled what is now Rajasthan in western India before the beginning of the Muslim conquests). The subject classes included the majority of the indigenous population (Magars, Gurungs, Limbus, Rais, etc.), whose tribal structures and occasional small chiefdoms had been only partly destroyed by the establishment of these Hindu kingdoms, and also the 'low caste' artisans and small farmers who came north with the more powerful 'Rajputs' as they migrated over the previous centuries into and within the Nepalese hills.

Different in certain respects from other petty states were the three kingdoms that had their capital in the fertile Kathmandu Valley. The largely Hinduised Newar rulers of these kingdoms were wealthy by virtue of the agricultural richness of the Valley itself, their control over the major long-distance trade routes and, at some periods, control over parts of the terai. Here, as nowhere else, flourished a genuine urban economy and society in which the production of such commodities as cloth and metalware was to be found, as well as the base for major trading operations between Tibet and India.

Around the beginning of the 17th century a junior member of the royal dynasty of Lamjung—a petty state in the western hills—was able to supplant the tribal (Magar) chieftain of Gorkha and establish a Hindu kingdom. The new rulers of Gorkha managed to consolidate and extend their control over the local population, enshrining their political domination in legal codes, and by the end of the century the Gorkha state had expanded to the north as far as the borders of Tibet, to the south virtually to the terai and to the east to the very edge of the Kathmandu Valley. It continued to expand and to strengthen its position during the first half of the 18th century until, in 1744, it was able finally to annex Nuwakot, a small trading centre through which passed a proportion of the long-distance trade between Tibet and the Kathmandu Valley, taking it from the Valley kingdoms. Control of Nuwakot enabled the rulers of Gorkha to derive significant benefits from the long-distance trade; increased revenues and superior military technology helped them to subjugate and control other areas further east, including the passes of Kuti and Kerung which constituted the main routes for the Tibet-Kathmandu-India trade. The conquest of Makwanpur in 1762 enabled them to extend their growing empire into the flat productive lands of the terai and also to control the southern routes between the Kathmandu Valley and India. Military expeditions sent against Gorkha by the Nawab of Bengal and the British East India Comany in the 1760's were repulsed, although the East India Company was able temporarily to retrieve certain areas of the terai. In 1767 the taking of Kirtipur gave Gorkha the first foothold within the Kathmandu Valley itself. Having established effective control over the territories surrounding the Valley, the expanded Gorkha state was able to impose a virtual siege and by 1769 the three kingdoms, Kathmandu, Bhadgaon and Patan, had been taken over. The subsequent transfer of the capital from Gorkha to take advantage of the peculiar location and agricultural wealth of the Newar kingdoms marked the establishment of central government in the Kathmandu Valley, where the centre of power has remained to the present day.

By 1775 the area controlled by the rulers of the expanded Gorkha state—now more meaningfully referred to as the state of Nepal—included the whole of the eastern terai, the eastern hill region as far as the Tista river bordering Sikkim, the central terai and a small part of the western hill region. Control over the rich terai and Kathmandu Valley and over the major long-distance trade routes through central and eastern Nepal enabled the new state to expand westwards. By 1789 all of the western hill states, which between them numbered some forty six distinct political entities, had been effectively annexed, conquered or reduced to vassal status; much of the western terai now also came under the control of the central government in Kathmandu. Thus, by the end of the 18th century virtually the entire area that is now Nepal had been incorporated into a loosely articulated hegemony that may be characterised as a tributary state. The centre of the new empire was Kathmandu, urban capital and traditional Newar town, but although some Newars were able to hold office the majority of government officials were of 'high caste' as was the ruling nobility. Newars remained for the most part in commerce (both as large merchants and petty traders) and in small-scale manufacturing. (See Chapter 9).

The state was maintained largely by the appropriation of surplus in the form of taxes from the direct producers, the peasantry (see Chapter 3)—often by local lords granted the right to collect those revenues and to appropriate for themselves a significant portion by the ruler himself as a reward for services rendered or to ensure loyalty in the future, but also by state officials. Those granted rights of local taxation were generally obliged to keep local law and order, to maintain the trails and ferries without which communications and transport would have been impossible (see Chapter 7), and to raise levies of troops when so required for the purpose of central government. This system resembles the European feudal system, in so far as it involved parcellised sovereignties under an overall monarch, each local lord able to appropriate surpluses direct from the peasants; but in so far as many areas were not under the jurisdiction of a local lord but consisted of an independent peasantry controlling the means of production and its distribution, save only for the obligation to pay taxes to the central government, and in so far as local lords were by no means always landowners, there are significant differences.

Agricultural production, in the hills in particular, was rarely sufficient for there to develop a regular marketable surplus over and above that taken in taxes; as a result, despite the existence of money in many areas, the extent of commodity production in the countryside was extremely limited as were the possibilities of accumulation by farmers. The local lords themselves were not legally landowners, but only granted temporary and alienable rights to appropriate surpluses produced in their domain; they were, as a result, not inclined to invest heavily in the land themselves, or even to promote, beyond a minimum, increased productivity among the peasantry. The opening up of new land or the exploitation of immediately available forest was far more attractive at this time. The terai, even at this early period, was a major source of animal and vegetable export to India (e.g. ivory and timber) and thus of revenue to central government, which imposed a form of trading tax on such exports as well as on imported goods, themselves becoming more popular among the privileged. The long-distance trade between Tibet and India which, of necessity, passed through Nepal, afforded further opportunities for the rulers of Nepal to line their coffers and maintain their control over the mass of the population through the state apparatus of army and administration and through the local lords, and over the local lords through grants and largesse.

During the 19th century, population growth and the spread of cereal cultivation (maize and rice in particular) were associated with a gradual reduction in the importance of pastoralism and a corresponding increase in more intensive agriculture, even in the hills. The difficulties faced by local lords and by central government, resulting from a low density of population, meagre agricultural production and the correspondingly low level of revenues to be extracted from the peasantry, grew slowly less, and there are indications that such institutions as slavery and forced labour became less necessary as the total number of peasants grew.

The expansion of the state apparatus and of conspicious consumption of imported luxury goods by the nobility was considerable during the 19th century; the surplus required increased accordingly. Land grants were made in increasing numbers throughout the century, particularly in the terai, so as to promote irrigation, settlement and the opening up of virgin land for cultivation. During the first decade of the 19th century, however, the State of Nepal came up against the limits to growth on the basis of territorial expansion, in the form of the Sikhs to the west and the British India Company to the south. The war of 1814-16 between the British and the Nepalese for example, in which the Nepalese conceded defeat, was over the control of areas of the terai, a major source of revenue for Nepal and India alike, and over the liberalisation of trade pressed for by the East India Company to allow it greater control over the north-south trade from Tibet.

The treaty of Sugauli, contracted in 1816 after the war, obliged Nepal to relinquish all her acquisitions west of the Mahakaii river, and east of the Mechi river; these rivers were then fixed as Nepal's boundaries. A British resident was to be appointed for Kathmandu and Nepal was not allowed to have direct communications with any western power except Great Britain. It was not until 1923 that this treaty was abrogated and the independence of Nepal fully recognised by the British government. For nearly a century, then, Nepal was a kind of political dependency of Great Britain; an arrangement that had benefits both for the British and for the rulers of Nepal. The former were guaranteed a self-manning buffer against possibly hostile powers to the north, a regular supply of soldiers from the hill regions of Nepal (the famous Gurkhas), a small but growing market for manufactured goods, and, probably even more important, a source of raw materials and primary products from both Tibet and Nepal; the latter were guaranteed a minimum of support and protection, and a degree of insulation from outside pressures for political change.

Within the tributary state, however, political changes were taking place. The weakness of the monarchy in Nepal during the first half of the 19th century was associated with the growing power of certain elements of the aristocracy, and the first forty years of the century were characterised above all by the control of Nepal by prime minister Bhimsen Thapa under a form of military dictatorship. After his death power was seized—following a short period of internecine strife—by one of the members of the powerful Rana lineage—(Jang Bahadur Rana) who thus initiated a century of rule by this one branch of the ruling class under the institutional form of a hereditary prime ministership but effectively through the creation of a new ruling dynasty, the Ranas. Administration under the Ranas had two main purposes: the collection of revenues and the maintenance of law and order, the latter primarily in order to facilitate the former. According to Goodall (1966) the revenues of the State were not distinguished from those of the Ranas and treasury surpluses were regarded generally as their personal income; and Kumar estimates that between 25% and 50% of total state revenue was appropriated personally to the Rana prime minister (Kumar 1967). Just as public revenues were treated as part of the ruler's private purse, so senior appointments in the bureaucracy, including the important post of district governor, were conferred personally by the prime minister. Districts were graded (A, B and C) according to such factors as distance from the capital, population and revenue potential, and the prime minister's closest kinsmen and most loyal followers were retained in Kathmandu or sent to govern the more important or turbulent districts, while those of lesser status, or whose presence in the capital was not desired, were assigned to the least soughtafter posts in districts of C grade.

The functions of the bureaucracy were primarily extractive and repressive, rather than productive, in the sense that it was concerned with the collection of revenue and the maintenance of law and order rather than with increasing productivity and improving the country's economic base. In many respect the structure of the administration under the Ranas in Nepal resembled that of the Moghuls in India (cf Barrington Moore 1969: 317-330).

Despite the lack of interest in the productive base demonstrated by the state bureaucracy, there is evidence that revenue to the state increased slowly throughout the 19th century and early part of the 20th, mostly as a direct result of the increasing agricultural production. Hodgson estimated that trade between Nepal and India, worth around 3 million rupees in 1831, had grown to over 30 million by 1891. Around the turn of the century it appears that rice accounted for nearly 40% of Nepal's exports to India, with mustard oilseed providing a further 20% (Rawat 1974: 67-55); from India Nepal imported a massive quantity of cotton cloth and yarn— nearly 60% of all imports—as well as other manufactured goods. A substantial portion of the profits accruing from increased foreign trade (in which it must be noted the balance favoured Nepal) was pocketed by the Ranas who had established monopolies over the trade in important commodities, either directly or else through contracted agents; where they did not effectively monopolise trade they taxed it heavily and amassed gold, silver and luxury goods for themselves.

The very substantial increase in rice exports from the terai in the last decade of the 19th century and first decade of the 20th century coincided with the extension of the Indian railway network to the very borders of Nepal, so that it now became increasingly profitable to exploit the forest and the cleared agricultural land of the terai; the railways connecting the Nepalese terai to the great markets of north India ensured that the revenue from forest and other land granted to members of the nobility by the rulers of Nepal was far greater than it could possibly have been in earlier periods. It is no coincidence that Rana palaces were constructed around the turn of the century on a far grander scale than any before, or that luxury imports from Europe came during this period to dominate the consumption of the nobility.

> "The growth of trade and to some extent small industries could not ....be maintained in the new terai towns after the extension of the Indian railways across the border. Grain surpluses passing through the new towns increased, but at a decreasing rate over the years. This was bound to happen for three socio-economic reasons. First, agricultural technology was then even more primitive than it is now. Therefore, once the potential agricultural surplus for the given level of technology was exploited further increases in production were at best very slow and come primarily through the reclamation of wasteland and forest area. Second...economic development was not then a national goal. The socio-economic structure was essentially feudalistic, and entrepreneurship among the people was frowned upon. The ruling class was not only afraid of technical innovation, but also feared changes in the values and aspirations of the common man. It recognised that the development of industries which would lead to a new awareness among workers regarding the sharing of political and economic power. Therefore no efforts were made to start consumer goods industries that could have potentially exploited the new monetization of the regional economy and the increased purchasing power of the people. Third, a trade treaty was signed with British India in 1923. The treaty allowed for practically unrestricted import of British goods to Nepal. Naturally it had the effect of discouraging the

> establishment of new industries and the continued operation of ancient handicraft and cottage industries. Thus the windfall trade gains from the extension of Indian railroads to a few points along the country's southern border were not able to generate forces of long-term growth and the region's economy finally seems to have followed the path visualised in the Ricardian Theory of the Stationary State" (Lohani 1973: 204-205)

But changes were taking place on a world scale that were to affect the future of Nepal. The Rana regime had become increasingly dependent on British India to the south and when in 1947 partition took place and India became independent, the basis for Rana rule was so seriously undermined that three years later they were removed from power and the monarchy restored as supreme authority in Nepal. Up until this time, the Ranas had relied on their special relationship with the British to prevent outside interference with the continuity of their regime—an effective alliance of interests between the ruling class of Nepal and British imperialism in India. However, the new popular forces that came to power in India were suspicious of the autocratic regime to the north, much as they were of the princely states in India itself, and established links with the small, but rapidly growing 'radical' movement within Nepal; at the same time there was considerable concern at the possibility of violent upheaval in Nepal, in view of the growing strength of China and its supposed ambitions in Asia, particularly after 1949. Thus, when the Nepalese king Tribhuvan, in collusion with individuals within the Indian Embassy sought asylum there and later in New Delhi, in 1950 identified himself with those opposed to the continuation of Rana rule (some of whom were themselves of Rana families) and thereby captured the leadership of the new democratic movement in Nepal, his action was warmly welcomed in India as substantially improving the chances for the emergence in Nepal of a reformist but relatively stable regime. Following Tribhuvan's move, armed insurrection broke out in Nepal with the active support of the Indian government, and the Ranas, unable to quell the disturbances and recognising the inevitability of formal political change, agreed to the return of Tribhuvan as king and head of state and the establish-ment of a 'democratic system'.

This formal break, marked by the restoration of the monarchy, was significant, but—as we shall argue later in this chapter—much less so than many have suggested. The degree of structural continuity between the 'tributary state' and so-called 'modern Nepal' is remarkable and explains many aspects of what we identify as 'the crisis in Nepal' (see Blaikie, Cameron and Seddon, 1979).

From Semi-Colony to Periphery

It might appear at first sight that Nepal's history is notable for the high degree of autonomy exemplified by the Nepalese state, even in the face of British colonialist expansion in the sub-continent during the 19th century. Such an impression is often conveyed by those who assert that Nepal's political autonomy served to protect it from outside influences, and thus to retain its 'isolated' and 'backward' state, until 1951. Such interpretations, apart from ignoring the very real evolution of economic and political structures within Nepal during the 18th and 19th centuries also generally rest on the premise that the appropriate unit for analysis is inevitably the nation state, conceived of as the crucial political formation and as effectively determining the allocation of resources within its own boundaries through the action of government but virtually powerless outside its border. In direct opposition to this is what has come to be known as the 'school of dependency' theorists, who see underdevelopment not as some primitive condition but as a process intimately associated with the expansion of capitalism and its domination of all other modes of production. This view argues that even where an underdeveloped economy and society is demonstrably not capitalist itself and retains political autonomy its incorporation into the wider international capitalist political economy subordinates it to the 'laws of motion' of capitalism. Most contemporary underdeveloped countries underwent a process of incorporation into the international capitalist system in which a vital stage was the establishment of a colonial state under the control of a metropolitan country. Subsequent decolonisation resulted in a degree of political autonomy (independence) but, it can be argued, failed to transform the underlying mechanisms of incorporation whereby underdevelopment continued to take place (i.e. what is often termed 'neo-colonialism'). One result of the establishment of the colonial state was, generally, the (limited and uneven) development within the colony of capitalist relations of production associated with certain infrastructural and other improvements. Not all pre-capitalist societies, however, were incorporated in precisely this fashion and some never experienced colonialism. Such societies, with a few exceptions, were however at least partly incorporated and altered. In an attempt to provide a convenient shorthand term for such societies, whose common characteristics were striking, Lenin coined the phrase: 'a semi-colony'. He used this term to describe those non-capitalist societies which managed to preserve a status of formal political independence, mainly as a result of international competition during the period of imperialist expansion during the 19th century. Countries to which this term could be applied include China, Japan, Turkey, Ethiopia, Thailand and Iran, whose existence as national political units largely predated the period of European expansion.

As we have seen, the treaty of Sugauli obliged Nepal to relinquish certain areas in the terai; a British resident was appointed to Kathmandu and Nepal was forbidden to have direct communications with any western power except Great Britain. It was not until 1923 that this treaty was abrogated and the independence of Nepal fully recognised by the British government. For nearly a century, then, Nepal was a kind of political dependency of Great Britain, an arrangement that had benefits both for the British and for the rulers of Nepal.

The decline of Chinese power during the latter half of the 19th century meant that Nepal was in no position to pursue a balance of power policy, and after 1850 Nepal could probably not have maintained her limited degree of juridicial independence without the concurrence of the British government in India. British policy with regard to other similar 'buffer' states, like Afghanistan and Iran, was not to incorporate them into the empire but to allow them a measure of internal autonomy in exchange for a preponderant influence in these countries' foreign and trade policy. The Rana rulers were convinced that they would be pressed hard to withstand a determined British assault on the vulnerable terai areas from which they drew so much of their revenue and they therefore acquiesced to the arrangement. Given this acquiescence on the part of the rulers of Nepal, there was little advantage to the British in occupying the territory. Nepal under the Ranas remained, therefore, a dependency, but never became a colony of the British. The preservation of these antique, semi-feudal or patrimonal states as the administrative and military substructure of imperialist exploitation at the same time discredited the old ruling order and provided it with the means of survival. Under these circumstances the state apparatus was quite incapable of laying down the technical and social infrastructure essential to national integration and development. At the same time, however, since the state embodied national continuity and was the repository of national traditions, it was frequently seen as the 'natural' framework even for anti-imperialist movements, as was the ruling class. Consequently, "the state became the expression and instrument of the coalition of imperialism with the traditional ruling class. In the absence of settlers or a colonial bureaucracy, the dynasty, big landlords, warlords, compradors and military elite themselves constituted the bridge-head of imperialism" (Rey, 1963: 70). The evidence of Nepalese history supports the case for regarding Nepal as a 'semi-colony'.

In the early period annexation was avoided partially due to the existence of competing imperialisms (viz. the British East India Company in Bengal and the Chinese in Tibet); however, terms limiting the autonomy of the Nepalese state were extracted by the British after the brief war with Nepal in 1816. The recognition of Nepalese independence in 1923 prevented any question of incorporating Nepal into India either before or after Independence in 1947 and by the 1960's the re-emergence of 'imperialist' rivalry between India and

China can be regarded as indefinitely perpetuating the semi-colonial situation. The situation within Nepal even after 'the restoration' still somewhat resembles that described by Rey:

> "The mortgaging of the national economy and resources to foreigners (treaties, concessions, abandonment of tariffs)... supported the regime and created the network of compradors, contractors, profiteers and complicit officials in whose interest the system worked. Thus the state became the expression and instrument of the coalition of imperialism with the traditional ruling class ...Local economic development ceased and in many sectors—especially the artisan—was wrecked... The state embodies national continuity and is the repository of national traditions. Hence the initial demand for a constitutional regime. Constitutional restraints... would, it was thought, without affronting the crown and the historic and cultural values residual in kingship... change the relationship of the state with the foreigners... No meaningful transformation took place... Moreover, gestures of anti-imperialism from the ruling elite, not entirely cynical, further confused the issue... The ruling elite... posed as the authentic hero of the liberation struggle. But this surrogate resistance achieved nothing except foreign irritation and rancour... Anti-imperialism in the semi-colonial period proper was thus socially and ideologically incoherent and the various options and complex conditions created... divergencies in the histories of each country."

The concept of 'semi-colony' is useful for two reasons. Firstly, it emphasises that underdevelopment is not a consequence of isolation from the world but of incorporation into the world. For a semi-colonial state this incorporation involved many of the disadvantages of colonialism (Rey's use of the term 'mortgaging' above is appropriate with its sense of formal title to property and postponement of crisis) with none of the advantages, e.g. those deriving from the productive investment of capital. Secondly, it illustrates the difficulties for the ruling class under these conditions of breaking away from self-rewarding dependence upon the imperialist power and the importance of chauvinist ideology incorporating a romantic sence of history in which the aristocracy plays the leading heroic roles, quite detached from considerations of economic development. This duality explains some of the seeming contradiction between passive complicity and fierce nationalism and suggests that nationalism is not necessarily a fundamental threat to the status quo. The semi-colonial nation-state thus stands peculiarly enmeshed in a world which it is incapable of altering; only under exceptional circumstances is it able to detach itself, except in rhetoric. It is to the origins and specific process of Nepal's enmeshment that we now turn.

From the Sepoy Rising to the end of the 19th century the rise of a domestic class of capitalists occurred in India, although managerial posts were still heavily dominated by Europeans; there was also an identifiable proletariat who relied on wages for income. Capitalism in India was both spatially concentrated (near Bombay and Ahmedabad) and sectorally concentrated (mainly cotton textile products), and its importance within the economy as a whole during the 19th century quite limited. With regard to the effects of these developments upon Nepal, railway construction in India produced enormously increased revenues from Nepalese timber sales and Indian urban growth meant that a buoyant market for foodgrains existed which was facilitated by transport improvements. Annual values of trade which approximately trebled in the fifty years from 1835 to 1885 had trebled again by the end of the century, with the value of Nepalese exports double that of imports. This strong trading surplus was produced with no internal transportation improvements and in a period in which emigration grew to the extent that in 1900 just under a quarter of a million people of declared Nepalese origin were recorded in the Indian census. This number had increased by over 30,000 in the period 1900 to 1911 with no increase in Indian army recruitment. An indication of the opportunity this situation represented is that using the balance of trade surplus to purchase textile mill machinery during these years would have employed all the net increase in numbers of Nepalese living in India in the period 1900 to 1911 (using contemporary Indian figures for finance capital required per workplace); in fact, the most notable act by the Nepalese rulers in this period was to mount a successful military expedition into Tibet (1904) which established a temporary tributary relationship between Tibet and Nepal. Population increase and an absence of any expansion in employment opportunities led to the physical expansion of subsistence farming in Nepal and to emigration. Over fifty thousand recruits offered themselves as recruits for the Gurkha regiments in World War I and when eleven thousand were discharged immediately at the end of the war only one third returned to Nepal. By the early 1930's about one Nepalese-born person in twenty was living in India according to Nepalese and Indian census estimates. This proportion has remained almost constant through to the 1960's, during which time the population of Nepal almost doubled.

The 1920's were notable for the first tentative steps by the rulers to develop the productive potential of their country by purchasing foreign expertise. The first modern college was set up, a ropeway was constructed linking the Kathmandu Valley with India and some mineral exploration was undertaken. The British proved willing to remove the restrictions on Nepalese diplomatic relationships with other nations and with the formal alteration of Nepal's political status in 1923 came the removal of all restrictions on trade between Nepal and India. Indian capitalists now had easy access to a growing market in a period when their productive capacity was rising fast whilst world trade was tending to become more restrictive. Nepal maintained an overall balance of trade surplus in the interwar period despite the increase in imports of mass-manufactured commodities. The declining size of the surplus however heralded the slide towards chronic deficit which has marked the post-World War II situation.

The virtual absence of local industries and the limited importation of foreign skills indicate that industrial capitalism was not able to make any significant headway in Nepal. The social changes that would inevitably have resulted, had there been a development of indigenous capitalism, would have threatened the position of the ruling class. The continued strength of this class relates to the relative autonomy of the Nepalese state despite the increasingly dependent character of its economy. This situation has not changed significantly over the past twentyfive yeara.

Nepal clay has a very substantial balance of trade deficit particularly with India, with whom 90 per cent of her trade is carried on, and her subordinate position is reinforced by treaties regarding trade and the transit of goods to and from Nepal which seriously undermine what few possibilities might otherwise exist for local mass production in the field of high value/low bulk commodities, such as fabrics, paper, matches, electrical goods and handicrafts for the tourist. As Rana has observed.

> "while the very small size of Nepal makes trade essential, the landlocked position of the country chokes its ability to trade. Not only is it land-locked, but landlocked in an extreme fashion. Other landlocked countries—Switzerland for example—may choose amoung several avenues of access to the sea through different countries. Thus the competition between the several countries offering transit facilities provides most landlocked countries with the ability to bargain for easy terms of transit. But in Nepal's case even the building of the Kodari road from Kathmandu to the Chinese border has not altered the Indian monopoly over access to the sea" (Rana, 1973: 223).

This dependence for trade and for transit on India, virtually to the exclusion of any other country, serves to reinforce India's monopoly position in the Nepalese market and her ability to perpetuate that monopoly through international trade agreements which Nepal. has little choice but to accept. As a result, Nepal's ability to improve her balance of trade position through the export of manufactured goods is strictly limited—by treaty and by the superiority of Indian industrial capacity from which the Nepalese government is unable to protect its own industries. Nepal is thus obliged to rely in trade almost entirely on the export of primary products, many of which are likely to dwindle rapidly over the next decade as population growth and the associated increased demand for cultivable land and for food continue.

Within Nepal, as a result of this unbalanced structure of trade, the majority of those in commerce are involved in the distribution of imported manufactured goods, only a relatively small number dealing in export items. Retailers, particularly those in rural areas, tend to be drawn predominantly from the local peasant population, coming into commerce either to supplement their farm incomes or, having raised the capital to open the business from savings or a loan, to run it as a 'subsistence' enterprise. Larger merchants, however, tend also to be members of the landowning class and in the largest private and semi-public enterprises members of the nobility and even of the royal family are heavily involved. During the last decade there is some evidence that Indian factories are increasingly tending to send agents to order direct from the large retailers, thus weakening the position of the wholesalers. This tendency is as yet relatively little developed, but merchants are aware of the possibility of their being bypassed by the factories, which are able through their financial strength and organisation to move into the distribution of the commodities they produce and thus increase the extent of vertical integration. Even the larger merchants are therefore heavily dependent on the Indian factories and the extent to which the latter are concerned to penetrate the peripheral market of Nepal through direct control over the distribution of commodities; the retailers, in turn, although possibly somewhat less restricted than previously, are still almost entirely dependent on the large wholesalers in Nepal. In the absence of large-scale commodity production in Nepal, merchants themselves bulk-up such commodities as are produced and sold on the market within Nepal—mainly by scattered peasant farmers—and export them to India. The possibilities open to merchants to move 'backwards' into production within Nepal are limited, for the bulk of locally produced commodities represent surpluses generated by small peasants concerned for the most part to produce first for domestic consumption and only second for the market, but in all cases involved in a highly disaggregated form of production. Nevertheless, the growing number of rice and oil mills, and the existence of some small-scale processing, such as ghee refining, suggests that under certain circumstances merchant capital may be invested in minor industrial enterprises.

In general, however, the commercial sector depends on the existence across the border of large-scale manufacturing and the penetration by Indian industrial capitalism of the Nepalese market, rather than on any development within Nepal in the production of commodities for export. It is certainly to India's advantage to have, on its doorstep, an economy which provides a market however small and peripheral for its manufactured goods, but which at the same time, by virtue of its own failure to develop any large-scale commodity production, is able to provide labour and primary products for the Indian economy and recruits for its army. The failure of Nepal to develop large-scale commodity production is thus in large part a result of the domination of the Nepalese economy by India in whose interests it is to maintain a relatively stable but undeveloped 'non-capitalist' economy in Nepal.

The relationship between India and Nepal can be expressed in terms of a relationship between metropolis and satellite or between centre and periphery. These concepts have been used to summarise the structure of exploitation and domination characteristic of relations between developed and underdeveloped countries and can clearly be applied to the case of India and Nepal. But if Nepal may be regarded loosely as a peripheral area vis-a-vis the 'centre' that is India, it is important to recognise that the relationship is not simply between two spatially defined regions, one dominating and exploiting the other, as the terms imply—although certainly crucial aspects of the relationship may be summarized as flows between two regions—but between complex structures representing differing and often conflicting economic and political interests, not only with regard to the relationship between 'centre' and 'periphery' at the international level, but also within both 'centre' and 'periphery'. For example, it is in the interests of Indian industrialists as a class in India to penetrate Nepalese markets and encourage their expansion, while at the same time ensuring as far as possible that competition from Nepalese industry be kept to a minimum; and, in so far as these interests do not conflict with the view of national interest held by the Indian government (itself representing the interests of several different classes within Indian economy and society), the realisation of these business interests is facilitated by the drawing up of treaties by the Indian government with the Nepalese government relating to matters of trade and tariffs. Within Nepal, the 'periphery', it is clearly in the short-term interests of the ruling class, if not of the economy and society as a whole, to accept the terms of such treaties in order to maintain amicable relations with India. They thereby ensure a substantial flow of foreign aid (India is the largest aid donor) which is largely diverted into enterprises not antagonistic to the interests of the aristocratic landowning class still in power in Nepal, rather than into investment to improve and expand the productive base, without which Nepal will remain a dependent economy or even collapse. The latter would introduce the risk of radical economic and political changes and even possibly the emergence of a new class—a national bourgeoisie—whose interests would conflict both with those of the present ruling class in Nepal and with those of Indian capitalism.

But the concepts of 'centre' and 'periphery' can be applied within countries as well as to summarise a relationship between countries, and it is instructive in this regard to consider the way in which Nepal's political independence over the last century or more distinguishes it from other areas, similarly 'peripheral' in many respects but politically and administratively a part of India—and before that a part of British India. Such areas may be said to have benefited from colonial rule and, subsequently, from their integration within independent India, in terms of infrastructural developments and investments in forest protection and agricultural production denied to Nepal by the very nature of the tributary state under the Ranas; at the same time it could be argued, this greater integration into national affairs led to a higher rate of exploitation of such 'peripheral' areas in terms of labour export or surplus appropriation. Formal political autonomy has made it possible for Nepal to seek aid and assistance other than from India, although its success in this has been relatively limited to date, and to maintain some degree of control over its own internal affairs. The corollary of this, however, is that citizens of Nepal have little control over decisions taken in India which, nevertheless, affect their lives to a considerable extent—they are, in a sense, disenfranchised by virtue of their belonging to another political system. The existence of a national frontier has had little effect in protecting Nepal's productive enterprises, and this, together with smuggling on a massive scale, makes the frontier a political rather than an economic boundary.

Nepal can, therefore, usefully be seen, in economic terms at least, as a 'peripheral' area with respect to the Indian 'centre' albeit a 'periphery' with certain characteristics which distinguish it from other peripheral areas within India itself. Key features in this relationship are the structure and balance of trade between the two 'regions' and the export of labour from Nepal in return for remittances, in a sense two sides of the same coin of surplus appropriation: the apparent 'exchange' of labour and primary products for wages and finished manufactured goods.

Centre, Periphery and the Class Structure

If the concepts of 'centre' and 'periphery' can be applied generally to refer to uneven development and to the fact that the 'centre' tends to appropriate surplus from the 'periphery', largely to its own advantage and to maintain the structure of domination and dependency, the concepts can be applied within Nepal itself. It must be recognised here again, that, as in the case of relations between 'centre' and periphery' at the international level, so within a given country we are dealing not merely with flows between spatially defined regions but also with complex economic and political structures involving relations between different sections of society with differing and often conflicting interests.

Under the Ranas, as under the Shah kings of Gorkha before

them, the ruling class of Nepal was concentrated physically in Kathmandu:

> "The rulers were absentee landlords in the terai, the income from whose forests and lands they derived through intermediaries such as the Jamindars. They were also absent from the hills from which they drew the manpower for their army. The provincial governors, revenue or judicial officials, represented the highest echelons of the aristocratic hierarchy. The hinterland (the rest of Nepal) was mainly assessed in terms of its capacity to serve the metropolis (Kathmandu Valley). This divorce between centre and periphery was not terminated even after the 1950 'revolution' (Malla and Rana 1973: 16).

Within Nepal today Kathmandu—the nation's capital and the heart of economic and political power in the country—is able to benefit or more precisely certain sections of Nepalese society resident primarily in Kathmandu or with close connections to those resident there are able to benefit from the fact that Kathmandu is the place where decisions are made regarding the appropriation, distribution and realisation of surpluses generated by production in peripheral areas, such as the terai and the hills outside the Valley, and regarding the use of foreign aid, now a very substantial portion of the national income. As Malla and Rana point out:

> "in terms of development expenditures, a disproportionately large part of the total investment in the last two decades has gone to Kathmandu and its surrounding areas and to a lesser extent to the eastern terai. This has gone so far that the gulf between Kathmandu Valley and the subsistance economies of the hills areas of Nepal is growing similar to the gulf between the developed countries and the underdeveloped 'third' world. To the problem of cultural heterogeneity mentioned earlier, the process of development is adding the problem of economic heterogeneity to such a degree that truly disturbing dualities may emerge in the nation. These differences between areas are echoed by differences between social strata. The two decades of development have seen the emergence of a privileged stratum which skims the cream of development opportunities and benefits" (Malla and Rana 1973: 20).

One obvious result of this is that in many respects Kathmandu is provided with better facilities (schools, colleges, health facilities, public works, etc.) than any other part of the country. This in turn accentuates and reinforces the inequalities that distinguish Kathmandu from the rest of Nepal.

Originally pre-eminent by virtue of its agricultural richness and its strategic position on the long-distance trade routes, Kathmandu became the centre of wealth and power in Nepal through the location there of the central state apparatus and the government, by means of which the king and the ruling class were able to control the appropriation, distribution and allocation of such resources as were available to the state. The appropriation of surpluses from the terai and the use of manpower from the hills, together with the control of trade, were always the bases for the maintenance of the tributary state. Remarkably little has changed, even today, and the state apparatus still essentially serves the interests of the aristocratic landowning class.

In Nepal today, the monarchy, the royal family and the various branches of the Ranas constitute the elements of the aristocracy which holds ultimate control of affairs of state and hence of formal politics in Nepal. Involved heavily in both the army and the administration, they are substantial landowners although some have taken advantage of their highly privileged position to invest in hotels, import-export businesses, tourist agencies and other lucrative enterprises in Nepal and India. The aristocracy is, in a sense, a section of a much larger ruling class of landowners, the majority of whom constitute what might be loosely termed the gentry. Whereas the aristocracy is closely-knit in the extreme and predominantly of Chetri caste (including Thakuri and Rana), the ruling class as a whole is more diverse in ethnic and caste background and more widely dispersed throughout the country. Most members of the ruling class maintain close relations with government and bureaucrats in Kathmandu, often by means of relatives actually in government service, and many have houses in the capital; but some are to be found living on, or near, their estates outside the Kathmandu Valley and in general, even when predominantly absentee landlords, they maintain a strong local attachment, employing tenants and sharecroppers to cultivate much of the land but also frequently involving themselves in the running of the estate when they are present. Many of these large landowners are active in local and regional politics and usually carry considerable weight with the local and regional administration, even if sometimes there are disagreements between the local gentry, with their generally conservative outlook and interests, and the more 'modern' of the bureaucrats in the regional administration; often they attempt to ensure that such difficulties do not arise by placing their relatives or 'clients' in the bureaucracy, using their contacts in Kathmandu and in the regional administration.

Inefficient in many respects in terms of its use of the trained and untrained manpower it recruits and employs, the bureaucracy demonstrates a strong bias towards certain classes, towards certain castes and ethnic groups and towards certain regions within Nepal. This bias is general throughout the country and throughout the administrative hierarchy, although it becomes more pronounced towards the higher grades and in Kathmandu. Pradhan has written:

> "the higher echelon of the bureaucracy is composed of the influential members of Nepalese society. It is composed of the elite groups who enjoy a monopoly over educational opportunity in a country where the literacy rate is very low and there are not many job opportunities available to the people outside the government. The education that a man achieves is also determined by the class in which he was brought up. Higher education, which is considered as one of the requirements to be in the higher echelons of the administration, is not available to all. The bureaucratic elite tends to have different values, norms and outlook compared to the rest of the bureaucracy, and particularly in relation to the common people" (Pradhan 1973: 162).

In fact, the upper echelons of the bureaucracy—both elected and appointed—particularly in central government and administration derive overwhelmingly, as do the higher ranks of the army, from the landowning classes, especially from the aristocracy; they also include a significant number of what might be termed 'traditional officials' (predominantly Brahmin and Chetri by caste) employed under the Ranas as civil servants but acting in effect as 'clients' of the aristocracy, and still in post despite the formal termination of Rana rule in 1951.

At the top, the power of the Palace has increased over the last decade or so until virtually all major decisions are taken by, or with the full personal knowledge of, the king and the Palace Secretariat.

> "During the past decade, the Crown has become the pivot around which the traditional interest groups, the sacred elite, the military, and the landowning aristocracy, still revolve. These groups gain access to the Royal Palace through their supporters and representatives on the staff of the Palace Secretariat. The Palace Secretariat has become the nerve-centre of administration and political structure in Nepal, even though its dominant policy and decision-making role is not defined via the law or within the Constitution of this country. The function of the Palace Secretariat can be closely compared with the previous, all-powerful function of the hereditary Rana Prime Minister's office. That is, the Palace Secretariat today functions not only as a relay station between the King and Government, but also as a decision-making component, frequently using the Central Government's Secretariat as an instrument for the implementation of decisions. This situation has led to a 'dual government' structure." (Beenhakker 1973: 23).

Distinct from the 'Palace bureaucrats' and of increasing importance, despite their relatively small numbers and uncertain position in the power structure, are what could best be termed 'modern bureaucrats' recruited from somewhat more diverse social backgrounds than other high officials and having in common their relatively advanced education and technical expertise. Even if some of these, however, come from the middle class, the majority are the sons of landowners who have received their education at university in Kathmandu or abroad and who thus might be expected to have conflicting values and interests themselves. The position of the 'modern bureaucrats' within the administration and the army is somewhat anomalous, and as long as the Palace retains control of the apparatus of state their role will be determined in large part by the interests of ruling class as a whole. In general, however, they are committed to a greater extent than any other element within the ruling class and machinery of state to the idea of economic—and hence inevitably to a certain extent of political—development in Nepal. Many would probably (covertly now that political parties are banned) support many of the objectives of the Nepali Congress Party, and some were even members in the 1950's. This group might be expected to hold an increasingly influential position in government as the crisis in Nepal deepens, for their technical and organisational attributes give them powerful qualifications for coping with many of the economic, and even the political, problems that will inevitably develop over the next decade.

The bourgeoisie is represented, in so far as it can be identified as a distinct class, almost exclusively by the larger merchants and those involved in such recent growth areas as tourism and construction. For the extent of industrial development is so limited in Nepal that it is misleading to speak of an industrial capitalist class with distinct interests, although there is a handful of industrialists who have a powerful influence relative to their numbers. Equally, in agriculture it is difficult to identify a distinct class of capitalist farmers, the number of those using new inputs and employing labour on a regular or seasonal basis with a view to producing for the market being extremely small. If the bourgeoisie is predominantly mercantile it is also difficult to distinguish members of this merchant class, particularly towards the top, from the aristocracy or the landowning gentry whose members also often indulge in similar activities; even among smaller merchants it is not uncommon to find families whose members bridge the division between classes. The existence of an important Indian business community, and the growing involvement of the state, through such institutions as National Trading and Salt Trading, in the distribution and marketing of imported goods (notably salt, sugar and kerosene), both serve to limit the scope of activities available to this class, and its importance in the economy as a whole remains relatively small. Historically, trade has been subordinated to the interests of the landowning ruling class, particularly the aristocracy, and elements of this remain today, including the allocation of a limited number of dealerships for goods manufactured in Nepal and the absence from the National Assembly (Rastriya Panchayat) of any representative of the business community, much to the annoyance of those businessmen without privileged access to the inner circles of government.

All of these classes, though analytically distinct, in practice merge through the involvement of families in several forms of economic activity and the dense network of marriage and family ties that have grown up among what, after all, is a very small number of individuals within the total population of Nepal. It is important to retain the analytical distinctions between classes, for only in this way can one begin to perceive the basis for growing contradictions between different class interests; but, at the same time, it is understandable that most commentators prefer to write simply of a 'privileged elite' having private and public control above all to maintain its wealth and power, even if they do sometimes refer to this elite as a class itself. Thus, Malla and Rana write:

> "This stratum has truly spread its net wide. The strategic heights of most institutions such as the bureaucracy, the judiciary and the university are held by the privileged elite. It has concerned most of the new industrial and developmental openings. Whether in the sugar lands of the Narayani zone, in the jute trade from the eastern terai, in the newly irrigated lands, or in urban real estate, the subtle but certain grip of this class is always in evidence. Most significantly, perhaps, this class has perceived that control over the opportunities of higher and foreign education provides the strategic means of consolidating and perpetuating its dominance over the new Nepal" (Malla and Rana 1973: 22).

The majority of familes included in this 'elite' which Rana and Malla see as originating in the 'client' families and land- owners subordinate to, but only a little less powerful and wealthy than, the Rana aristocracy prior to 1951 and benefiting from the termination of Rana rule:

> "come from either the old 'Bhardar' groups of Brahmins and Chetris or the higher caste Newar groups. Geographically, most of them are inhabitants of Kathmandu or have become Kathmandu-based with their entry into the charmed circle" (Malla and Rana 1973: 22).

The middle class in Nepal, consisting of the educated and professional self-employed (doctors, lawyers, etc.), the bulk of university and college teachers, journalists and those in the administration, is small but it is from this section of society that some of the most vocal criticism of present government policy and action (or inaction) comes. Even here, however, there is evidence to suggest that, given the degree of state control over employment for such individuals—in teaching and the administration in particular—the criticism is often muted by self-interest, with only those in exile and the minority willing to risk official displeasure managing to maintain a constant opposition, if only in verbal form, to the continued authoritarian form of government behind a facade of democratic popular participation and the failure of the government to implement successfully a programme of agrarian reform and broad-based economic development.

The petty bourgeoisie, notoriously difficult to define, may be seen as comprising two distinct elements: the small commodity producers and shopkeepers in the urban areas, on the one hand (see Chapter 9) and petty officials, minor bureaucrats of clerical grades, school teachers and lower-level trained personnel (including what is usually termed, in Nepal, 'middle level manpower') on the other (see Chapter 8). These stand in an ambiguous and ambivalent position vis-a-vis the mass of the population—peasants and workers—on the one hand, and the ruling classes, on the other. Unwilling to lose that little they have that distinguishes them from the mass of the population, they tend to be conservative and obedient to demands from above; but at the same time they feel themselves exploited and oppressed by those above them or with control over greater resources than themselves, and in this sense may come to feel sufficiently aggrieved to oppose the status quo, particularly if, as in the case of the so-called 'untouchable' low castes, they are discriminated against socially despite legislation to prevent such discrimination.

The vast majority of the population of Nepal are peasants owning their own means of production (land, livestock, implements) and producing primarily for their own consumption. It is possible to distinguish strata within the peasantry on the basis of resources owned and the employment or sale, or labour in agriculture (the conventional division is between rich, middle and poor peasants) but it is the 'middle peasant', who neither employs nor sells labour as a commodity, that characterises the peasantry as a class. Rich peasants have much in common with the small commodity producers of the urban petty bourgeoisie, while the poor peasant (see Chapter 3) is often virtually indistinguishable, except by the land he owns, from those almost totally dependent for their livelihood on working for others, such as tenants and sharecroppers on the estates of the large landowners, the agricultural labourers employed by the larger farmers and rich peasants (see Chapter 6), or skilled artisans dependent on the system of annual fixed payments from other peasant households in return for services for a livelihood (see Chapter 4).

In fact, the rural proletariat, in the sense of a free labour force with no ties to the land and no other means of livelihood but the sale of their labour is relatively limited in size; the vast majority of those primarily dependent on wage labour for their income do have access to some land, however small a plot, and indeed, as has been said, it is often difficult to distinguish the agricultural labourer from the poor peasant selling his labour for a part of the year on a temporary or seasonal basis. The number of those depending largely on wage labour in agriculture is, however, very considerably greater than that outside agriculture, where the employment possibilities are limited. Among the major sources of employment outside agriculture, menial jobs in government service are probably more important than any other; also portering, construction work, employment in the hotel business or in casual labour of various kinds account for relatively small numbers. Those employed in fairly regular work in industrial concerns, the industrial poletariat, is very small indeed, and restricted almost entirely to the terai, in particular to the eastern terai, where the larger factories are situated (see Chapter 8).

The interests of the different classes outlined above are distinct and in some cases in contradiction with each other. Ethnic and caste differences remain of major importance for the majority of the population and serve to obscure the class differences they cut across; social and political discrimination on grounds of caste or ethnic group arouses greater antagonism than does the less overt discrimination in terms of unequal control over resources. It is, however, important, that correspondences do exist, and are seen to exist, between social inequalities and class differences, particularly among the poor. For the present, the ruling class, through the state apparatus—particularly the administration, the police, the courts and the security service, and through the operation of patronage on a massive scale—maintains overall control and the level of oposition remains, for the time being, relatively low, although there are indications of growing unrest. Unrest within the state of Nepal reflects the response of different sections of society to the progressive underdevelopment of the economy and to the specific pressures that this exerts on different classes and social groups. Detailed discussion of the economic crisis Nepal currently faces cannot be undertaken here, and in any case has been presented elsewhere (cf Blaikie, Cameron and Seddon 1979). Nonetheless it is important to note here certain central indications of the extent and severity of this crisis. The implications of this general situation and prospect for the most disadvantaged groups in Nepal—the lower classes, will constitute an essential component of the discussion developed in the following chapters.

Politics, Economics and the Coming Crisis

Today there are increasing signs of unrest within the country as a whole both in the hills and in the terai, as well as in the Kathmandu Valley itself, albeit deriving from different immediate situations and taking different forms. It seems likely that before long, if economic and social conditions do not improve rapidly, such unrest will become more pervasive and better organised. The ruling classes confront a basic dilemma; that of promoting the economic and social changes without which the country as a whole will collapse, bringing their own downfall with it, but at the same time preserving the essential political stability in whose absence their own privileged position becomes rapidly of no significance. Other countries in which somewhat similar situations exist or have until recently existed include Morocco and Ethiopia. In such cases, unless radical changes take place, both in the extent of popular participation and, correspondingly, in the relations of production (the class relations) associated with the various forms of production that together constitute the economy, through a major shift in the distribution of power and of resources, the chances of achieving either political stability or economic and social development remain extremely small.

In this regard, the period between the official re-instatement of the monarchy in 1951 and the banning of all political parties and assumption of absolute powers by the king in 1960 marks a restless interlude, somewhat similar to that experienced by many ex-colonies immediately after independence, during which popular democratic forces struggled for supremacy against the forces of conservatism and autocratic rule, and for the time being have lost.

Indian independence in 1947 and the evident power of the Indian Congress Party had a major political repercussions within Nepal. The Nepali Congress Party, for example, grew significantly in strength and ambition during the period between 1947 and 1951, finding considerable support not merely among the petty bourgeoisie and intellectuals, but also among peasants and the tiny body of workers, and among disaffected members of the nobility, some of whom became leaders in the Party. When King Tribhuvan returned from India early in 1951 he was obliged to recognise this growing 'radical' movement and expressed his intention to act as constitutional monarch and to create an elected advisory body to draw up a new constitution for Nepal along democratic lines. In the meanwhile, the Interim Government Act of 1951 restored legal and constitutional powers to the king. The Ranas, though officially ousted from power retained very considerable influence in the circles of government and in the army. This was reflected in the composition of the first Cabinet created by the king—a coalition of Ranas and members of the Nepali Congress. The attempt to forge a political alliance between such fundamentally opposed camps was doomed to failure, and the next Cabinet consisted almost entirely of Nepali Congress members, the Ranas retiring from the limelight of formal politics to strengthen their position elsewhere in 'the corridors of power'.

During the next decade numerous political parties sprung up, many of them essentially the personal following of a particular political figure rather than popular movements in any sense, and experimentation characterised Nepalese government as Cabinets were formed and dissolved, Advisory Assemblies established and re-established, and parties created and fragmented. This served primarily to strengthen the power of the Palace and those who had the ear of the king. In 1954 the King proclaimed that supreme rights in the legislative field should be vested in him pending the drawing up of the Constitution.

After the death of Tribhuvan in 1955 his son and successor, Mahendra, declared his concern to hold general elections as soon as possible; when drafted in 1959 the Constitution allowed for a parliamentary system of government with party representation but provided for a monarchy with residual and emergency powers. The elections of 1959 gave an overwhelming victory to the Nepali Congress, which tood 74 of the 109 seats; a Cabinet was formed under B.P. Koirala and the first popularly elected government officially took power. But not for long.

The uncertainties of government during the previous seven years had made the implementation of major reforms, had they been strongly desired, very difficult, and the economy had remained largely stagnant while the various parties and pressure groups struggled to mould the future political system of Nepal.

The notion of economic planning had been accepted early on and the first Five-Year Plan was drawn up for the period 1956 to 1961; but overall the results were not satisfactory. No new industrial venture of any significance came into being during this period and indeed several of those industries established in the terai during the Second World War had gone into liquidation. In 1950 Nepal had signed a trade and transit treaty with India which assured that country's virtual domination of Nepal's economy, and a perpetuation of the unequal relationship between the two countries. (In the period between 1956 and 1963, for example, Nepal's imports from India rose by about Rs. 430,000,000, while her exports rose in the same period by only about Rs. 190,000,000, increasing the balance of trade deficit from Rs. 72,000,000 to Rs. 310,000,000, the burden of maintaining the balance of payments being borne entirely by 'invisible' earnings from India, through the export of labour in large part). In the field of agriculture, attempts were made to alter the very complex structure of land tenure, with the primary objective of increasing revenue from the land, and only incidentally to improve productivity and the condition of the producers.

The government that came to power in 1959 was openly concerned to implement radical reforms, designed to 'modernise' the administration and to encourage economic and political development to take place through popular participation. Its objectives included radical agrarian reform, a fully planned economy, the elimination of discrimination and privilege in recruitment to the civil service, the army, and in other walks of life, and the reorganisation of the administration. Among its credentials as the party and government of radical change the Nepali Congress had observers' status at the Socialist International and was a member of the Asian Socialist Conference.

In the upper house or senate, the eighteen royal appointees who constituted half of its membership systematically opposed the programme and actions of the Nepali Congress party and its government, while outside official political circles the comparatively radical views and intentions of the government aroused considerable fears among the nobility and other more conservative sections of the populations, including the Palace itself, and pressure groups began to prepare the defence of traditional vested interests against proposed government policy (cf Pradhan 1973: 146). In December 1960, the king, with reference to article 55 of the Constitution, revoked the Constitution itself, dissolved parliament and the Cabinet, suspended the Fundamental Rights and promised to institute 'a more suitable form of democracy' than that based on parties and parliament. The Prime Minister, Koirala, was arrested, as were many other local and central party officials, and all political parties banned. Higher ranking officers of the army and the police, as well as the secret service, were on the king's side, but not the overwhelming majority of the younger officers and civil servants. Given such a fundamental rift even within the State apparatus, it was inevitable that the next fifteen years were to see the monarchy performing a dangerous tight-rope act to maintain political stability and yet encourage a modicum of economic and social development. However, since the assumption of absolute powers by the king and the institution of so-called 'panchayat democracy', the economic situation of Nepal has deteriorated significantly, despite the increasingly large volume of foreign aid provided by India and other countries.

In 1974 a UN report on Nepal opened with the bleak statement: "Nepal is poor and is daily becoming poorer" (ARTEP 1974: 1). It has been pointed out that, during the years 1956 to 1965, "the limited available economic data suggests that overall national output...grew at the average rate of about 2 per cent per annum, while population growth tallied about 2.5 per cent per year" (Beenhakker 1973: 3), and figures for the period 1961 to 1969, relating to the annual rate of growth in per capita food production—a crucial indicator in a country where over 90 per cent of the population are dependent on subsistence agriculture—suggest that, at best, Nepal attained a zero rate of growth during that decade (OECD 1972: 105). The IBRD/IDA Bank Atlas gives a decline of GNP per capita of 0.1 in the 1965-73 period.

But Nepal in the late 1970's is not just a very poor country (one of the world's 'poorest twenty-five' according to the UN and probably in the poorest five) that is increasingly unable to provide adequately for its rapidly growing population: that would be an over-simplification and in many respects an under-statement of the problem. The country now faces a crisis whose major components include serious over-population, ecological collapse in the densely populated and highly vulnerable hill areas (where 30 per cent of the cultivable land supports some 60 per cent of the population), the elimination of certain important 'natural' resources (such as timber), and overall declining yields in agriculture (for a fuller discussion of the crisis in Nepal, see Blaikie, Cameron and Seddon, 1979). This is likely to lead to a general and rapid economic decline, associated with growing local food shortages as subsistence production fails to keep pace with population increase, a retreat from the production of commodities for the market into the 'domestic' economy, and an increasing inability to pay for imported commodities (including foodstuffs). Only massive increases in the already enormous flow of foreign aid could then conceivably prevent the collapse of the Nepalese economy and the emergence of widespread political unrest, both threatening the continuing viability of the Nepalese state as presently constituted.

> "The financial support of the four major aid-giving nations (India, China, USA, USSR) has been accompanied by the rhetoric of change. However, their aid has assisted the monarchy both directly and indirectly to create a better-equipped and better-trained army and to put a large number of potentially restive youngmen on the bureaucratic payrools. It is true that aid-giving agencies of several nations have pressed the king for reforms, but aid programs have been maintained despite the continued absence of significant reforms because, for these nations, change had a lower priority than maintenance of the status quo, which they all found to their advantage for different reasons. Thus, in the short run at any rate, foreign assistance has enhanced the monarchy's chances of survival and has inhibited the growth of pressures for fundamental change" (Gaige 1975: 200).

In this context the failure of the government to identify and overcome the inherent weaknesses and contradictions of the

Nepalese political economy is crucial. The explanation lies in the fact that, whatever its relative autonomy, the nature of the state apparatus and its functioning is ultimately determined by the political economy as a whole: the contradictions within the political economy are largely reproduced within the state apparatus, of which the government is but one element. Whether the government and the state apparatus is able, in the future, to intervene more effectively to transform the condition of the lower classes, thus depends in large part on the changing alignment of classes within Nepal.

CHAPTER 3

POOR PEASANTS

The Peasantry in the Nepalese State

The role of the peasantry in the political economy of Nepal since the unification of the Nepalese State until at least the first quarter of this century, has been to provide the bulk of the surplus on which a ruling landed aristocracy relied. Although this is no longer the case, the development of a tributary state following the unification of Nepal during the 18th century as a means of extracting and converting this surplus into use for the ruling class has been instrumental in the development of the crisis which the peasantry faces today. Simply, the crisis faces both the peasantry itself as well as the viability of the Nepalese State, since Nepal is overwhelmingly a peasant economy (albeit significantly supported by foreign aid). This economy is under severe pressure due to increasing population and declining productivity, and the Nepalese state is unable to transform itself from an essentially tributary state into one that can effectively intervene in the production process. On the one hand the taxability of the peasant is reduced to near vanishing point, and on the other the interests of the landed aristocracy are still broadly in line with policies pursued by the institutions of state—inspite of considerable pressures from a local bourgeoisie and a small group of intellectuals and technocrats in the university and government who are fully aware of the situation. The interests of the ruling class coincide with (or at least do not significantly diverge from) most policies of development aid agencies, the main aim of which can be summarised as one of preserving the peasantry, which from the point of view of the ruling class itself is of importance only in as far as it appears to guarantee the political stability of the Nepalese state. In the last twenty years, and particularly in the last five, alternative sources of revenue to those extracted from the peasantry through the traditional means of tribute, enforced military service, slavery and corvee labour, have been sought (and frequently found) in the form of international aid, which has provided funds for a small circle of influential families to set up services for rich tourists, such as luxury hotels, an airline, large-scale merchanting and a few industrial enterprises. Thus Malla and Rana write:

> "This stratum has truly spread its net wide. The strategic heights of most institutions such as the bureaucracy, the judiciary and the university are held by this privileged elite. It has cornered most of the new industrial and development openings. Whether in the Jagir lands of the Narayani zone, in the jute trade from the eastern terai, in the newly irrigated lands, or in urban real estate, the subtle but certain grip of this class is always in evidence" (Malla and Rana 1973: 227).

By and large the bureaucracy, which has grown enormously during the past eight years (partly to lend credibility to requests for international aid), likewise has a very limited capability for achieving the positive developmental effects which the 'rhetoric of development' would lead prospective aid-givers to believe. Thus, as will be argued here, the peasant today is faced with a crisis of production, increasing impoverishment and eventual destitution, and a state which, for all its developmental institutions, is unable and too frequently uninterested in providing the necessary reforms, information, credit, and inputs.

After the unification of the Nepalese State during the 18th century, the means of appropriation of surpluses from the peasantry were strengthened. Local rulers who had been conquered by Prithvi Narayan Shah, members of the royal family and favoured generals were given grants of land or given the right to tax the produce therefrom, thereby altering the relations of production existing at the time. Certainly the previous immigration of Indians into the lower valleys of the Nepalese hills from the 12th century, bringing with them rice culture, including terracing, irrigation and the plough, had introduced different relations of production from those prevalent in the predominatly pastoralist economy of the hill peoples (Bista 1967). However, with the unification of Nepal and the establishment of a tributary state, the privatisation of land was further enhanced. Each local lord had the responsibility and opportunity to collect tribute on his own and central government's behalf. (The efforts to secure these surpluses prompted the royal ministers to write to local rulers advising them not to tax the peasants so harshly that they (the peasants) would flee into the jungle and attempt to find their subsistence elsewhere).

However, forest lands during the 19th century were not appropriated and were still considered communal in all but title (since they belonged to the Government), and the right of usufruct was free to all those who cared to avail themselves of it. Many of the peasants' requirements came from the forest —through fishing, hunting, collecting wood for fuel and construction, and most important, herding of buffalo, cows, goats, and on the higher pastures, sheep. As population grew, and with it the extent of arable land, forest lands declined in area, and hence private ownership and control was extended over an increasing part of the economy. The land, however, was frequently worked by communal labour arrangements based upon reciprocity (called in the hills, *parma*). Population growth also had the effect of preventing the poor peasant without sufficient land to support himself, to clear the jungle and increase his arable land. In fact labour shortages to work the land were one of the primary problems which the ruling class encountered. Thus both the peasant and the land-owning class both found that at least up to the latter part of the 18th century labour was the scarcest resource.

It is difficult to establish with any degree of accuracy and provide specific data for the onset of some of the effects of population growth which was to transform the situation. It is likely that falling yields due to the extension of arable land to steeper and less suitable slopes, and a disturbance in the forest-arable ratio, started to have a considerable effect in some areas at the turn of this century, but the effects of the First World War probably disguised this process in the following way. Emigration had long become one of the responses to oppressive taxation and the inability to earn a subsistence in Nepal. In addition, employment in the British army offered relatively high earnings and a security in old age in the form of a pension. During the years 1914-18, no less than 56,580 Gurkha soldiers served overseas (Mojumdar 1973), and of course remittances and pensions thereafter tended to mask the crisis in productivity.

What is important was that the tributary state, established by Prithvi Naravan Shah, continued to fritter its remaining resources upon an extravagent life-style which reached its most ostentatious at the turn of the century, for the benefit of a handful of families who were either oblivious or uncaring of the crisis of the peasantry which would eventually become the crisis of all classes in Nepal. During the 'twenties vast stocks of timber (*shorea robusta,* or sat in Nepali and Hindi) were sold to British contractors who were engaged at the time in railway construction and required timber for railway sleepers (Buchanan 1934). Here already, the source of tribute was shifting from the labour of peasantry on the land to a non-renewable resource— at least in the context of a tributary state, to which the idea of replanting forests or replacing them with productive agriculture never occurred. However, population growth and an increased demand for foodgrains led to an increase in the cultivable area at the expense of the forest in the hills of Nepal (the terai being unsuitable for widespread settlement until the eradication of malaria there in the early 1960's). The present situation is summed up by recent writers about the Nepalese rural economy:

> "visual evidence of already existing over-population, includes deforestation, erosion and silting. Within the last decade wooded

hill-tops have been cut doom or severely depleted, terraces have been extended to the tops of hills, and cattle have had to graze further away. In some cases, hill-top terraces have leached out, have been abandoned, and have started to collapse on terraces below. Villagers often have to go much further to cut fodder for animals. The complex interaction of wood for fuel, cattle for manure and draught, and manured terraces for rice etc. is becoming increasingly vulnerable to overcrowding of the hill areas. If conditions worsen, areas now cultivated will have to be abandoned." (Enke 1971: 20).

"Population growth in the context of a traditional agrarian technology is forcing farmers onto even steeper slopes, slopes unfit for sustained farming, even with the astonishingly elaborate terracing practised there. Meanwhile, villagers must roam farther and farther from their homes to gather fodder and firewood, thus surrounding villages with a widening circle of denuded hillsides." (Eckholm 1976: 77).

"Two Nepalese scholars, Pashupati Shamsher and Mohammed Mohsin have completed an interesting study of leadership in the eastern hills in which 59% of the 243 village leaders they interviewed stated that productivity of their land was declining." (Gaige 1975: 64).

Excerpts from a recent report on the state of the eco-system in Nepal referring to the west central region describe the relation between population growth and accelerated erosion:

"Sheet erosion on outward sloping terraces as well as gulley erosion due to denudation of slopes is quite widespread. In general, south-eastern and eastern slopes are more eroded than others because of more intensive land use in these locations".

"...In Tansen town, a spring supplying the population with 50 litres per head per day was destroyed by a recent landslide". "...The Tansen area is remarkable for the almost complete absence of efficient terracing. Most of the dryland activites are carried out on steeply sloping fields, thus leading to extensive erosion". (Rieger et al. 1976: 58 and 73).

Oral histories given to us during our own investigations reveal a similar syndrome of declining yields, soil slips, landslides and the failure of perennial water sources; and frequently wholescale morphological changes in the landscape (increased drainage densities, talus formation and denudation of upper slopes etc.).

The declining yields in the hills result from an increasingly serious energy crisis in which a sufficient transference of fertility from forest to arable land (through the collection of fodder for stallfed animals, whose manure is composted with their straw bedding and applied to the fields) can no longer be maintained. Even with a static population, aggregate yields can only be maintained by a further clearance of forest producing a vicious circle. Soil erosion too is not confined to cultivated areas, but also affects grasslands (areas which used to be forest, and occupy ridge tops and land over about 5,500 feet) and scrub and secondary forest. In fact our own statistical analysis using aerial photographic data in the hilly areas of Kosi Zone (Lesslie 1974) indicates that unhealed soil slips and landslides are concentrated in these latter areas. Thus it is widely recognised (not least by the Nepalese peasantry itself) that environmental stress is widespread throughout the hills of Nepal, and is systemic in its nature.

The emergence of this crisis, varying across space and in its timing, is the most recent manifestation of the changing relationship between population and the political economy. In the past-population for the ruling class of unified Nepal represented a source of agricultural surpluses, corvee labour, and recruitment into an army which was used to coerce further peasantries. When land was plentiful it was easier for peasants to flee oppressive taxation and the requirements of forced labour by escaping. Slavery became the appropriate relation between ruling class and peasantry which in a situation where labour was scarce, had some degree of independence and the means of evasion. By the turn of this century population growth meant that slavery was no longer required by the ruling class (and was officially abolished shortly after World War II).

The Peasant Economy

The economy of the peasant is essentially a domestic one

in which production is for the use of household or kin, and surpluses, such as they exist, are redistributed by payments to the temple, festivals, poor relatives, etc. (In the past production by the peasantry also had to produce a surplus for the local lord who had been granted rights of taxation or usufruct over the land). There was undoubtedly considerable inequality within the domestic economy, but both a redistribution mechanism within it, as well as the social and physical accessibility of communal resources of the village (the forest), prevented the process of differentiation of the peasantry from being inexorable and increasing. As a result of population pressure producers within this economy found that the fundamental aim of self-sufficiency in food staples required both more land to be taken into cultivation and also other crops to be displaced (particularly cotton and tobacco), as productivity per unit of land and labour declined through time. This led to a situation where, to purchase the goods which were hitherto produced within the domestic economy, a source of cash had to be found, thus causing contradictions within it. Thus a tightening of the availability of land, loss of grazing and declining levels of plant nutrients, and an increasing privatisation of these resources, all started to cause certain disadvantaged households to seek sources of subsistence outside the purely domestic economy described. A process of differentiation, already in existence since the introduction of the package of new agricultural techniques during the 12th century' (the plough, terracing and *padi* cultivation, private control over land and a caste hierarchy by Indian immigrants) thereby was accelerated. However, it was not only a result of a *transfer* of resources from one section of the peasantry to another, but also of a *decline* in the productivity of land and labour—although both processes were and are present. Thus differentiation of the peasantry in the hills was (and still is) very slow, and in an important sense, deriving from *internal* processes.

The peasantry in the terai had a much more recent history and differs in some respects from that described in the hills. Endemic malaria in the terai limited settlement in the area to indigenous groups, of whom the Tharu are the most numerous, and some immigrants from Oudh (in what is now Uttar Pradesh) during the 19th century. The importance of the terai nonetheless grew with growing numbers of migrants from India, and through the encouragement by the Rana regime of the settlement of hill people there. Large grants of land were distributed to military personnel, senior government servants and others in favour with the ruling families, creating a class of semi-feudal (and frequently absentee) landlords. It was only after malaria eradication that larger numbers of hillmen started to settle in the terai in the mid-1960's. Some purchased land from the indigenous peoples and from the semi-feudal landlords who were created by the then deposed Rana regime (particularly after the Land Reform Act of 1964). Others settled (and still settle) illegally, squatting at the edges of the uncleared jungle and attempting to evade the efforts of the police and the Ministry of Forests to evict them. It is perhaps here that the struggle is at its most acute between. the marginalised peasant and the state (which directly reflects the interests of large landowners, contractors seeking licences; to fell and sell timber, and senior bureaucrats who stand to gain enormously through the granting of licences). Police brutality, and the practice of local officials demanding a share of the crop produced by these squatters (*sukumbhasi*) in return for turning a blind eye to their continued occupation of the land have been a continuing problem for the poor peasant of the terai, and a symptom of the action of the state in attempting to safeguard (what there is left of) its last non-renewable resource for the benefits of its ruling class.

A recent paper (Feldman and Fournier 1976) has provided an analysis of the social relations and agricultural production in the terai. While much of the general prognosis for the decline of agricultural surplus and its effects upon the viability of the Nepalese state is similar to that taken in this book and elsewhere (Blaikie, Cameron and Seddon, 1979, in press), their analysis of the relationship between the landless labourer and poor peasant of the hills and the agricultural surplus of the terai differs from our own in a number of ways. These authors maintain that the terai was settled by a package of possessors of capital and a rural proletariat, the former influential families from the hills and a few from India, and the latter indigenous swidden cultivators now forced to clear the forest. Although there is little evidence of a secular increase in the concentration of land ownership today, historical conditions of settlement ensured a very substantial concentration of ownership. The development of the agricultural surpluses derives from the seasonal nature of the demand for agricultural labour (since there are few irrigation facilities, agricultural operations being dominated by monsoon), which is met by the migration of submarginal farmers in the hills, who make up the deficits from production on their own farms by obtaining wage labour in the terai during harvesting (and to a lesser extent other) operations. Therefore, in Feldman and Fournier's view it is wrong to conceptualise the phenomenon of seasonal migrations and the coexistence of small subsistence holdings alongside the large surplus producing enterprises as one either of a dualism in which the former representing the 'traditional' sector 'withering away' in contradiction to the expansion of the 'modern' development sector; or of two forms of production (capitalist and domestic) which articulate in some common social formation—the latter conceptualisation, it is claimed; implying an independence 'which is not a reflection of reality' and the forcing of inappropriate categories. Our own view differs partly in its emphasis—a detailed analysis of the economy and society of the hills we feel is important but should not exclude its relation with that of the terai and of India; but also as a result of a difference in the perception of the concrete situation. First, the contribution to the supply of seasonal agricultural labour made by peasant households in the hills is very small—it is mostly met by peasant households with sub-marginal farms and landless labourers in the terai itself and in India; hence the accumulation of surpluses by large rural capitalists in the terai is not underwritten by the hill peasant (the cost of the reproduction of his labour being largely born by his labour on his own farm). Secondly, the importance of the large farmer in the terai has been over-played (the authors admit in the appendix that their (very small) sample was probably biassed towards the large farmer). Larger surveys (of 300 households in the terai) indicate that the agricultural surpluses are actually produced by a much larger number of small farmers or advantaged peasants, only some of whom hire labour seasonally. This is a particularly important issue in the analysis of future trends in the polit-ical economy of Nepal. The agricultural surpluses have steadily been declining (our traffic and production surveys reached independent estimates of the exported surplus of the terai in the west central region as being presently of the order of 60-80,000 tons per year). This decline we see is due to a number of factors: declining yields (where the stored up fertility in the soils recently cleared of forest is not being replaced); the reduction in the size of holdings due to population pressure; and the failure of newly established farms in the cleared jungle to contribute to marketed surplus (due to the fact that it is largely the poor peasants from the hills and India who are the active colonisers here).

A counter-trend to the declining marketed surplus in the terai might be the extension of capitalistic behaviour on the part of the more advantaged farmers. The transition in the terai could be characterised by aggressive expansion and deepening of the forces of production by an emergent class who would tend to purchase land and force cultivators off their tenancies, and invest in machinery, chemical fertiliser and high yielding seeds.

It has been widely recognised for some time that capitalism has been penetrating Indian agriculture for twenty years or more, and a new class of farmer has emerged where production is specifically for the market; where profits are reinvested to improve the efficiency of the means of production; and where relations of production involve the landowner employing wage labour. Without becoming entangled in essentially logical positivist diversions into the recognition of a capitalist as a 'pure' type (since it is a process of transition, in which its elements are in constant and changing contradiction), it is clear that this sort of revolution has made little headway in Nepal.

Statistics on the distribution of land holdings, amount and distribution of the adoption of new inputs, marketable surplus and the relations of production of the farm, indicative as they may be in a general sense, require a detailed analytical treatment which is not appropriate nor relevant in an essay on poor peasants, (and has been tackled elsewhere, see Blaikie, Cameron and Seddon, 1979, in press). However, a brief review of some indication of these changes is in order. Nepal as a whole has the lowest contributions of chemical fertilisers to cereal production in South Asia (at a response rate of 10:1, the percentage of total cereal production contributed by fertilisers was estimated to be 1.17 in Nepal, 7% in Iran and 19.4% in Pakistan, IBRD Annex. 8:19). Furthermore the significance for the west central region of average Nepalese figures is further reduced since the spatial distribution of fertiliser use is extremely uneven, over half the fertiliser sales taking place in the Kathmandu Valley. The estimated use of fertiliser per ha in the hills excluding the Kathmandu Valley is about 4 kg, and only double that in the terai. The increase in the use of other new inputs is likewise very sluggish, and various estimates of yields in both the hills and terai suggest that they are declining (Blaikie, Cameron, Feldman, Fournier and Seddon 1976). Data on yields through time cross-classified by farm characteristics (e.g. farm size) are unfortunately not available. However, our own scanty data show no evidence at all of any marked increase in yields nor marketed surplus produced by larger farms. Lastly, there is little evidence of a differentiation in the size of land holdings. On the other hand, evidence in India points to an aggressive purchasing of land by both capitalist landowner, as well as merchant/rentiers by means of foreclosing upon the debts of the poorer peasants. Our own records of sales of land (elicited by interview of 667 farmers in the west central region) show that over the last five years, in the terai, nine per cent of households have made a sale of land and in the hills thirteen per cent. However, the majority of sales were in effect merely an exchange of one plot in order to purchase another (often more conveniently located). Only seven distress sales occurred. Also purchases of land were made by households of all size categories of existing land holdings.

The implications of the foregoing discussion for the poor peasants in the terai are threefold. First, there is little evidence of the poor peasant being forced off his land (or land possessed by him under verbal tenancy agreements) by an expansionary class of rich peasants or larger landowners. The process of differentiation derives not from the development of an active capitalism in agriculture from within but from the enervating effects of capitalism from without (linked with the interests of the ruling class in Nepal). This process is described in more detail below. Secondly, the labour market still retains some pre-capitalist characteristics (see Chapter 6 on Agricultural Labourers). Although wage labour is by far the most widespread type of employment household servants are frequently employed, sometimes on a yearly contractual basis, sometimes on a permanent one where the employer will accept some responsibility for workers' dependents. Thirdly, wages rates are not forced down to the level necessary for the survival and reproduction of labour. The customary daily rate in the terai is four *kuruwas* of paddy (2.48 kg), and is estimated to support a working man and a child of between five and ten years old. The rate is well above that paid across the border in India, thus encouraging large numbers of landless labourers in India to migrate to the terai at times of harvest seeking employment. Another reason for the maintenance of particularistic relations of employment in the terai was, and continues to be that trusted servants and local labour are very important in a 'frontier' area in the terai, where law and order is frequently tenuous. Armed bands of robbers (*gundaa*) are common, and their most frequent targets are landlords' houses.

Responses

Having located the peasantry within the political economy of contemporary Nepal, it is now possible to turn in more detail to the responses of the poor peasant to his environment which we have described, namely declining yields, environmental decline, ineffective state apparatus, and the absence of any significant and rapid progressive developments in the productive base. At the outset, it is important to remember that the middle peasant today is the poor peasant of the next generation, and the labourer the generation after (or maybe even sooner), although little aggressive action on the part of other classes is necessary—merely that of population growth itself and its compounded effects. Therefore an answer to the question 'what can the peasant do?' must be firmly rooted in a time dimension as his changing demographic environment, which is at present fundamentally stable over the next ten years or so (although definitely deteriorating). It is the underlying assumption of this approach that the poor peasant can only respond as an individual to a political economy, the shape of which has been, and is still quite outside his control.

The general process of impoverishment of the peasantry outlined above has prompted peasants to seek on an individual basis means by which their domestic economy can be maintained or supported from other sources. A large number of possible choices are open to the individual household, although the ability of a particular household to choose one or more may be limited. The basic problem of the domestic economy is the increasing difficulty of producing sufficient foodstuffs from the farm, creating the necessity either to increase the productivity of the land worked by the household; to produce a small amount of commodities for the market in order to finance the purchase of these shortfalls in grain and other household requirements; or to sell the labour of the household, either locally, or by migrating for a period of time. The choice between these responses and various combinations of them will be determined by what is termed here the *access position* of the household. (We indentify the household as being the relevant social unit, defined as being a group of individuals each one of whom either contributes to its earning capacity (by direct productive labour or via remittances of cash or kind), or eats at a common hearth). The access position of the household is derived from (a) control over the sum of various physical assets, both private (land, labour, livestock, implements) and public (forest and water for irrigation purposes); and (b) from the sum of social assets (e.g. the household's membership of a certain caste which enables the individual to have a better chance of obtaining a post in the army or the administration, or merely a predominance of the male gender in the household opening up many more employment opportunities outside the home than exist for women). The definition and nature of an 'asset' is determined by the political economy, and developments within it will alter the importance of each asset (and with such a change the class position of all households).

There is a considerable problem in combining the analytical category of household and of class. Both are useful, and in important senses are merely different ways of looking at the same sets of relationships. Households and even individuals within the household (particularly those of the "Third World") are involved in a number of modes of production. Hence the individual or household may well have a number of different class positions. The way in which economic and social decision-making units (households) combine these various activities is determined by their access position, which in turn is defined as the bundles of assets they have at a particular moment, and the uses to which these various assets can be put in combination with others. The *distribution* of these assets across a population of households, as well as the broad pattern of responses is determined by the logic of the domestic economy with its characteristic relations of production, approaches to the market and use of surpluses.

From Table 1 which lists possible responses on the part of the peasant, it can be seen that there will exist a set of possible responses which each household can make. That response which the household chooses at a particular point in time will determine the way in which the relevant assets will be combined. To give two examples, a possible response to an inability to meet cash needs for household goods is to start petty commodity production and to sell at a local market. One product which is commonly sold is milk. Thus the relative location of the household to a market becomes important since fresh milk has to be carried into the market early every morning. However, the household must not belong to an 'untouchable caste' or else it would be unable to market the milk. Thus membership of a specific caste, plus a favourable location and the physical assets of a buffalo, and the labour to look after it together determine how each of these assets are combined, and therefore which characteristic of the asset is of importance. (In this example a low-caste status would have prevented sale of milk and most other foodstuffs, so neutralising the effect of a possible favourable location, and ownership of a buffalo). A second example can be given where the use of chemical fertiliser might be a possible response to declining yields and the inability of the household to grow sufficient foodgrains. The assets required for the household to avail itself of chemical fertilisers are sufficient cash income (implying already the existence of non-agricultural income, and/or the sale of commodities produced by a farm in considerable surplus), and the availability of extension advice (a probability determined by geographical proximity to a road and the personal acquaintance of the agricultural extension agent, called the JTA or Junior Technical Assistant). In this case, a location near a road greatly increases the probability of technical advice as well as a reliable delivery schedule for the fertiliser. However, the lack of any one of these assets in a particular household reduces drastically the probability of using chemical fertilisers, and thus will alter the way in which existing assets are used—e.g. non-agricultural income may be spent instead upon increased consumption.

In summary, the assets which each peasant household possesses, and the general logic of the economy and society of which it is a part, defines its access position, and gives it a range of options open to it at any one point in time. The household's access position changes through time, and decision-making both affects the position at a later point in time and is affected by possible futures.

Having presented a simple analytical scheme to explain the distribution of resources (here termed 'access position')

TABLE 1

1. Accumulation Opporltunities

1. Buy land
2. Buy assets
3. Buy irrigation
4. Buy animals
5. Lend money
6. Start business
7. Arrange investment loan
8. Buy education for children

2. 'Maintenance' Opportunities

1. Use chemical fertiliser
2. Grow cash crops
3. Join army
4. Get post in administration
5. Obtain land for share-cropping in

3. Opportunities to Make Good Chronic Shortfalls

1. Sell labour locally (workers still live at home)
2. Partial migration of household (e. g. work in India)
3. Downgrade consumption levels.

4. Opportunities to Make Good Acute and Desperate Shortfalls

1. Total migration of household
2. Obtain loan for current consumption
3. Close business
4. Sell assests (houses, implements etc.)
5. Sell land
6. Sell livestock

of the peasantry in terms of the political economy, it is pertinent here to return to the logic of the domestic economy itself in order to understand the objectives of the peasant household which are pursued in the face of the constraints implied by each household's access position.

The domestic economy is defined by its characteristic relations of production, relations to the market and use of surpluses, which have already been outlined. Hence the objective function of a peasant will tend to be such that there arise no contradictions between these three defining characteristics. For example, if an advantaged peasant household wishes to accumulate on a continuous basis for the purpose of extending and broadening its basis of production (a classic 'rich peasant' response to the availability of the new agricultural technology), a number of contradictions arise. First, the obligations to the destitute, the occupational castes, and the temporarily unfortunate will have to be reduced or abrogated, with considerable embarrassment and loss of status. Secondly, the household wishing to employ labour will attempt to keep its costs down to a minimum (so as to reinvest profits), and so reciprocal labour arrangements, customary payments, a range of 'perks' and extra gifts, interest-free loans, gifts of old clothes, food and drink at festivals, all tend to be reduced or done away with altogether. Relations of production will start to alter from reciprocal to market relations. Now, avoidance of these contradictions is not sufficient of itself to ensure the domestic economy against the penetration of market relations, nor from productive capitalism in general, but acts to slow down the transition, and to provide the basis and form for the differentiation of the peasantry. However, when, as is the case in Nepal, the impulse of the market is transmitted in a mercantile form and indigenous capitalism is dwarfed and enervated, those impulses that do exist (stronger in the terai for reasons of both proximity and its suitability for the use of the new technology) find responses which tend to avoid these contradictions within the domestic economy. Thus, the domestic economy tends to prevail, accumulation on a continuous basis is not at all common and does not lead to a revolution in production, and the objective of most households remains to provide for itself and fulfil its customary (and usually reciprocal) obligations. However, for those few households that do have the ability to accumulate, their transition (however slow) tends to occur because the alternative to accumulation is a fairly rapid slippage into laboring to make up shortfalls in farm-produced goods, and eventually to virtual landlessness.

Thus, for the great majority of peasants, the objective of economic activity within the domestic economy is to ensure sufficient foodgrains for its members and cash for items not produced by the household (the most common being salt, spices, kerosene, shoes and cloth, the latter being by far the biggest item of expenditure in poor households), and to fulfil customary obligations to others. Further, from empirical evidence of household budgets and from interviews with poorer peasants, any shortfall in these requirements is made up to balance the household budget exactly, if there is the combination of assets available in the household to do so. It is impracticable, except in a few extreme cases, for a household to be able to accumulate from labouring alone, particularly in situations where labouring contributes over half of the income of the household. A few cases where there are an exceptional number of youngmen and few dependents, can save (in the sense of 'putting something by' rather than accumulate) and do exist in our sample. (The issue of the relationship between earnings from laboring and consumption at the margin is not tackled here, and is briefly dealt within Chapter 6).

The discussion can now turn to the responses of the peasantry itself, and the access qualifications of each of these responses in more detail. The most common are discussed first at some length, (new inputs, non-agricultural employment and cash cropping) linking them and their access qualifications to the processes of the political economy and explaining why in general, these qualifications have become increasingly severe, threatening an ever-increasing number of peasants' ability to support themselves at all. Then a list of other responses, less widespread but nonetheless important in aggregate, is given with brief comments. Lastly, we describe in empirical terms what proportion of peasants can take up these responses, and the processes which are working to change these proportions—some relatively independent of the actions of the peasantry itself, and others ironically, *as a direct result* of some of the responses taken.

Because of the abundance of labour, and its low productivity due to low levels of technology and the surplus which is extracted by the employer, it is quite impracticable to accumulate on a continuous basis where earnings from labouring form a major part of a household's income, and thus it remains only as a means of subsistence. Thus the only means of accumulation lie either in ownership of land or in the availability of non-agricultural employment. Both new inputs and advice from extension agents require considerable access status as earlier discussion of the relationship of the peasants to the state apparatus shows, and therefore the *productivity* of the land itself can only be raised by 'traditional' means—levelling, irrigation and composting, the latter two requiring increasingly scarce resources. Irrigation in the terai is only possible from a tubewell or a pump set (using the water of small, usually ephemeral water courses which are deeply dissected into the terai); while in the hills physiographic constraints, as well as those deriving from deforestation and the failure of perennial water-sources, are very severe. Composting requires a transference of fertility from forest (public) land to arable (privately-owned) land as has already been described, and the decimation of forest reserves puts this source of plant nutrients under severe strain. Hence an increased productivity in small farms sufficient for continuous accumulation is extremely difficult indeed, and, in order to accumulate (and stay ahead of the inexorable growth of the household's population), ownership of a relatively large amount of land is necessary. It is difficult to suggest a threshold area of farm which gives possibilities for accumulation, since these depend upon many other factors, but to give a very approximate order of magnitude, these thresholds would be 1.5 ha for the terai (unirrigated, but capable of growing *padi* in the rainy season); and 4 ha unirrigated, or 1.5 ha irrigated, or a combination of the two in the hills.

The availability of outside income as a means by which continuous accumulation can take place, is also problematic for the (already) poor peasant household. First of all, there is little to be had—part of the whole syndrome of under-development. Secondly, the access qualifications needed to avail oneself of these opportunities are frequently severe—not surprising since most of them require social networks or other assets not associated with the domestic economy at all (e.g. formal education, contacts with the bureaucracy with a view to employment, capital, and links with wholesalers to set up a shop etc.). One of the least demanding in terms of access qualifications is the opportunity to serve in a foreign army (Indian, and decreasingly to almost vanishing point, British) where tribal peoples (in the west-central region Magar, Gurung and to a lesser extent Tamang) are almost exclusively recruited into the British army, and in much greater numbers than other castes into the Indian army. However, there is a distinct impression from pension records that there is very considerable clustering of recruitment within families and within villages. This is especially marked in the distribution of Gurkha officers—a Gurkha officer is frequently the son of one, and will have a brother similarly placed. Similarly some villages will have most families placing sons in foreign armies, while others have none at all. One could hazard a guess that the recruiting officers themselves prefer aspiring recruits (there are usually hundreds of applicants for each vacancy) who come from families or villages known to them, but it is very difficult to confirm. However the implication is that even this opportunity, which is the most important in propping up the ailing domestic economy, is open to only some castes, and is concentrated within villages and households within them.

The last response to be discussed at some length is the production of cash crops. The constraints of land, sometimes labour and new technology are usually problematic, and there must always be a trade-off between the returns from land used for subsistence crops, and that for cash crops. Access qualifications of course vary for each crop; and, under conditions of choice, considerations of comparative advantage to a particular household will apply. Many of these qualifications have a geographical dimension (i.e. there is a *spatial* order to the aggregate of individual households' qualifications), and maps of the production of some of those various crops and products (calculated from traffic flows and origin-destination data) show marked regional variations. Perishability and cost per load/km. by the mode of transport available to the producers are the major distance-related considerations of comparative advantage for different types of land use (and for the households located within zones of feasability in which the product can be produced and marketed), while irrigation and forest reserves are the major "on-site" considerations. In the hills manufactured products or crops for cash include ghee (clarified butter), ginger, goats, buffalo, chickens, eggs, milk, curd, vegetables, tumeric, bamboo mats, winnowing fans and baskets, and in the terai, paddy, wheat, pulses and sugar cane.

By taking two contrasting farm products sold on the market, ghee and ginger, some indication of the effects of access qualifications upon the production of these exports can be given. Ghee production relies overwhelmingly upon buffalo milk. The buffalo lactates only one year in two (without a carefully managed environment), and so two are usually kept to ensure continuous production. The buffalo is fed on grass and tree fodder fetched from the forest. They are usually, although not invariably stall-fed, since they frequently damage themselves if allowed to roam freely on the hillsides. In the terai, they are often left to graze the paddy and wheat stubble. Hence some of the resources required to keep the buffalo are not privately controlled ones, but public. However, the labour requirement is very high indeed, particularly where the forest is poor, and great distances have to be covered to collect fodder. A back-of-the-envelope calculation of returns to labour show that this is frequently Rs. 1.00 or even Rs. 0.50 per day where the forest is far from settlements.

Table 2 shows a number of characteristics of ghee and ginger producers. It must be emphasised that, since our rural survey included only a handful of ghee and ginger producers, statistical inference was impossible. Instead, a purposive survey of thirty ghee producers and forty ginger producers was used as a basis for comparison. However, since it was impossible to know anything about the universe of these producers from which these samples were drawn, the sample was not made on a random basis, and conclusion suggested here must be treated with some reserve.

TABLE 2

Characteristic	*Ghee producers*	*Ginger producers*
% undertaking any labouring or portering	19	10
% receiving remittances or pensions	14	18
Mean holding of unirrigated land (ha)	0.178 ha	0.351 ha
Mean production in kg paddy from irrigated land	224 kg	383 kg
Mean number in household	5.77	6.32
mean number of males in household	3.43	3.59

Ginger is grown exclusively on unirrigated (*pakho*) land, and is for reasons of comparative advantage not grown in the terai, only in the hills. Before the introduction of roads, the ginger was dried (*sothi*) and portered to Butwal on the edge of the terai and sold there. But after road provision, fresh ginger could be sold to dealers who had set up near the major areas of production (Palpa and Tanahun districts) at road-side locations. Fresh ginger is far more paying than dried ginger, even if the costs of collecting firewood to dry it are excluded. The secular price of ginger too has risen sharply during the years 1973-76, and many households are starting to grow the crop. Seed has often been difficult to procure, particularly during seasons when there was an expansion involving many households in the same area. Storage of seed ginger and widespread insect attack make a reliable income from ginger difficult. Although some larger farmers have been able to negotiate loans to grow ginger in large quantities, the Agricultural Input Corporation has done little else to mitigate the high risks of the crop or offer technical advice (one farmer in the forty interviewed had received advice, and he had travelled to the District headquarters to obtain it).

Ginger is frequently planted under a crop of maize (thus the only crop foregone is the millet crop which is raised in a seedbed and transplanted under the maize when the latter has grown to about a foot high). There is, however, an opportunity lost in terms of the millet crop, and a reduced maize crop. Because of the extreme uncertainty of the revenue from ginger, very small landholders tend to avoid this crop. It is labour-intensive, particularly because of the large amounts of compost and forest litter (often applied in the form of whole branches and leaves placed on the soil a month or so before planting). Ginger can be marketed by any caste and therefore does not have the same access qualifications of caste as the sale of ghee. The simple comparison offered in Table 2 indicates some of the implied access qualifications for the two products. Ghee producers tend to have a smaller land holding and a high worker land ratio. This is reflected in the ability of ghee producers to use the 'public economy', and not to rely on land which is privately owned by them. Although our data are not sufficiently comprehensive to test it, a tempting; hypothesis is that ghee production is, (for families with rather small landholdings, with physical accessibility to a forest less than three hours' walk away, and a caste status other than untouchable) a life-cycle phenomenon. Families with a large number of children who can help with gathering fodder, but are too small to sell their labour or migrate, are particularly hard-pressed to find sources of cash income, but can deploy their children in such a way as to offset this.

To return to a more general view of the range of possible responses, Table 1 shows four groups (accumulation, maintenance, to make good chronic shortfalls, and to make good acute and desperate shortfalls). The four groups are only intended as a guide to the long term implications of the responses within them. Of course, selling land (response 4.5) may well be in order to finance a more paying enterprise, while response 1.4 (purchasing animals) may in many circumstances be a decision to maintain the household's consumption levels, and not represent an accumulation opportunity at all. Furthermore, the arrangement of an investment loan (1.7) usually implies other decisions too (e.g. 1.3, or 1.6).

It will be clear that peasants who make responses in the latter two categories do so because of the accumulated inability from previous time periods to respond either to invest or even to keep pace with their (usually) increasing numbers and (usually) declining fertility of their land. In fact the peasants who are only able to respond in category two (maintenance opportunities) today, are those who must make responses in categories three or four (making good chronic or acute shortfalls) within a decade or at least within a generation. Under the present distribution of access there is simply no other course. Of the 660 households interviewed, forty-seven per cent followed strategies in group three (including thirty-eight per cent selling their labour), and eighteen per cent in group four. These responses are the result of poverty, are a manifestation of it, and a guarantee of further (and more profound) poverty in the future. Accumulation is impossible since even with semi-feudal characteristics of the labour market still surviving, the surpluses extracted from labour of low productivity in a super-abundant labour market, leaves the labourer with enough grain for himself and a child with the prevailing kind payment in the terai, and rather less in the hills. Deteriorating access positions of households almost everywhere make this response the most taken in the longer term (and some of the more disastrous ones for the long-term viability of the household such as desperate sales of assets). Because they are forced to make these responses (both sale of assets, as well as labour), these households are poor—and the implication of these decisions for their future is that they will remain so.

Consumption

While the cause of poverty lies in the level of development of the productive forces and in relations of production, poverty is experienced as a level of consumption, and it is to this aspect we now turn.

A grouping device was used in the analysis of consumption data which assumed that the consumption level of a household was related to its relations of production, its involvement in producing for the market, and its access position to non-agricultural income. Hence the entire sample of our rural survey was grouped into five (wage labouring, wage labouring with domestic production, domestic production, small employers and large employers). These were further subdivided into those with and without non-agricultural income, and again subdivided into those above and below a rupee threshold of marketed goods, as can be seen from Table 3, which also gives the numbers in each category within our sample of 660 households. This classification has an analytical purpose based upon the theory and analysis outlined above and elsewhere in the book, rather than an empirical one. Households are continually in transition, and the analysis of inequality between them implies a dynamic through the creation and resolution of contradiction within the forms of production in which these households are involved. However, it is useful to be able to resort to some appropriate units of aggregation, to be able to generalise about these units and understand orders of magnitude. The groups discussed here are those whose access position is so poor that the responses they can make fail to arrest the decline of their fortunes.

In Chapter 6, we discuss the case of the agricultural wage labourers, and here the wage labourers who also work their own land, and domestic producers. Table 3 (reproduced from Blaikie, Cameron and Seddon 1979) shows the cell, row and column total in percentage terms of households in these categories. It will be clear that almost half the households sell less than Rs. 250 (c. £ 10 at 1975 exchange rates) of produce on the market, and secondly that about 447 (186 and 103 households, or 289 domestic producers altogether) of the households are still largely within the domestic economy (buying and selling negligible amounts of labour, and, excepting a handful of households, selling under Rs. 850 of produce on the market). Also those who are obliged to supplement their income from their own land by selling their labour to an appreciable degree (i.e. more than 50 man days labouring per household per year but amounting to less than half the total income of the household), are also numerous (totalling 119 households, or

19%), and will become more so, if the general analysis of the direction of the political economy suggested here is correct. It is also very clear that the existence of non-agricultural income precludes the necessity to produce for the market (i.e. the objective of households within the domestic economy appears to be to balance the household budget, and access to a number of non-agricultural income sources provides sufficient means to do it), or in other words, non-agricultural income is not spent on increasing production on the farm for sale. A comparison of each pair of columns (with or without non-agricultural income) within each category of household (wage labouring, domestic producers, small employers, etc.) shows that the amount sold on the market is appreciably more for those without non-farm income (such as a military pension, income from an office job or a small shop, etc.).

Figures 1 and 2 are two sample household budgets of two groups which are particularly vulnerable in terms of present living standards and their inability to even maintain their position in the future. The first sample household budget shown as Figure 1 (of those households in the domestic economy, with wage labouring, without non-agricultural income, and with sale of produce less than Rs. 250) shows the mean, standard deviation and median measures of income stream (in cash and kind) and expenditure for this group. First of all, most households are in debt (total cash earned minus total cash spent for the sample year 1974/75 was a negative amount (Rs. 662.7 cash income minus Rs. 993.5 cash outflow, giving an average deficit of Rs. 331)). Their cash earnings are largely spent upon foodstuffs (both shortfalls in grain from their lands and other items not produced by the farms, such as salt and spices). Other expenditure upon investments such as improved seed and fertiliser is clearly precluded by household's inability to save in the short-term, and for expenditure upon consumer durables it is one of the lowest of all groups (x = Rs. 137 or about £ 6 p.a.). The lack of sources of cash other than labouring is also outstanding, sales of agricultural produce being negligible, forcing the household to resort to the only reasonably easily available means of

TABLE 3

Sales of Farm Produce	Wage + Labouring		Wage labouring Domesitc Producers		Domestic Producers		Small Employers		Large Employers		
	With*	Without	With	Without	With	Without	With	Without	With	Without	
250 Rs	44	68	24	39	103	12	9	1	4	0	304
250-499 Rs	2	5	9	15	26	10	3	1	0	0	71
500-749 Rs	0	7	2	8	14	12	3	1	1	0	48
750-999 Rs	0	4	0	7	16	21	4	4	0	0	56
1000-1999 Rs	2	5	3	7	19	29	7	7	3	1	83
2000-5000 Rs	0	1	0	5	8	17	9	20	4	9	73
5000 Rs	0	0	0	0	0	2	4	4	4	11	25
	48	90	38	81	186	103	39	38	18	21	660

*With = with non-farm income.
Without = without non-farm income.

supporting subsistence, wage labouring. It can be seen that the 'profile' of access qualifications of these groups practically defines the group itself, although, of course, the episodic or once-and-for-all decisions (e.g. sale of assets) are not reflected in a budget statement of this kind.

The other sample household budget presented here (Figure 2) is for households wholly within the domestic economy (hiring or selling no or negligible labour), with non-agricultural income, and with agricultural sales of less than Rs. 500. These households are not 'poor' in a sense relative to others in west-central Nepal and are not part of the process of differentiation in which they have surplus extracted from their labour to be realised by another section of the peasantry.

However, a brief discussion of this category of household is relevant to the analysis of the poor peasant. The household within the domestic economy today does not accumulate and cannot have any prospect of reliably and continuously doing so. Any small surpluses (average Rs. 265, median Rs. 428) are spent upon items typical of a redistributive society: religious festivals, life-cycle ceremonies, consumer durables and an enhanced level of daily consumption. If further detailed data of the latter items are used (Blaikie, Cameron, Fleming and Seddon 1976), it can be seen that meat, fish, eggs and milk are consumed in larger quantities than other groups without non-agricultural income, and that rice is substituted to some extent for millet and maize. Improved seeds, fertilisers and other investments attract negligible funds (average Rs. 5 and 9 respectively) funds which *could* perhaps be squeezed out of the present range of productive resources of some of these households, if a reduction in consumption levels and non-productive (in a narrow economic sense) expenditure was eliminated. However, access to non-agricultural income clearly transforms the economy of the households, but inhibits any productive response to the continued failure of the farm to provide income (the cash crop production of these households is negligible, although some slack resources of land and labour could be made available for this end). Thus it is pertinent to turn to the reliability and future of such

FIG. 1

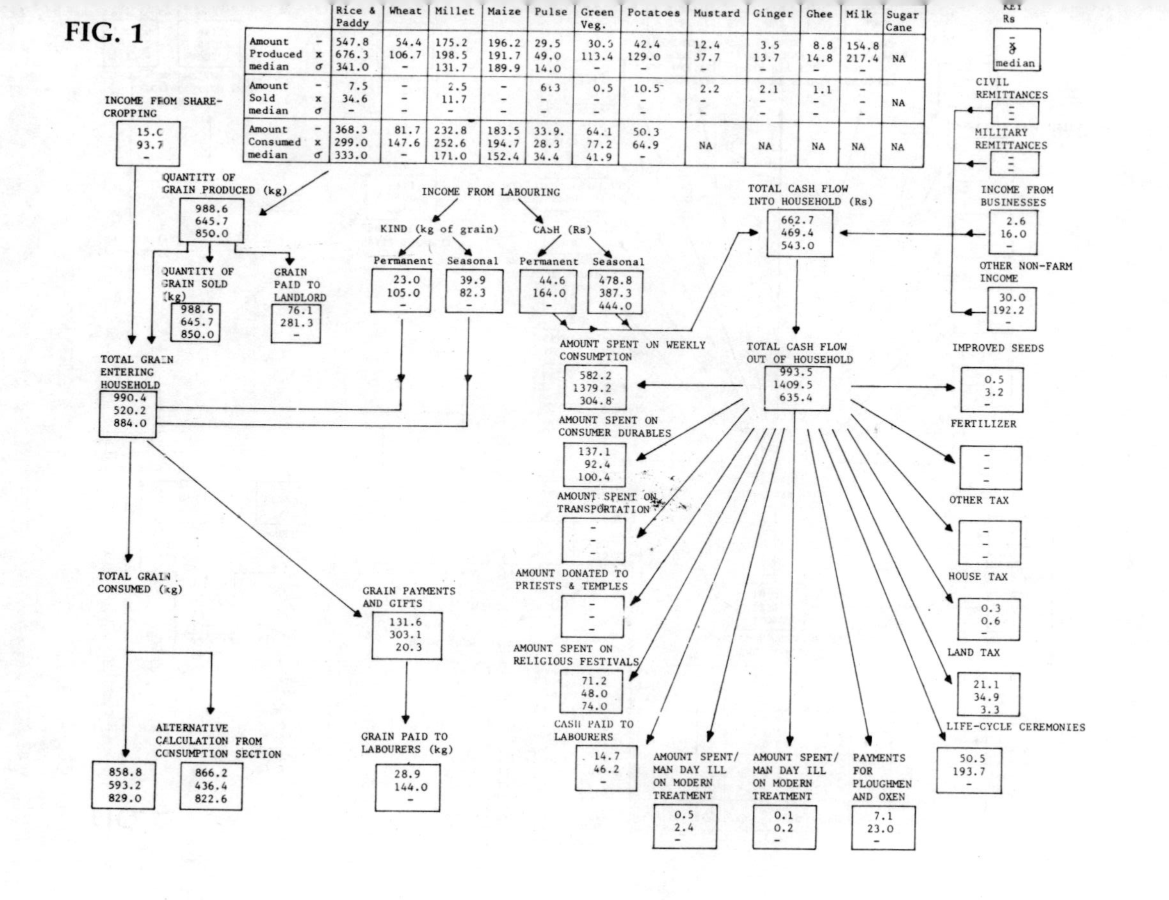

		Rice & Paddy	Wheat	Millet	Maize	Pulse	Green Veg.	Potatoes	Mustard	Ginger	Ghee	Milk	Sugar Cane
Amount	-	547.8	54.4	175.2	196.2	29.5	30.5	42.4	12.4	3.5	8.8	154.8	
Produced	x	676.3	106.7	198.5	191.7	49.0	113.4	129.0	37.7	13.7	14.8	217.4	NA
median	σ	341.0	-	131.7	189.9	14.0	-	-	-	-	-	-	
Amount	-	7.5	-	2.5	-	6.3	0.5	10.5	2.2	2.1	1.1	-	
Sold	x	34.6	-	11.7	-	-	-	-	-	-	-	-	NA
median	σ	-	-	-	-	-	-	-	-	-	-	-	
Amount	-	368.3	81.7	232.8	183.5	33.9	64.1	50.3					
Consumed	x	299.0	147.6	252.6	194.7	28.3	77.2	64.9	NA	NA	NA	NA	NA
median	σ	333.0	-	171.0	152.4	34.4	41.9	-					

FIG. 2

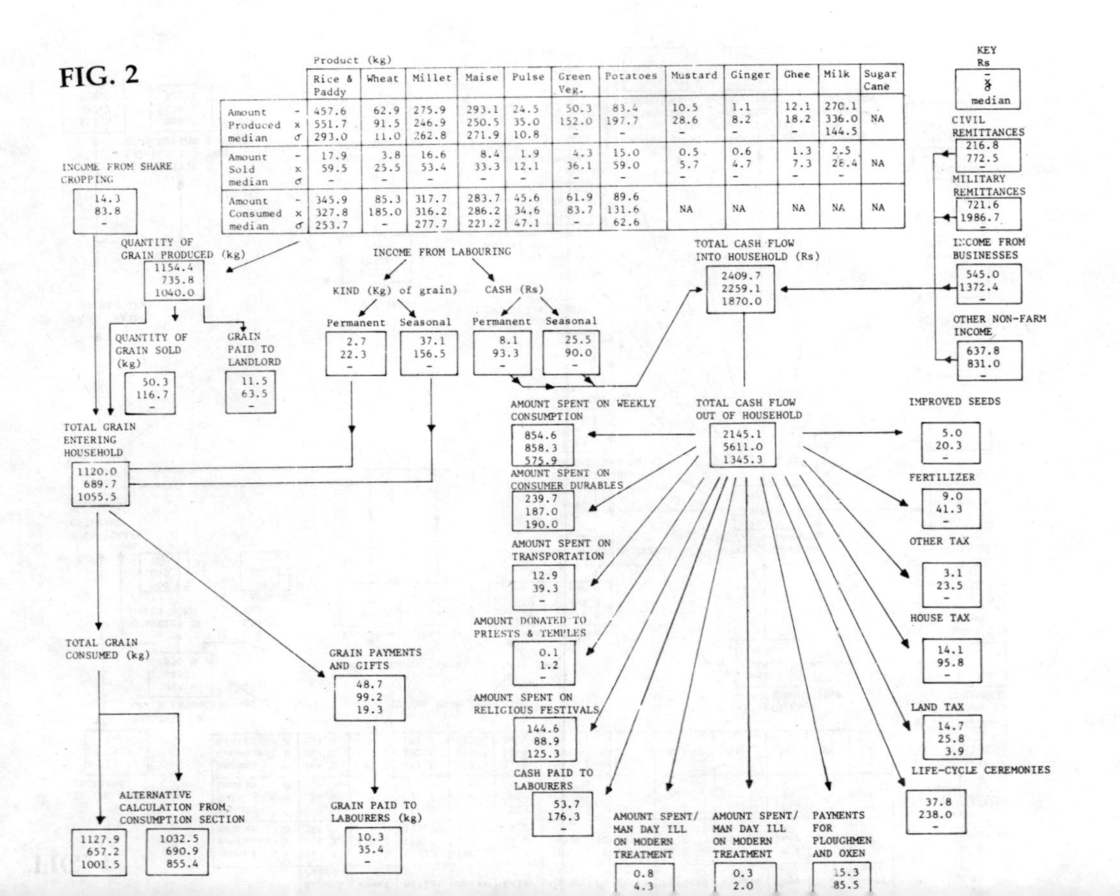

Product (kg)

		Rice & Paddy	Wheat	Millet	Maise	Pulse	Green Veg.	Potatoes	Mustard	Ginger	Ghee	Milk	Sugar Cane
Amount Produced	$\bar{x}$	457.6	62.9	275.9	293.1	24.5	50.3	83.4	10.5	1.1	12.1	270.1	NA
	σ	551.7	91.5	246.9	250.5	35.0	152.0	197.7	28.6	8.2	18.2	336.0	
	median	293.0	11.0	262.8	271.9	10.8	-	-	-	-	-	144.5	
Amount Sold	$\bar{x}$	17.9	3.8	16.6	8.4	1.9	4.3	15.0	0.5	0.6	1.3	2.5	NA
	σ	59.5	25.5	53.4	33.3	12.1	36.1	59.0	5.7	4.7	7.3	28.4	
	median	-	-	-	-	-	-	-	-	-	-	-	
Amount Consumed	$\bar{x}$	345.9	85.3	317.7	283.7	45.6	61.9	89.6	NA	NA	NA	NA	NA
	σ	327.8	185.0	316.2	286.2	34.6	83.7	131.6					
	median	253.7	-	277.7	221.2	47.1	-	62.6					

income sources. Here again, the dependent nature of Nepalese society upon processes outside Nepal altogether is very apparent, and there are signs that non-farm income which serves as a prop of the domestic economy, is under considerable threat. The great majority of non-agricultural incomes (43 out of the 191 domestic producers who have non-agricultural incomes) are from the military, and the volume of cash is often quite large. The run-down of the British Gurkha brigades has particularly affected certain hill peoples' economy, and it could be argued that India's interest in maintaining recruitment of Gurkhas is prompted as much by strategic objectives (that is to keep the hill economy collapsing, inviting instability in a sensitive geographical zone) as by purely military objectives. Civil remittances accounted for 13% of all remittances and these too are under threat, since the various constituent sources are either in decline, and certainly are not going to increase commensurate with an increasing population. Income from businesses too is ultimately dependent upon the disposable income of customers, and, in any case there is considerable overprovision of small retail outlets (see Chapter 9) and the failure rate of such establishments is consequently high. In summary of Figure 2, the households of this group are the poor of the next decade, and will be found after ten years or a generation in other groups with a less advantaged access position (e.g. as shown in Figure 1). Or to put the passage of time in reverse, many of the households within this group ten or fifteen years ago are those now in the wage labouring/domestic production group, or even wage labourers. As these families become increasingly vulnerable, a disaster or a series of disasters usually overtake the household, e.g. the death of a young male adult, a landslide, an expensive piece of litigation, hail damage to the maize crop, etc., and force it to respond in a reactive manner, often ensuring that it will never recover. At points such as these there occurs a decisive shift in the household's fortunes.

As to the prevalence of serious shortage of food and malnutrition in these groups, our data are not detailed. A series of questions on seasonal periods of difficulty and securing enough to eat, a measurement of the reduction in food intake, any substitutions in food type, and the extent of desperate consumption loans made were devised. Thirty per cent of the total sample recorded at least one month in which such problems existed, and other smaller surveys also reported serious problems of under-nourishment (e.g. of the forty service caste households surveyed, thirty-one reported such problems). Furthermore, the amounts of foods high in protein (pulses, fish meat, milk, ghee) are consumed in significantly lower amounts by these groups.

Collective Action

This analysis of the situation of the peasant must beg questions as to the possibility of collective action to change the processes which seem to drive inexorably the peasantry into becoming a landless or near landless proletariat. In order to halt these processes of quickening decline, it would indeed need a fundamental shift in the nature of the Nepalese state—the replacement of the landowning aristocracy which controls the institutions of state, an end to the dependent nature of Nepalese economy and society upon powerful interests within India, and a discipline on the part of the peasantry to institute radical soil conservation measures, re-afforestation, resettlement, and of course, entirely new relations of production. A "peasantry-perpetuated" policy (whether or not within the constraints imposed by Nepalese state institutions) can now no longer have credibility as a medium or long-term measure. While in a more stable ecological situation, an effective policy of this nature might buy time, it will be of little efficacy here and now. Hence the need for fundamental change arises not so much because there is potential class cohesion and action in the face of exploitation and differentiation of the peasantry brought about by the aggressive action on the part of the more advantaged sections—there is little evidence of that anyway; but because the whole peasantry itself faces a collapse due to a failure to produce enough. However, some of the very reasons for the crisis are the same which inhibit any collective action to avert it by fundamental changes in property relations and relations of production. There are few completely landless in Nepal, and therefore, even for households which largely rely upon selling their labour, a further retreat into their disappearing domestic economy is to be preferred in times of hardship, to militant demands for better conditions of employment or an alteration of the terms altogether. Other alternative sources of income deriving from the essentially labour exporting economy of the hills too, tend to reduce the absolute necessity of confrontation with employers in Nepal itself. Secondly, terms of employment are frequently mollified by a number of gifts between employers and employee—meals, alcoholic drink, and sometimes old clothes at the end of the longer labouring contract. The employer frequently knows the worker and lives nearby. Such a relationship is not lightly thrown away for the sake of a solitary complaint when the alternative is competition in an abundant labour market elsewhere, where no preferential treatment by the potential employer can be expected. Thirdly, the spatial and temporal characteristics of the labour force mean that there is seldom a large concentration of workers in one place for more than a fortnight or so. (When the situation does arise in peculiar circumstances such as road construction, organised protest quickly ensues, see Chapter 7). Fourthly, there is little evidence of really aggressive purchase of land by more powerful landlords as a result of foreclosed mortgages and distress sales on the part of others. There are, however, some exceptions to this, almost invariably in the terai, where superior access to the bureaucracy during the major period of land registration from about 1960 to a few years after the Land Reform Act of 1964, allowed the literate and already powerful to cheat those who had had customary usufruct of the land for many generations. The Compulsory Savings Scheme introduced by the Nepalese government during 1969 (Economic Intelligence Unit Quarterly 1969) excited riots and unrest where there existed a single, easily identified, scandalous issue (including alleged irregularities in the collection of funds and their improper use). Other reported uprisings include an attempt by the untouchable caste (predominantly leatherworkers, blacksmiths and tailors) to be allowed to read the holy scriptures at religious ceremonies, a privilege hitherto reserved for Brahmins. (After a few deaths, and a brief and brutal police and army action, the uprising subsided). But all of these tended to be local, ephemeral and not focused upon the fundamental economic condition of the poor peasantry and landless.

It will be clear that the different components of the analysis of the poor peasantry—a coming crisis of production, the lack of development of productive capitalism and of an aggressively impelled differentiation of the peasantry, and the lack of strong, organised class action—are not static, but must 'react' in the future. A total collapse of the hill economy (endemic famine, large-scale out-migration) can hardly occur without a change in the consciousness and response of the victims. When there is little scope effective for private action (as suggested by the series of responses discussed) to alleviate hunger and in the longer term oppressive poverty, collective action becomes more likely. So far, a number of hunger marches to Kathmandu have been made by victims of crop failure and landslides in 1973, and it is likely that these will continue—less sporadic and ephemeral than the small uprisings already mentioned. The viability of the Nepalese state itself may soon be called into question, since as the opening paragraphs of this chapter suggest, the mobilisation of its (limited) physical resources within the country will call for changes of a fundamental and rapidly successful nature. Such changes must be associated with political 'uncertainty', and Nepal's two giant neighbours will hardly standidly by. Thus the turning point in the future of the poor peasantry will be instigated by their inability to feed themselves, but decided, as has long been the case, by interests outside Nepal.

CHAPTER 4

RURAL ARTISANS

The History of Rural Artisan Production and the Influence of Caste and Market

Ideas of caste and the division of labour associated with these ideas were introduced into the territory of the present State of Nepal from the 11th century onwards by Indian immigrants fleeing from the Muslim invasions and from associated discrimination and persecution, moving north and eastwards into the hill regions of Nepal. The immigrants from the south were led by people claiming descent from Rajput families who ruled Rajasthan before the Muslim conquests, bringing with them not merely Hindu notions of religious status, but also a new technology of production and of warfare and retainers possessing new skills. The prevailing systems of farming prior to their arrival had consisted of transhumant pastoralism and shifting cultivation using hand implements only; the new arrivals brought with them the techniques of wet rice cultivation and the plough. The hill peoples of Nepal had previously relied in war primarily on light bows and arrows, easily fabricated within a peasant domestic economy; the newcomers brought swords and other metal weapons, requiring special skills and techniques in manufacture and repair as well as in use. Superior technology and socio-political organisation allowed the gradual supplanting of local tribal chiefs or the reduction of their petty chiefdoms to vassal status.

The establishment of small Hindu kingdoms in the hills of Nepal meant a significant development in technology and in the division of labour in society throughout the areas under their control, increasing productivity in agriculture and the development of new methods of surplus appropriation by the new ruling classes strongly associated with 'caste' ascription of roles.

The nobility of these petty states were 'high caste' immigrants and local chiefs—the two gradually becoming indistinguishable as caste divisions came increasingly to permeate the fabric of economic and social life for all ethnic groups. The courtiers, officials and high ranking military officers that surrounded the nobility and constituted the highest echelons of the state apparatus were also given 'high-caste' status, even in those cases where the strict endogamy rules had been broken. The majority of the indigenous population, previously organised along tribal lines or scattered in smaller groups united only by a common ethnic identity, were now reduced increasingly to a subordinate peasantry, despite retention of ethnic and tribal identities largely separate from the caste system. Also part of the subject classes were many small farmers originating from India claiming 'high caste' status, and the 'low caste' or 'untouchable' artisans who had joined the migration north and who constituted an integral part of north Indian economy and society effectively imported, with modifications, into Nepal. These groups invariably were given access to little land so that ritual low status and poverty have always been closely associated together.

It would appear that, in the late 18th century,

> "in the hill regions, occupational castes were generally limited to tailors, leather-workers, blacksmiths, goldsmiths, etc. The list is larger in the Terai districts, with dairymen, gardeners, washermen, oilmen, carpenters, blacksmiths, traders and shopkeepers, etc." (Regmi 1971: 23).

That the existence of a division of labour associated with the caste system in the hill regions is a consequence of the insertion into these regions of populations from India bringing with them a distinctive mode of economic and social organisation is not in doubt. The only uncertainty relates to the extent to which the 'low caste' artisans were able to move independently of their patrons and clients. There is some suggestion that artisans were able, even in these early periods, to move to take advantage of opportunities caused by the development of new settlements or demands from communities lacking particular skills. Regmi writes, for example, of labour shortages in Limbuan in the eastern hills, and of 'low caste' artisans moving there to find work. Thus,

> "occupational castes such as those of tailors, blacksmiths and cobblers had not developed within the Limbu community, and this social gap must have been another important factor resulting in the migration of non-Limbus to Pallokirat even in the absence of official encouragement from Kathmandu" (Regmi 1971: 53).

A difficulty resides in the usual confusion of formal caste status with actual occupation and class position. Even in earlier periods it seems likely that there was not a complete coincidence of caste status and occupation; it is probable that the economic division of labour in the Nepalese hill economy and the division according to membership of caste groups were related but by no means identical at any given time. Almost certainly, members of specific 'occupational castes' were obliged, by virtue of the inherently limited demand for their products in the hill peasant economy, to supplement their livelihood by carrying out tasks other than those which their caste alone assigned for them. Blacksmiths (*kamis*), for example, were involved, occasionally if not more or less permanently, in agricultural labouring, portering, farming and construction work, in addition to blacksmithing.

The non-Hindu people in west central Nepal were generally included within the imported caste ideology, although there were no specific 'occupations' associated with their position within the hierarchy except in Newar society; they can be regarded as having caste status only in the sense that they were considered, and came to consider themselves, in terms of 'the caste system', to be above the 'untouchable' castes and below the 'highest caste' elements of caste practice, although always in an attenuated and simplified form. Thus, these particular ethnic groups followed the Buddhist faith when they recruited artisans from outside, incorporated them within the peasant domestic economy on a basis of 'low caste' status and near landlessness similar to that in Hindu society. The activities of the artisans constituted an integral part of all village economies by the mid-nineteenth century. Payment for what became specialist services, even if perhaps not originally, were now fixed locally in relation to the economic and social position in the village of the peasant household making the payment as much as to the actual labour time involved in production. The artisan was enmeshed in a complex network of social relationships which tied him to the households which customarily paid him; he was not free to work for others, once the relationship was established and perpetuated, nor was he free to alter his 'price' as in a market relationship. Throughout Nepal, in 'Hindu' and 'non-Hindu' villages alike, each artisan was involved in what is known in the hills as a *bista* and in the terai as a *juga*, an arrangement whereby peasant households could call on the artisan for his special skills, as needed, and whereby the artisan households were assured of a payment, after harvest (once or twice a year) in the form of a fixed amount of grain, thereby guaranteeing a basic subsistence from year to year. But this income was only part of a wider relationship characterised on the whole by the disadvantage of the artisan. This relationship also included specific rights and obligations at times of festivals and life-cycle ceremonies and also arrangements surrounding agriculture and construction activities where there was an obligation to labour and a right to foodgrains or building materials on the part of the artisan in the relationship.

The penetration of market relationships into Nepal since unification, has tended to redefine the spatial aspects of social and economic relations, and a geographical analysis thus provides a way of understanding some of the important variations in which the artisan relationship is transformed by the market. But we cannot understand how the artisan relationships are affected without looking at the changes in the whole peasant economy into which the artisan is completely integrated. Relative location is of importance in terms of the accessibility to productive resources such as land, water, forest, pastures and also perhaps of inaccessibility from the point of view of tax-collectors to the source of potential surplus output. Regional economies have existed for a very long time, even outside the Kathmandu Valley, in terms of local barter between valley-bottom (rice surplus) and hill-top (animal products, fruits and jungle products), and transactions involving sales from petty commodity production and purchases of salt or cloth, kitchenware and jewellery (produced by Newar craftsmen in the small towns). However, these transactions did not materially alter the relations of production within the domestic economy. Spatial relations (themselves defined by the mode of production), although they did exist between household, village and the region, did not lead to marked differentiation between areas in a social division of labour. Of course, comparative advantages did allow certain villages to develop as trading centres, entrepots, and others to take advantage of a particularly plentiful resource, but there was no force acting through the spatial relations defined by the pre-capitalist relations which systematically led to the transformation of the domestic economy. However, the development of markets due to the expansion of capitalism redefines space and the location of producers. A blacksmith wishing to augment his income from casual work rather than from his bista is obliged to capture passing trade, itself made possible by the use of money, and to locate himself so that he can do this. Thus the concept of this potential will occur at roadside localities, near inns where people stop for a while and will consider having their sickles sharpened, have their shoes repaired or give an order for a shirt to be made up, and in towns where the concentration of higher incomes and a more extensive use of cash add to this potential. Hence, the sons of poor artisans will tend to migrate at least temporarily and commute to such locations in the hope of "poaching" off the established *bista* catchments nearby. In fact such displaced artisans can *only* utilise these openings (where 'impartial' market forces operate and where he is 'free' to participate), since appointment to a *bista* requires long-term connections with the local leaders of the village, which are virtually impossible to secure at a distance and outside the special long-term economic and social relations of reciprocation. On the demand side too, a client who wishes to slip out of a *bista* arrangement has to have an alternative source of supply. Thus it is in areas which are particularly close to towns (e.g. the whole of the Pokhara valley), on or near roads, and in the terai (where physical proximity to India as well as its internal and external accessibility are important), where there are the opportunities for both supply and demand to be met through market rather than through customary relations. In Nepal where the artisans are the poorest members of the village it may be expected that any pressure on the village economy will thus produce out-migration which then displaces other artisans' work and makes the process cumulative.

The penetration of the market implies, too, a logic of price surfaces where the manufactured product has to compete at the point of consumption with the locally made goods. This suggests that areas relatively inaccessible to the merchanting networks which stretch from the Indian border, through the terai and up to the petty retailers in the hills, tend to feel the effect of the manufactured goods from India rather less. But some manufactured commodities have been moving for well over a century into almost every village in the west central region. Whilst our detailed price surveys for twenty locations in 1974/75 still showed very significant price rises with increasing distance and the related number of links in the marketing chain, only one middle hill village in eastern Syangja far from metalled roads and the terai visited on the rural survey exhibited characteristics of a domestic economy relatively untouched by the market. Cotton yarn was still woven in the village and a recent application by a merchant to open a retail outlet was turned down by the village council since it was thought that the presence of a shop would undermine customary arrangements within the village. But in general artisan production has not been protected from competition both with nearby petty commodity producers and mass-manufacturers as production relations changed and markets have developed. To answer the question how this process will continue into the future, it is useful to consider how the peasant ecomomy is changing and the place of the artisan within this change.

Artisans and Peasants

The term 'artisan' is the central analytical concept of this essay. The use of this concept rather than the more apparent categories of caste and *jat* is deliberate. Not only does the socio-economic category of 'artisan' suggest possible comparisons with situations outside south Asia but also the apparent immutability of the caste system, enforced by strong endogamy rules, denies change to the extent which the term 'artisan' does not. Careful observers of the caste system have discovered that movements do occur within certain bounds but nevertheless it is the sense of stability rather than change which dominates much of the discussion on caste.

Lenin recognised in Russia that 'the first form of industry to be separated from patriarchal agriculture is artisan production, i.e. the production of articles to the order of a consumer' (Lenin 1967: 335) and that the 'closeness of artisan production to the natural economy of the peasants sometimes leads to attempts on their part to organise such production for the whole village, the peasants providing the artisan with his keep, he undertaking to work for all the inhabitants of the village concerned' (Lenin 1967: 338). The inclusion of the artisan form of production within domestic industry and handicrafts, and the emphasis on its closeness to the natural ecomomy of the peasants—the artisan producing use-values for specific clients, or sets of clients, in return for 'payment', often in kind, within a relatively closed nexus of non-market exchanges—has obvious parallels with our description of the situation in west central Nepal.

Lenin suggests that, in the face of the spread of commodity production (goods produced for sale on an anonymous market in its pure form), the artisan as a category disappears through a process of 'differentiation'. This process can take one or more of three major forms. Firstly the artisan becomes a petty commodity producer attempting to find a protected niche in the market system which may grant a temporary monopoly and an opportunity for limited accumulation. This will allow the former artisan to become a small capitalist and extend his activity in order to take advantage of increased division of labour including the introduction of machinery. This development is hindered in Nepal by the socio-economic position of artisans in all villages, which limits access to the resources needed to set up a business elsewhere. In the town of Pokhara, about ten Newar tailors have set up small enterprises with a few employees but the conditions for accumulation by former rural artisans are very few. Secondly, artisans may be forced to take out-work from a merchant who can extend credit on input purchase and/or output sale. Out-work has tended to be replaced sooner or later by factory production and, for the Nepalese market, the technology of commodity production has moved workers into the factory before any outwork system developed. The phase of out-work as a transition between artisan and proletarian categories is not available for Nepalese villagers. The first two forms utilise the acquired skills of the artisan and modify them to meet the needs of the market, the third form occurs when the artisan simply is forced to give up his craft and become a general labourer. In our rural survey of west central Nepal we found only one quarter of those 36 households with a family name (*jat*) identified by a common particular craft occupation in the *jajmani* system were practising their craft. All the rest were farmers/labourers which suggests that the third form of the process of 'differentiation' is dominant in Nepal.

Thus we consider that the title or *jat*, which simultaneously defined an occupation, endogamy group and virtual status as 'polluting' for any artisan, is being eroded in terms of minimal economic security but not in the realm of social discrimination. This breaking of the link between the *jat* as the description of the craft of the male members of a household and *jat* as a position in the caste-system with specific 'polluting' attributes does not produce great tensions in villages since the artisan relationship has probably always included agricultural and construction labouring tasks for patrons. How far this process will diminish the meaning of *jat* as a divisive influence among the poor and increase the collective sense of caste discrimination remains to be seen but by concentrating on the category of 'artisan' rather than *jat* and caste it is possible to understand fundamental change processes which are already well advanced, and begin to see the apparent stability of the caste system as a vulnerable temple not a massive fortress. The caste system is, however, a real problem for social democracy in Nepal because it identifies the King as a divine monarch, legitimates the aristocracy in politics and forms a rallying point, not only for the entire ruling class, but also for large numbers of relatively poor but 'high-caste' farmers and petty traders. The question of whether the nettle of caste discrimination must be grasped directly or left to wither away as its economic soil is eroded resembles that of whether a separate women's movement is necessary in the social democratic movement.

The category of artisan is in the process of disappearing as an ascribed right for sons belonging to one particular *jat*. But this does not mean that peasant households have completely entered the market for services previously provided by artisans. In the rural survey we asked households how they obtained the services normally associated with some of the more common *jat* artisan names. Many of the replies received were expressed in terms of an annual payment of foodgrains. The proportion renumerated in this form varied across occupation and space as shown in Table 4.

Below we shall consider the reasons for variations between services but here we wish to establish the large proportion of households who are still paying for services in a form more appropriate to artisan than market ralationships. This impression was reinforced when our survey also revealed that (i) all households paying at an annual kind rate obtained these services from people situated in the same panchayat, (ii) variations between households within villages appeared less than those between villages and (iii) in those cases where blacksmith and tailor services were both obtained by a household on an annual kind payment basis the amounts paid to the blacksmith and the tailor were almost invariably the same. The survival of many such relationships plus the possession by all households of some land means that the decline of the artisan has taken particular forms leading to generational and partial, rather than total, migration from the village.

TABLE 4

Location	*No. of cases*	*Black-smith*	*Tailor*	*Shoe-maker*	*Barber*	*Other*	*Notes*
Hills	238	204	183	8	1	101	All 'other' are paid
Pokhara Valley	98	87	58	8	1	26	
Terai	330	169	36	1	124	47	26 of 'other' are paid to priests

Source : Rural Survey 1974/75.

In a specific survey of fifty members of so-called 'occupational castes' in the hills and terai of west central Nepal, about 75% of blacksmiths and tailors said that their *bista* or *juga* had declined (in terms of the amount of income derived from it) dramatically over the last ten years. Usually this was related to a decrease in the number of peasant households involved, but other factors mentioned included a decline in the real value of the payment, not only as a result of the effects of relative price changes on a fixed kind payment but also through quite clear reductions in the total amount paid by peasant households. The reduction was sometimes achieved through the outright refusal of a peasant household to continue at the present rate, sometimes by a process of bargaining between peasant and artisan and sometimes through a general 'village policy'. Often, additional customary provisions for artisan households have been reduced or discarded altogether;

the widespread discontinuation of the custom of providing clothing for blacksmiths and tailors, given as 'presents' at festivals, is a case in point.

Some examples will illustrate the severity of the decline in the *bista* system and illuminate the difficulties that many artisans—or former artisan—households now face. In one case, a decline from 80 households paying in all 25 *muri* of unhusked rice to 7 households paying a mere 2 *muri*, within a single generation; in another, a reduction over twenty-five years from 80 households of peasant clients to 15; in yet another, a decrease in the number of client households from 25 to 3 and in the gross payment from 8 *muris* of maize and millet to about 1 *muri*. In this survey, three general tendencies emerged clearly: an overall reduction in the number of peasant households involved in the *bista* system, a general reduction in the size of payments made by the remaining households, and a general shift from payments in kind to payments in cash, reflecting the increasing importance of 'market' considerations in relations between peasants and rural artisans. It also becomes apparent, however, that these general tendencies affect peasant households unequally, depending upon their economic and social standing. For the relatively affluent peasant households maintenance of customary payments and continuing involvement in the bista confer status in so far as they represent a repudiation of encroaching market forces and a maintenance of dependency within the village. This dependency includes relationships of generosity and largesse, which enhance the reputation of the wealthy and provide a minimum of 'social security' for the relatively impoverished. But in general, the transformation of the domestic peasant economy and society through the extension of the market for products and for labour is profoundly affecting the condition of artisans and craftsmen. In an analysis of economic and social change in a hill village immediately to the north of Pokhara, Macfarlane identifies.clearly the implications for the rural artisans:

> "...much of the former work of the village Blacksmith, Tailors and Cobblers is no longer necessary because of the growing market for cheap tools and clothes at Pokhara. In practice, such

> lower-class groups have become landless agricultural labourers working for their Gurung patrons. Each Blacksmith family has between ten and twenty households for which he mends and makes a few agricultural tools; almost all cooking utensils come from Pokhara nowadays. Probably one day per household is the maximum of work a Blacksmith can expect; his yearly fee, partly irrespective of work done, is between three and ten *pathi* of rice. Thus there is probably something like 90 man-days of work to be shared out between the six practising Blacksmith households. The Tailors have even less caste work to do, they just sew and make a few children's clothes. One of the Gurung households has a sewing machine and others do a little stitching, which further reduces the work available to the Tailors. Probably less than 25 man-days of work per annum is available to all six Tailor households combined. The Cobblers (sic) who live just outside the borders of our hundred sample households have no caste work to do at all. One of them has become the best village carpenter, however, and carves doors, makes furniture and similar jobs." (Macfarlane 1976: 139).

As manufactured commodities become increasingly available, particularly in relatively wealthy villages, such as the one studied by Macfarlane, where a significant cash income is available to many of the peasant households, there is a growing discrepancy between the work available for the artisans and the customary payment in kind. As Macfarlane points out,

> "the rewards for Blacksmith's work are far higher, almost double (a ploughman's wage) in fact... Until a few years ago, each Blacksmith and Tailor did a considerable amount of work for his client family and a fixed amount of grain varying between 3-10 pathi (worth Rs. 20-70 now) was paid for this, mainly after the harvest. This traditional amount is still paid; all those I asked saying that it is normal to give about 5 *pathia* of rice to the family Tailor and the same amount to the Blacksmith. But the amount of work done, especially by the Tailors has decreased rapidly with the increased purchase of readymade clothes and hardware at Pokhara. How long the Gurungs will be prepared to pay the old rates is difficult to say. Probably as long as they have adequate supplies of grain for themselves, plus a small surplus for the service castes. Thus, when cereal shortages begin to occur, the service castes will soon lose up to a quarter of their total income" (Macfarlane 1976: 154-155).

Our surveys also showed that many villages have already reached the situation that Macfarlane foresees, where declining yields and reduced per capita incomes from farming and from other 'outside' sources for peasant families has already reduced them to a position where they can no longer make the regular fixed payment for the services of the former artisans. The crisis facing the peasantry as a whole is, therefore, felt particularly acutely by those who have, in the past, derived a certain crucial proportion of their income from artisan production and involvement in a bista.

Variations Between Major Groups of Artisans

All artisan relationships are under pressure but as Table 4 shows there are significant variations within occupations in so far as this pressure is indicated by form of payment. An example of the variations within particular services is clearly shown in the column for tailors in the table. These variations do not only depend on commercialisation but also on the historical distribution of *jat* names and the specific nature of the relationships. For instance, in some areas of the terai there were relatively few households of either blacksmith or tailor *jat*. Attempts to attract blacksmiths to these areas involve elements of *juga* relationships as well as straight cash payments for work done. Also, in the hills, payments ostensibly for particular services are more likely to involve agricultural and construction labouring arrangements. The results for Pokhara Valley, which is as open to outside influence as most areas of the terai we visited, show the same pattern as the hills with over 60% of households making annual kind payments to tailors; however for many households this was augmented by cash payments on a market basis. Thus, both the hills and the terai show a range of individual experiences from relatively pure artisan to varying mixtures of artisan with labouring and artisan with petty commodity production. These variations occur within all types of service in which artisans are involved but there are also considerable variations between occupations. For instance, practising blacksmiths have remained within the annual kind payment system to a great extent but shoemaking and repairing is very rarely obtained in this way.

A survey of forty blacksmiths revealed the least deterioration in both work derived from the *bista* as well as casual work on a cash basis. While both tailors and shoemakers manufacture consumption items, which are most vulnerable to peasant economising and competition from capitalist manufacturing, blacksmiths provide and service the tools for agriculture. Since capitalism has hardly penetrated agriculture (in terms of large-scale production, employing wage labour, constant accumulation and reinvestment in productive capacity and/or at the intensive and extensive margins), the tools of production have changed only slowly and have remained within the capacity of the local blacksmith to manufacture and repair. The close proximity of a local blacksmith to the production process itself (to repair ploughs, sharpen sickles, repair hoes etc.) means that the bulk of his work cannot be taken away from him by relatively distant large scale production units. However, it is important to note that in the past, blacksmiths also manufactured and repaired kitchen implements (particularly the large copper or brass *gagri* or water carriers).

These originally locally-made products as consumption items of relatively high value and low bulk were replaced in a number of stages. First of all Newar craftsmen started to diffuse from the Kathmandu Valley, particularly after their persecution and discrimination at the hands of Prithvi Narayan Shah after his annexation of the Kathmandu Valley kingdoms in the late eighteenth century, built small settlements and set up workshops throughout Nepal. Their superior skills quickly started to sap that part of the local blacksmith's income. Copper and tin ware continued to be mixed and smelted locally but cash payments tended to be substituted for kind and the local domestic economy was in this respect integrated into a regional one. Mass manufacturing in India was not able to penetrate this market until the late 1920's when the design of the traditional *gagri* was copied and mass-manufacturing was started on a factory basis from cheap alloys in India. The craft industries of towns such as Tansen collapsed almost overnight. The blacksmith in the hills today does not manufacture *gagri* and most have forgotten how to repair them. We visited a village in west central Nepal which had previously mined copper but this had stopped due to competition from India and the shortage of fuel for smelting as deforestation proceeded.

The Tailors during the last twenty-five years or so have suffered a more severe depletion of total work time available—both within the *bista* and on a casual basis. The sewing machine was introduced in appreciable numbers sometime soon after World War II (although our survey data gives a wider range of dates of introduction of the machine into villages, ranging from about twenty-five years ago to one year with a modal figure around twelve years). The productivity of labour increased about six-fold, and it was inevitable that many tailors would be pushed out of work. Some tailors were lucky in obtaining sewing machines before other tailors in their villages, and thus enjoying the transfer of many clients from these other tailors without machines. It is clear from historical evidence provided by interviews of older tailors still carrying out their occupation, that there was a de facto reduction in the implied rate of payment per garment upon the introduction of the sewing machine. The consequent process of differentiation between tailors did allow the more fortunate to maintain or increase their bista to off-set reduction in rates. However, the readymade market (as a logical extension of capitalism into this sector—first via yarn, then cloth, then printed cloth ousting the local hand-printed product) has seriously undermined the tailor's income, particularly since richer clients prefer the more fashionable clothes for sale at cloth and clothing shops on the trails and in small towns. Even fewer rural tailors will survive this second wave of capitalist penetration.

The *jat* Sarki is commonly identified with leather-working and this ranks very low in the caste system. Leather-working has virtually disappeared from villages and the most appropriate symbol of the destruction of rural artisan work in Nepal might be the rubber sandal (*chappel*) which is manufactured in Indian factories but sold throughout Nepal. However, it seems likely that people unfortunate enough to be born into families of Sarki *jat* in Nepal have always been expected to perform general out-door labouring tasks for more powerful patrons and their leather-working was only a relatively minor activity. In some contrast to the continuing plight of the Sarki is the survival of the barber as artisan in the terai (the *jat* Nau associated with barbering is virtually unknown in the hills). The barber benefits by not being replaceable by a mass-produced substitute and requiring so small a payment that economising is hardly worthwhile. Similarly the task of village watchman in the hills (not associated with any particular *jat* but commonly a man of 'low-caste' *jat*) is likely to survive as a tiny vestige of 'artisan' relationships into the future. Other examples of survival may be found in the terai, where many occupational *jat* names are found, including milk-sellers, sweet-makers, fishermen, vegetable growers, carpenters, oil-pressers and washermen. But successful survival as artisans will be localised and anachronistic and our analysis and observation suggest that one of the three processes of erosion, differentiation and collapse which we have described for blacksmiths, tailors and leatherworkers respectively will assert itself wherever the activity is significant in the local ecomomy. The category of artisan is disappearing but the individuals who at present gain income from artisan activity will not and it is to their possible responses to the loss of this income to which we now turn.

Responses to Change

We have seen above that the decline of the village artisan is in progress in Nepal at differing rates depending on the particular occupation and location involved. The historical context of this process is such that those most vulnerable to this change are least able to find new opportunities outside wage-labouring. The conditions under which artisan production takes place, production within the household working directly for a particular client, are hardly conducive to resisting pressure either individually or, to an even greater extent, collectively. But these same conditions plus possession of even a tiny amount of land means that the household is unlikely to migrate completely, whilst elements of protective patronage exist. The opportunities which exist within the village are circumscribed by limited economic activities outside agriculture and by the rules of the caste system. In most rural areas casual labouring is available in agriculture and construction either for a daily wage or by extending the labouring component of a *jajmani* relationship as a transitional stage. Location near a road or a centre of population may give some additional income from portering and other labouring but caste restrictions operate in any activity where handling cooked food is involved.

The pressure of declining artisan work finds its outlet in movement by younger members of the household. The occupational mobility of children is restricted not only by caste but also by limited access to education. Even primary education does cost money for writing materials and to this is added the opportunity cost of labour and the problem of learning in a home where advice is not available. There were thirty-six households with the 'low-caste' names Kami, Sarki or Damai in our rural survey, of whom thirty had spent nothing in the previous year on education and in a hill village visited near Pokhara less than ten per cent of these groups had spent any money at all on educating children under fifteen up until 1974. The absence of formal schooling and basic literacy ensures that jobs in the administration, at even a menial level, are effectively barred to people with 'low-caste' names without any need for active discrimination in selection. Recruitment as craftsmen into the Indian army (the British army does not recruit from people with these caste names) is very limited and, in general, young men must join the casual labour force, perhaps seeking employment in the very factories producing the commodities which contributed to their original displacement.

The destruction of the artisan relations in west central Nepal has been a long historical process and will continue into the future. The particular circumstances under which artisan relations were structured by the ideology of *jat* and caste has meant that independent development of forces of production by artisans was difficult, if not impossible. The creation of a proletariat from displaced artisans without the simultaneous coming into existence of local manufacturing capital was thus not only possible, but more arguably, probable in Nepalese conditions. Any future attempts to develop the rural areas on the basis of local resources and skills must come to terms with recent erosion of both the physical environment and the human environment. Deforestation produces a hydrology which tends to work to the detriment of the productive potential of the ecology; caste produces flows of resources and cooperation which tend to work to the detriment of the productive potential of all people, most critically in the case of rural artisans.

CHAPTER 5

PORTERS

One of the most important characteristics of portering in the west-central region of Nepal is that it is overwhelmingly an activity which men undertake only as one part of earning their subsistence. The occupation of porter in this region, implying a particular activity which is pursued as the only or the dominant source of income by an individual, is almost unknown. Thus a characteristic set of relations of production and conditions of work which are at the root of class relations do not emerge from portering alone, but merely as one of a much wider set of which porters are a part. Of course multi-income households or individuals are not exceptional, particularly in non-capitalist social formations, and also different relations of production may often exist in each of a number of productive activities which an individual may carry out (e.g. the peasant farmer who migrates for seasonal employment in mining or manufacturing). However, the implication which follows is that particular attention must be paid to how these various activities relate to others in which these individuals are involved. It is only then that decision-making on the part of the individuals or households which do portering can be fully understood, and the conditions of work, levels of earnings, employer-porter relations within portering itself be explained. Very simply, since portering is only a fairly small part of some households' income in west-central Nepal, the analysis must also look outside portering to explain its specific attributes.

Most loads being carried in the hills of the region belong to the carrier him/herself. Either the carrier has produced the load itself and is carrying it to a market for sale, or he/she is carrying purchases of household goods back for home consumption. In the loosest sense, these carriers are 'porters', but it is not these who concern us here. A very much smaller proportion of loads on the trails in the hills are carried by wage porters, usually calculated per unit weight for a fixed distance, and it is with these that the discussion is concerned. However, the preconditions for a demand for porterage of all types is first necessary to understand why the distribution and characteristic of paid porterage occur as they do. Paid porterage in the terai is very much less common than in the hills for a number of reasons. First of all, the bullock cart is utilised as a means of transport in the plains, and is very much cheaper than the porter. (Estimates of costs in dollars per ton-kilometre by Hagen give some idea of orders of magnitude, and are for the bullock cart $ 1.60, the mule $ 4.40 and the porter $ 9.40). Furthermore, most of the terai is accessible to trucks at least from October to May, and large-scale consignments from merchants as well as the larger producers of exports themselves (overwhelmingly this refers to paddy, rice and to a lesser extent to wheat and sugarcane) travel by this means of transport. It now remains to explain the place of porterage in Nepalese society, what factors determine the proportion of porterage as paid as wages (as opposed to being carried out by individuals), and lastly why wage porterage is carried out by individuals who almost invariably earn most of their subsistence by other means.

Although evidence is scanty, it is likely that wage porterage has existed for a very long time in Nepal, since medium and long distance trade between India and Tibet, and Nepal and both these countries has long been established. There is evidence too of corv e labour being used to porter military supplies, luxuries and grain—but this was discontinued during the last part of the 20th century (Regmi 1971). Grain and cotton goods used to move north from the plains of India, and wool, salt and medicinal herbs south from the plateaux of Tibet, and merchants employed porters to carry them. In many localities trading establishments were set up to the north of the Great Range, but still inside Nepal. Here, traders owned large storage facilities which were used as a entrepot; since when the lower hills were passable outside the months of the monsoon the Tibetan plateaux were covered in snow, and when the Tibetan plateaux were passable in summer the lower hills to the south of the Great Range were impassable because of the effects of the monsoon. Long-distance trade has gradually declined, partly due to the by-passing of the major trading routes which went through Nepal (and helped to support the Malla kingdoms of Central Nepal and later on the unified Gorkha state (see Chapter 2) by the opening up of the route through Darjeeling by the British; partly by the discovery and wide distribution of salt deposits and the wider use of 'Western' medicine in India which depressed the demand for herbs and minerals for medicinal purposes which constituted an important element of the trade; and lastly by the increasing restrictions from the 'fifties onwards upon trade across the Tibetan border. Today therefore, although the circumstances of trade (as a prerequisite for the demand for porters) still exist, they are very different from those of the 19th and early 20th centuries' (Fürer-Haimendorf 1975). The present circumstances are as follows.

First, the hills of the west-central region (as of all Nepal) have become a grain deficit region (for reasons already outlined in Chapters 2 and 3). In 1976, it has been estimated that the hills have a total deficit of 96,000 tons. In addition, the increasing inability of the domestic economy to produce other household requirements (e.g. tobacco, lamp-oil, shoes, textiles, kitchen utensils) has encouraged importation from India. To give some idea of the volume and value of goods which are currently being imported into the hills (which can, in a different analytical context be converted into a quantity of portered traffic generated), an excerpt from our trade and traffic surveys, shows the major imports and exports for a number of 10 km^2 regions in the hills (see Table 5 and a reference map for location of regions, Map 3).

TABLE 5

Region	*Population*	*Major imports*		*Major export*	
I. 12	26,700	Cloth	Rs. 1,468,240	Livestock	1,861,680
		Rice	Rs. 362,534	Ghee	179,669
		Millet	Rs. 107,328	Firewood	97,020
		Total:	Rs. 2,533,586	Total:	2,434,457
I. 10	16,342	Rice	517,000	Ghee	531,452
		Cloth	200,000		22,562 litres
		Maize	132,000		
		Total:	900,000 (approx.)	Total:	610,000 (approx.)
H 17	9,553	Cloth	80,800	Rice	293,360
		Ghee & edible oils	60,000	Livestock	201,400
		Total:	350,000	Total:	1,516,110
L 11	9,046	Rice	96,133	Ghee	338,620
				Potatoes	42,965
		Total:	638,759	Total:	382,965

Source : Traffic Survey 1974/75.

TABLE 6

Region	*Population*	*Imports total (kg)*	*Exports total (kg)*	*Total exports and imports per head in region*	*Imports per head in region*
I. 12*	16,342	350,736	193,053+ 7123 goats & oxen	33.28 kg	21.46 kg
I. 10	26,700	230,725	25,374	9.59 kg	8.64 kg
H.17	9,553	119,024	521,524	67.05 kg	12.48 kg
L.11	9,046	123,315 +Rs. 528,350 *kirane* goods	53,259	19.52 kg	13.63 kg

*Inclusive of the road-side administrative headquarters of Syangja District.
Source : Traffic Survey 1974/75.

MAP 3

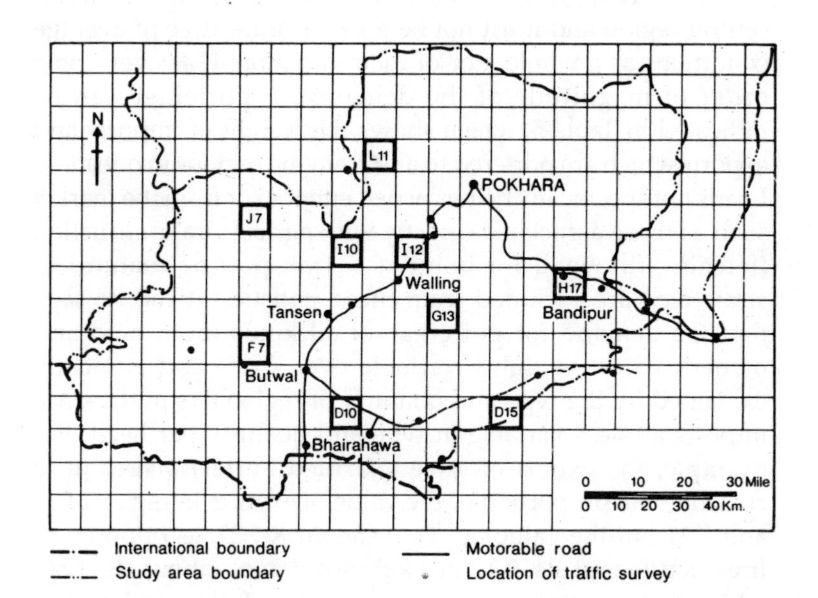

D 10 : Population 29,550 Exp. 8,861,016 (Rice/Paddy-7,159,079, Wheat-444,474, Molasses - 471,420)
Imp. (purchased in Nepal) 1,084,582 (Rice-573,146, Kerosene-109,107)

D 15 : Population 13,233 Exp. 461,426 (Rice/Paddy-438,926)
Imp. 425,040 (Cloth-350,000, Salt-68,640)

F 7 : Population 13,000 Exp. 941,320 (Ghee-598,001, Bamboo goods-255,405, Citrus fruits-70,320)
Imp. 1,230,427 (Rice/Paddy-1,019,050, Cloth-131,400)

G 13 : Population 3,885 Exp. 449,059 (A11 Ghee)
Imp. 346,302 (All Rice)

H 17 : Population 9,553 Exp. 1,516,110 (Rice-293,360, Animals-201,400)
Imp. 823,780 (Cloth - 80,800, Ghee and Edible Oils-60,000)

I 10 : Population 16,342 Exp. 610,000 (Ghee-531,452)
Imp. 900,000 (Rice-517,000, Cloth 200,000, Maize-132,000)

I 12 : Population 26,706 Exp. 2,434,457 (Animals-1,861,680, Ghee-179,669, Firewood-97,020)
Imp. 2,533,586 (Cloth-1,468,240, Rice-362,534, Millet-107,328)

J 7 : Population 31,043 Exp. 1,183,195 (Ghee-1,156,195, Oranges-27,000)
Imp. 1,150,000 (Rice-620,000, Maize-208,000, Cloth-180,000)

L 11 : Population 9,046 Exp. 382,405 (Ghee-338,620, Potatoes-42,965)
Imp. 638,759 (Rice-96,133)

Exp. = Total Export Revenue, Imp. = Total Import Bill.

These regions are chosen at random within the west-central region and must not be taken as indicative of average conditions as a whole, nor of their variation. However, some order of magnitude of the demand for porterage can be indicated in Table 5, which shows the weight of imports and exports which are portered to and from the regions in question. Loads not specifically being carried either to or from the market such as those associated directly with agricultural production (fetching firewood for home use, transporting manure or straw etc.) are excluded from these statistics. It can be seen that the demand for porterage of all kinds (both paid and owner-carrier) is highly variable over space and is mostly explained by the type and quantity of regional exports, since imports are less variable in type and quantity per head. For example, the export of ghee (clarified butter) makes up a considerable proportion of the value of exports in regions I.10 and L.11 but the value per kg. is about Rs. 22, as opposed to firewood (about Rs. 0.17 per kg) or potatoes (about Rs. 1.50) which form a major part of the exports of regions I.12 and L.11. An explanation of the regional variations of exports and imports is not relevant here, apart from the fact that trade and hence porterage to and from markets are still a most important element in the hill economy, so much so that in three out of four regions, at least one porterage load (and in one case two) is required for exports and imports per head of the total population living in each of these regions per year. It remains, however, to explain the proportions of these loads carried by wage porter (rather than owner-carriers), and the reasons for it.

Two further developments affecting the demand for porterage have occurred during the last ten years or so—the rise of the bureaucracy creating large centres of demand in the hills which has to be met by the importation of goods from India and the terai (the only areas able to respond productively to the growing markets created by the huge inflow of cash wages at administrative centres); and the construction of metalled roads which has occurrred during the last ten years in the region the Siddartha Rajmarga finished in 1968 joining the hills (as far north as Pokhara) to the Nepalese terai and India via Bhairahawa (see Map 2), the Mahendra Rajmarga finished in 1976 joining Butwal with Narayanghat, all of which runs through the northern terai, and the Prithvi Rajmarga, opened in 1971, wholly aligned within the hills joining Kathmandu with Pokhara.

Table 7 shows the expenditure by officials in six administrative centres of the west-central region, upon *(a)* locally produced goods, *(b)* those within the study area but not local, *(c)* and those from the rest of Nepal, *(d)* India and *(e)* abroad. To give an idea of the size of this implanted source of demand, the annual wage bill for the administration in Pokhara (the Gandaki zone headquarters) is, at 1975 rates, Rs. 475,000; for Baglung, (the Dhaulagiri zone headquarters) Rs. 135,000: and for other District level centres about Rs. 70,000 each. In addition, other expenditures causing a demand for porterage of imported items are very considerable (e.g. stationery and buildings). From Table 7, it is quite clear that the propensity to import is substantial for all salary groups, and particularly the higher salary earners. The phenomenon of long-distance importation as opposed to short-distance hauls from local areas of production is significant, particularly since the introduction of roads, and because they usually involve merchant and retailer, rather than local producers who may market directly and porter their own produce (since, as Chapter 3 has indicated, they will tend to be petty commodity producers and therefore tend not to employ wage labour in production of transportation to market). This tendency for long-distance importation therefore, tends to stimulate trade of a particular sort (implying the hiring of porters to carry in goods which belong to a middleman of some kind), and not of encouraging local petty commodity production (implying the transit of goods to the market by the producer himself or his unpaid kin).

Many of the imports into the hills have been directed from porterage to road transport, but there is good evidence that price reductions in most imports at the point of consumption were quite small after the opening of the north-south road in

TABLE 7

Income per month range Rs.	*Number interviewed*	*Average No. of declared dependents*	*Average income per month Rs.*	*Local Expenditure Rs.*	*Study Area Non-location*	*Rest of Nepal*	*India Rs.*	*Foreign not India Rs.*	*Sav Rem.*
91-400	15	0.3	242.5	91.7 (70)	87.3 (65)	7.9 (6)	39.7 (31)	20.4 (16)	
401-600	15	0.8	514.3	204.1 (113)	105.3 (60)	9.4 (5)	60.5 (33)	27.3 (15)	90 (5)
601-1300	15	1.7	835.0	316.1 (117)	230.1 (85)	22.2 (8)	92.1 (30)	46.2 (16)	127 (4)

N.B. Figures in brackets are expenditure per caput of officials and their dependents.

1968, and certainly were not sufficient to lead to any recordable price-led increase in demand (coil 1971: Schroeder and Sisler 1971; Blaikie, Cameron, Feldman, Fournier and Seddon, 1976). Road provision reduced the transport costs enormously but, because of secular relative price increases of manufactured products and a restructuring of the merchanting and retail network, the net improvement in the terms of trade of imports was small and shortlived. There was no price-led surge in demand for imported goods (and the dearth of slack productive resources locally prevented a rise in exports which might have become easier to transport to market, and yield more profit to the producer), and so the aggregate demand for porterage following the effect of road provision upon prices remained largely unaffected.

Thus in summary, the five factors affecting the demand for porterage as a whole are therefore: the decline of the domestic economy and the financing of imports by the export of labour; the virtual extinction of long-distance trade between Tibet and India; rapid population growth leading to a greater aggregate demand for imports and porterage; the rise of the numbers of administrative staff and consequent centres of demand both on and off roads; and the construction of motorable roads. It is almost impossible to show conclusively that the demand for porterage per caput or in aggregate has not declined appreciably during the last fifteen years, but this author would speculate that such a demand has not decreased —certainly not in aggregate, and probably not per caput.

It now remains to analyse the distribution of wage porterage (as opposed to owner-carrier porterage) and the circumstances which determine it. The first major distinction to be made is between the porterage of exported and imported products. The hills have preserved, albeit in an attenuated and precarious manner, a domestic economy where exports for the market have usually resulted from petty commodity production (see also Chapter 3), and therefore porterage to the market was carried out by the producer or his (unpaid) kin. In pre-road days, such exports were often carried large distances to the trading centre at the foot of the hills and exchange would take place (frequently without the use of cash except as a balancing factor in some transactions) between the hill exports (e.g. ghee, tumeric, dried ginger, livestock) and Indian-made imports (textiles, soap, matches and increasingly during the 20th century a whole range of household goods, (see Chapter 9). After motorable road construction into the hills, entrepots were set up by traders moving nearer to the points of production and consumption, locating themselves on motorable roads so that petty commodity producers would porter their own goods to these centres, which would be bulked up and consigned to the large merchants in the old trading towns at the foot of the hills (such as Butwal and Narayanghat in the west-central region) or direct to points of consumption in India. Thus it is both the nature of landholdings and relations of production in the hills (predominantly small scale owner-cultivation), and the topography which has inhibited what feeble impulses there might have been towards large-scale commercial farming, which have ensured that transportation of exports remain largely an extension of the characteristic relations of production of the domestic economy itself.

As distinct from the circumstances of export production one of the dominant features of the political economy of Nepal is a condition of increasing dependence for imports upon a mode of production located outside the country itself, from which mass-manufactured commodities tend to replace local production and stifle the development of an indigenous capitalism. Thus, by the nature of production of these imported goods, they are consigned in large batches, usually by rail to the Indo-Nepalese border, and from thence by truck to the break-of-bulk locations already mentioned for retailing there to local markets and for onward transmission by porters to other centres off the roads. Thus the hierarchy of trading establishments is characteristically from large (usually nearer points of production, and India) to small (usually in off-road, inaccessible hill areas), and the off-road transport linkages are served by wage porters. In the terai imports are generally taken by truck to the major towns, and from thence by truck, or horse or bullock cart to the major *haath bazaars* (literally 'hand markets'), or periodic markets where goods used to be bought to and from the market. Timing of these bazaars usually allows middlemen (usually Indians) to purchase goods and transport them by horse and bullock cart for resale at the smaller village bazaars. Wage porterage is limited to distances under about 10 kms and to consignments which are small, high value: bulk ratio, or episodic (which discourages carts and trucks because of inordinate waiting or turnabout time). Our traffic survey records for Bhairahawa show a wide variety of such consignments, e.g. fresh vegetables from across the border in India being portered to the weekly Bhairahawa vegetable market; porterage of bricks from a local kiln to the site of housebuilding some 1 km distant; or porterage of a sack of rice from a local market to the house of a senior administrative officer in an off-road location. However, the number of such paid porters in the terai is much smaller than in the hills, in spite of much higher incomes.

Having assessed the demand for porterage, it is necessary now to see how it is met, and to explain the fact that there is no professional porterage, only porterage as a part-time activity. There are three inter-related reasons for this. First of all, the domestic economy has been under severe pressure from declining yields, stagnant technology and increasing population pressure as Chapters 2 and 3 describe, which means that increasing numbers of men are seeking outside employment to supplement their incomes, (and how this particular decision amongst the many others available to the peasantry as a whole is reached depends upon the access position of the household). Of course there are sufficient landless labourers in aggregate in both the hills and the terai to meet the demand for paid porterage, but these are in competition with the far larger numbers of peasants who work submarginal farms. It is the latter who look upon portering as a paying but highly strenuous activity, to be taken on occasionally when the demands made by the farm are not severe. However, the heterogeneity of peasants who can undertake wage porterage prevents there being any reflection of the seasonal demand in agriculture in the rates paid to porters, except in isolated instances.

Secondly, there is a super-abundance of labour for most porterage jobs, which means that the demand for porters is usually met at once, but aspiring porters are obliged to wait at points of demand (either at break-of-bulk points at roadside locations, or at large wholesalers). These periods of waiting for a load can be as long as five days (and often three) which tends to limit those who are able to take a regular porterage assignment to those who live close-by, enabling them to return home at meal-times and at night, and to assist in some of the day to day running of the holding. This spatial limitation upon the demand of paid porters to within a few hours walk of break of-bulk points and other links between middlemen in the import retailing chain sets special problems for those who are looking for a casual portering assignment, leading to a wide dispersal of available work amongst the sub-marginal peasant farmers and landless labourers who have reasonable physical access to origins (and less often, destinations) of consignment of goods.

Thirdly, porterage is extremely strenuous work, and even the fittest find that five or six journeys (say, up to twelve days per month during the six months of the dry season) are about as much as is physically possible. This limitation provides the upper limit for the amount workers can rely upon porterage as a means of subsistence. However, most men work as paid porters very much less time than this per month for the other reasons outlined above. The mean number of portering assignments for a population of thirty porters interviewed at Nandanda (Syangja District) and Majhua Khaireni (Tanahun District) is eighteen times per annum (usually concentrated in the dry months when transportation is most practicable (i.e. from October to April). It is interesting to note that from our sample of 667 households from five Districts of the west-central region (not from porters interviewed at major trans-shipment points who predominantly live in the vicinity) only 1% had undertaken any paid porterage at all, and, judging by their earnings, only managed several trips a year. With one exception in both surveys, all porters also undertook casual agricultural labouring (*mazdoori*) as well. Porters interviewed said that they considered portering as a particularly lucrative method of earning wages, but could only afford to attempt to get the work a few times a year because of the difficulties already mentioned, namely opportunity costs of the porters' time in agricultural operations; other commitments to perform labouring for a particular employer over a period of time; the sheer physical strain of portering; and the proximity of a centre of demand for portering near home which would allow a reasonable probability of getting assigned a load within two or three days.

The hiring of porters is done in a variety of different ways. In the few cases of portering agricultural exports (usually confined to the terai), the relations of production under which the crops are grown generally extend to their transportation as well. Labourers are hired on a daily basis, and there is no marked advantage on the part of the labourer to be local and known to the employers when the work is harvesting or weeding. However, the transport of vegetables to market requires a degree of honesty and commitment not to be found invariably on the open labour market, and hence most of the porters in this activity are from the same village as the employer (who is also the landowner), who will habitually employ a very small number of landless labourers or sub-marginal farmers known to him to undertake the job. In the west-central region, the portering of vegetables is confined to Bhairahawa, and to a much lesser degree Taulihawa.

In the more common situation of wage porterage, the merchants themselves or commission agents hire porters at break-of-bulk locations. These locations are either at the foot of the hills where bullock carts can no longer ply (e.g. Patharkot, Zimzimia, Tribenighat, see Map 2), or within the hills themselves where lorries can transport goods to trans-shipment points (e.g. Tansen, Walling, Syangja, Naudanda, Pokhara, Dumre, Bimalnagar and Majhua Khaireni). A merchant will travel to Butwal or Bhairahawa and purchase a lorry load of merchandise (or a number of smaller merchants will combine to make up a load) return with the lorry or by bus before the arrival of the lorry, and will supervise the unloading of the goods. At the time of unloading, he will hire porters—usually those whom he has used before and trusts, since there are reported to be a few cases of porters disappearing with their loads *en route*. A rate will be agreed, while unloading is in progress. There is some degree of bargaining, but the porters are not in a strong position since there are usually far more porters waiting than there is demand for them. However, there is a 'going' rate which applies more or less universally, and is calculated on a per unit weight basis between origin and specified destination. This rate is almost constant during the the dry season as a whole, and only changes very slowly from year to year. During the wet season there are fewer porters and the rate rises (see Table 8), and during one or two feast days, those merchants.fortunate enough to want their goods portering, often have to pay over double the usual rates.

TABLES 8

		Dry Season	*Wet Season*
From Naudanda to			
	Seti Dobhan	Rs. 5/- per quintal	Rs. 7-8/- per quintal.
	Karkineta	Rs. 0.75-Rs. 1.00 per dharni	Rs. l-1.25
	Kusma	Rs. 1.75-Rs. 200 per dharni	Rs. 2.25
	Baglung	Rs. 2.25-Rs. 2.50 per dharni	Rs. 2.50-4.00
	Beni	Rs. 2.50-Rs. 2.75 per dharni	Rs. 4.00-4.50
	Dharban	Rs. 4.00	Rs. 5.00

dharni = 2.39 kg.

Some merchants do, however, attempt to bargain below the accepted range of rates by obstructing the efforts of the porter to weigh the load, and by trying to persuade the porter to accept the merchant's (under) estimate of the weight. This ruse sometimes is resignedly accepted by porters. The merchant then pays the porter an advance if he asks for it (to purchase food and drink on the trail, and sometimes to pay back the local merchant who has sold the porter grain while he has been waiting for a load), dispatches the porters, and walks up the trail himself to his shop to supervise unloading and final settlement.

Some merchants who do not have shops in the hills and are not familiar with the porters of the route they wish to use, employ commission agents, of whom there are a few in most of the centres. They charge the merchant a rate of approximately Rs. 0.10 per *dharni* on top of a rate of Rs. 2.50 (to Baglung), and a *pro rata* percentage rate of 47 applies to other hauls. The agents also know porters by name, and tend to use a fairly small clientele. Thus 'knowing' the commission agent is considered important, although not essential, by porters. Men from outside do come to these centres to find porterage work and happen to be present when a load needs carrying, and conduct their own bilateral bargaining with the shopkeeper or other individual (e.g. a soldier on leave with household belongings, an official returning to his quarters with produce and purchases from his home town etc.). But outsiders are generally lucky if they can pick up a load if they are unknown to the shopkeepers or commission agents.

The porter will himself decide how much he can carry. In spite of some unsubstantiated stories of enormous loads, most porters carry loads which are remarkably standard (about 24 dharnis or 57.4 kgs). Thus a porter walking from Naudanda to Baglung will earn gross Rs. 60, or about Rs. 20 per day: two days, or a little more to Baglung loaded, and half or three quarters of a day back, unloaded, (reflecting the deficit in the balance of trade between the hills, and the terai and India). The rates applying to short hauls (e.g. to Seti Dobhan where a porter can carry a quintal down the hill from Naudanda, taking 1 hours, four times or perhaps five times a day, earning himself Rs. 5 each time) tend to work out to very similar daily rates (although rates are seldom offered on a per *diem basis*). These rates do vary somewhat from place to place, but remain remarkably constant within the same circumstances of hiring of porters. Very much lower rates are paid under different conditions of employment and relative strengths of contractual position.

A few porters work for a shopkeeper to discharge a debt, and rates under these circumstances are frequently derisory. The few cases that have come to light have all occurred in places far from established porterage tracks and roads. It is tempting to speculate that a well-informed and free market in porterage rates tends to be eroded where opportunities for porterage are infrequent and rates are not known and discussed otherwise the indebted would prefer to earn a better wage on the open market to pay his debt, rather than submit to rates offered by his creditor which frequently do not even provide for subsistence on the trail. However, such cases are thought to be rare.

There is very considerable evidence, however, that real porterage rates have increased, and not decreased since road provision—an interesting, counter-intuitive finding. Before the opening of the Siddartha Rajmarga from Bhairahawa to Pokhara in 1968, the rate was Rs. 4.00 per *dharni* from Baglung to Butwal, taking about 10 days (or a daily rate of about Rs. 8.75 including one extra day for turn-around). Thus with a standard 24 *dharni* load, daily rates have increased in nine years from Rs. 8.75 to Rs. 20.00 in the same time as inflation has been in the order of fifty per cent for foodstuffs (by far the largest expenditure item for poor families—up to eighty per cent—Nepal Rashtra Bank Agricultural Credit Survey, Vol. II, p. 150). Almost every porter who has worked in pre and post-road eras says that daily equivalent rates have increased, and that average journeys undertaken are shorter. Other historical data of pre and postroad porterage rates all support this contention, and agree in approximate order of magnitude. Why is this so?

There should be no reason why merchants and commission agents should not be able to force the price of porterage down to the opportunity cost of a would be porter's time—which in the slack season is very low, and certainly near to the level of remuneration of casual agricultural labouring (Rs. 6-8 in cash or equivalent in kind) plus some reflection of the extra expense of the porter's purchase of food on the trail, and of the extra physical effort involved. The argument that the high rate represents waiting time and return time (since backhauls are almost impossible to secure) likewise is vulnerable to the fact that there is hardly ever a shortage of porters. The ability of merchants to haggle, and to pick and choose porters demonstrates this. The explanation offered here is not a particular satisfactory one, and it is difficult to offer empirical evidence for every causal link. From our price surveys and interviews of commercial establishments in the region it is clear that merchants do not act in a simple labour-cost minimising manner but follow a "cost-plus" approach to pricing of merchandise. Since the clientele of many retailing as well as wholesaling establishments (the latter implying other small retailers) are maintained by relations of credit, reciprocal services and exchange and other 'non-market' considerations, and many merchants follow other prices in the vicinity, rather than attempt to undercut competitors in an aggressive way, it is perfectly possible for an employer of porters to survive in wholesaling or retailing and to pay his porters at levels higher than that to which the employers as a group could reduce wage rates, if they acted in an aggressive, competitive manner. One obvious objection to this explanation is that while it allows rates to rise in general, it does not explain why they did not do so before road provision. However, the increase in the number of retailing and wholesaling establishments in the hills has been particularly rapid after the opening of the Siddartha Rajmarga, and the very large numbers of small commercial establishments (often yielding little more than a means of subsistence without accumulation for the owner—see Chapter 9) are a very recent phenomenon. Therefore, there has been an explosion in the phenomenon of hired porterage and the number of traders who are using porters. Furthermore the knowledge of rates of hire will definitely be better distributed amongst porters themselves and therefore be in a better position to resist isolated attempts of rate-cutting. This explanation lacks an incisive cause and effect mechanism, and takes on the less satisfactory form in which such a disturbance in the wholesale and retail structure of the hills following road provision allowed the upward tendency in porterage rates to assert itself since fierce competition between employers do not exist. It is clear that further research is required to provide a better explanation of the phenomenon of rising porterage rates after road provision.

To turn now to the net earnings of the porter himself, the expenses of the porter on the trail will very greatly with his personal circumstances, and acutely affect his net earnings, If he travels alone or with a small group of others not from his village, he cannot easily carry his own grain and cooking utensils, and so has to purchase ready-cooked food on the way. Porters' estimates of the cost of wayside meals and tea at 1974 prices vary between Rs. 6-8 per day, and thus net earnings in these circumstances are reduced to between Rs. 12-14. If, however, the porter is able to secure a load with many of his fellow-villagers (say, a minimum of six or eight), one will carry cooking utensils and food for the party, as well as a small load, hence saving at least three or four rupees per head on provisioning expenses. This situation is rare in the case of hired porterage, although it is usual in the case of parties of owner-carriers travelling over long distances to sell their produce (e.g. ginger growers in Palpa District travelling to Arya Bhanjang on the Siddartha Rajmarga to sell their produce); or in the occasional portering contracts which the government may arrange through a trader or village panchayat to transport materials for a public works programme in a particular village.

In summary and conclusion, the phenomenon of paid porterage today is an expression of the inability of the hill population to produce for itself and the export of labour from the declining hill economy. The population pressure which is one of the manifestations of such a stagnation in the productive capacity of the hill economy, also provides the supply of porters —by progressively creating far greater numbers who are unable to support themselves from their own land, and who are chasing fewer and fewer jobs in the region. Paid porterage in this context has a special irony—the outcome of a collapsing economy, but also an infinitesimal contribution to the employment problem which such a collapse causes. The response of the state to the general crisis too has an ironic implication—its inadequate stimulation of production and its only capability of providing some employment in the form of transporting imports to feed its bureaucracy. As such, porterage is merely a symptom of underdevelopment.

CHAPTER 6

AGRICULTURAL LABOURERS

The History of Agricultural Labouring

Very few people in west central Nepal have never laboured in a field, only the most privileged have completely avoided the hard physical labour required to cultivate the staple food-crops of all the Nepalese people. The growing of paddy in the valley-bottom and on the plains requires many labourers at the critical times of transplanting (in about July) and harvesting (in about November) working in the mud of small 'trays' often in heavy rain. On the hill-sides are small terraced fields growing paddy where irrigation is possible but primarily producing maize and millet as a double crop. The latter two crops, and many of the inter-cropped and catch-cropped products such as mustard, groundnuts, soyabeans, and many varieties of pulses are not so demanding in terms of labour peaks but the heavy demands on paddy growing and the general effect of small field sizes ensure that much labour is critically required in agriculture at several times between April and December. Relations embodying the need to meet this demand for labour time to be applied to agriculture have varied across time and from place to place. For the purpose of this section we will briefly describe some of the major variations.

A form of relationship which is still common and has probably existed for centuries is that known as *parma* in the hills and *juga* in the terai. For instance, in a situation where the ecology allows some staggering of operations such as in terraced agriculture and almost all households own roughly equal amounts of land there is the possibility of exchanging equal numbers of labour days without either partner in the exchange feeling disadvantaged. For instance, a household whose fields are situated three hundred metres above another's with a more northerly aspect may well find the optimum time for its operations more than a week behind thus allowing both households to work in both sets of field cooperatively and sequentially. This form at its purest reflects no division of labour between households and, when marginal uncultivated land was available further up the hill or in the next valley, there appeared to be the possibility of an egalitarian community existing with little class or status differentiation. Open access to the many resources of the hill-top jungles including the raw materials for clothing, shelter and fuel reinforce the idealised picture of simple or primitive communism which has so attracted Western observers. Even the sexual division of labour within the household for such groups appears to have been limited to an extent which leaves women relatively unoppressed. Of course, such an image does require qualification but cannot be simply dismissed especially when it forms a moment in the consciousness of so many people by revealing the possibilities of some co-operation in a fragmented society and concealing the processes which are leading to the destruction of its original economic base, especially in the form of ecological decline. Agricultural labouring in such a situation unites everyone in the struggle against nature, expressing a common position.

As is so often the case in Nepal an apparently opposite situation appears virtually alongside and vying for equal attention. In contrast to the 'natural equality' ideal of some hill communities is found the 'natural hierarchy' ideal of many valley-bottom and plains' villages. In such a system the performance of certain tasks in agriculture are either formally proscribed by caste rules, e.g. ploughing for Brahmins, or covered by a rigid sexual division of labour. But the amount and timing of general labour required in agriculture does not seem to permit the designation of groups specifically for this task and thus all castes have been heavily involved in agricultural labouring including virtually all women and many men of Brahmin caste. The 'grain-pile' of the village from which each draws according to the custom of his station is the distribution ideal which corresponds to the term *jajmani*. But important in the structure which ensures that non-labourers receive a share is that the decision is not simply left to the discretion of the direct producers but is enforced through unequal division of land which reinforces the religious right with a private property right. Thus from the viewpoint of the person who works as an agricultural labourer the situation is often a complex mixture of both relatively independent craftsman (in his or her sanctioned place in the general division of labour given by caste-name and/or sex) and employee on another person's land. It seems likely that the total self-image of caste, so powerfully expressed in so many actions, would dominate in such circumstances. Agricultural labouring under these circumstances thus tends to suggest reinforcement of the consciousness of 'homo hierarchicus' but offering the possibilities of relations developing into wage-labour forms where caste would serve as a mask, not an expression of economic relations. Both these idealisations of relations of agricultural production contain their own dynamic which predisposes the systems to move in different directions. One moves towards common ruin in a situation of ecological decline and the other more directly towards changing production relationships as available forces of production develop, both changes to the relative disadvantage of weaker groups in the village.

But whilst the village systems do demonstrate internal change processes when seen as bounded unities, it is vitally important to also move beyond the village and see how other factors have been introduced to alter the conditions under which agricultural labouring is performed. Certainly since unification at the end of the 18th century, the Nepalese state has been used by a national ruling class as an instrument to penetrate even relatively closed village systems in order to extract tribute directly as labour services, indirectly as food-grain and other kind taxes and (in exceptional circumstances) through cash payments relying on price manipulation to maximise their advantage. The ruling class thus managed to ensure its own survival and some growth in numbers by actions which exacerbated the tendencies for the direct producers in agriculture to suffer without their sacrifice yielding any prospects of future break-throughs in land and/ or labour productivity.

But whilst systems may crumble, the threatened individuals involved respond to avoid personal disaster usually by migration. Throughout the 19th and 20th centuries Nepalese history is marked by attempts of the rulers to maintain control over movements of population. Attempts at exercising control over population movements whilst minimally disturbing existing production relations have been a consistent feature of central State policy. Problems that appointment of local leaders as tax collectors tended to reinforce local rather than central power structures, were met by the appointment of itinerant central officials, but this often led to over-zealous collection and the fleecing of the very population who produced the surplus. Similarly the granting of stronger owner-cultivator rights with the intention of creating an immobile peasantry made extracting surplus relatively difficult whilst slavery and forced labour were reputed to produce relatively little surplus even if the surplus was easily appropriated. Also adjusting the border-line between labourer and peasant through legislation on share-cropping and tenants rights in favour of the direct producers, produced problems when the need to increase the surplus arose. For almost two centuries the Nepalese ruling class walked a cliff-edge seeking policies to ease extraction of existing surplus but failing to develop the conditions needed to produce new surplus and in the 1950's found that the resolution of its conflict was based on the tendency to continuously 'extract' surplus labour without having resources to apply that labour productively. The existence of increasing numbers of households unable to find a secure niche in a village system or full-time work outside this system, is a process within the Nepalese crisis which could be labelled "marginalisation" if such a term did not suggest that these households lay outside the central processes of society. But this process is properly seen as typical not exceptional or peripheral and it is to agricultural labouring largely shorn of its 'community' attributes that these households are forced to look for survival.

Thus discrimination along caste and ethnic lines at the village level is associated with exploitation by a ruling class, based upon town and cities, legitimated and coerced through the agency of the national State. Apparent opposition between, for instance, town and village and class and community, are revealed as aspects of a unity which reproduces the subordination of the most vulnerable groups in agriculture. As capitalist relations have penetrated Nepal over the last one hundred years the agency of subordination has changed from the coercion of being excluded from the village (with the probability of becoming a slave) to the coercion of the labour market where wages are apparently free to be accepted or refused. To make a moral choice between forms of subordination is not the purpose of this discussion and to describe the present situation as any more critical for the poor than the past is itself problematic; but it would be misleading to idealise either past local communities or present national liberties without recognising that both conceal the real essence of subordination and that the reproduction of subordination is always a crisis process although the nature of crisis changes. In the past the provision of agricultural labour to produce surplus for appropriation by the ruling class was met through attempts to directly extract forced labour and the administering of taxes in forms compatible with various types of reciprocal labour relationship. The periodic crises this produced have now been replaced by a development which places the strain of adjustment even more firmly on the subordinated themselves. A central characteristic of the present crisis is thus the creation of large numbers of households who have little alternative but to look to agriculture for wages and who are thus almost totally excluded from any control over how that work is conducted. Unlike other societies where the 'free' industrial urbanised working class have been able to lead the struggle for better conditions for all workers, in Nepal the farm labourers individually and collectively must find their own methods of survival in unfamiliar social territory surrounded by the monuments and trappings of former relationships whose form partially conceals the reality of the wage-bargain.

Current forms of Employment

Any household with control (identified in west central Nepal with ownership as share-cropping and renting are relatively rare with much less than ten per cent of households even marginally involved) over more land than it has the labour to cultivate itself is likely to use labour from other households rather than leave it uncultivated. Often the amount of labour involved will be small, being less than fifty days extra labour on top of what can be provided by the household members. As an indicator of the relative concentration of the demand for labourers we can quote figures from our own survey of 667 rural households in west central Nepal in 1975. In this survey we found 116 households which employed more than fifty labouring days a year, of whom 39 bought more than a year equivalent. This can be compared with 267 households who sold more than fifty labouring days, of whom half could be considered to be heavily dependent on labouring to the tune of requiring more than half their food-grains from this source. Thus, whilst only 27% of households were heavily engaged either as an employer or employee, 567 of households were involved on one side or another of a significant labour hiring situation. The variations in this relationship can be classified into three basic types.

The first type is closest to the variations in reciprocation which characterises *parma* and *jajmani* relationships. Households requiring relatively small amounts of labour, which cannot be met from parma exchanges between households, can obtain labour through exerting pressure on other essentially non-market artisans whose incomes have become increasingly vulnerable as their position has been eroded by the penetration of massmanufactured commodities from India. This has allowed households requiring agricultural labour to extend the relationship, which has always included agricultural labouring, further and further into the area of agricultural work which thereby disposes of the little independence that village artisans may have once possessed. This development may involve other elements of a patron-client nature especially loans to meet individual crises. Loans with little security and interest rates of less than 207 (relatively low by South Asian standards!) appear to be significant features of relationship between rich and poor in several villages visited. As we have suggested for village artisans, the processes we observed in west central Nepal suggest that the trend is towards confirming the rights of the rich and the obligations of the poor. Resistance to this trend is unlikely to develop since the relative social and spatial isolation of the poor, the close ties with their patrons, and the genuine impoverishment of much of even the more advantaged peasantry, all militate against effective defensive action. No individual household would willingly lose its tiny share of protective patronage even though this process involves not only an increasingly subordinate position but also an increasingly precarious one. Thus, this method of obtaining agricultural labour is crucial to maintaining many households intact on small plots of land but is being displaced by more open market relationships as village economies come under increasing pressure.

In many villages there are no households needing to employ labour beyond a marginal amount. In such situations the most desperate households split and migrate leaving the small employment base to be shared among the remaining members. Many leave with the intention of returning as the life-cycle of the family moves into a new stage but few will return to find sufficient employment available in their home village. However, in some villages the degree of inequality of land distribution is such that aspects of an embryonic full-time labour market exist. This situation is more common in the terai than in the hills where the settlement pattern was created on the basis of substantial land grants which have not yet been completely reduced to subsistence holdings by successive divisions through inheritance or sales. At least one farm of more than twenty hectares therefore exists in most villages. These farms will have a demand for a few years equivalent of labour time each. A proportion of this labour is often employed on an annual basis. Both in terms of regularity of work throughout the year and the tendency for the arrangement to be renewed this form of employment may be called 'permanent' labour. One day a year in the agricultural slack season is widely recognised as the time for such annual contracts to start or be confirmed. The types of work to be undertaken by permanent labourers are not specified at this time and, although much of the work in practice could be regarded as farm labouring, the labourer finds himself on the wrong side of a very open arrangement to the advantage of the employer. Permanent labourers who previously could be characterised as 'retainers' are being changed slowly to farm mechanics. The process is continuing at different rates depending on local conditions and it will be a considerable time before a few 'salaried' employees on all the larger farms become the norm but there are no structural obstacles to this tendency. We shall return to the problem of proletarianisation in agriculture below but it is worth noting here that the conclusion to Chapter 8 on urban workers which draws a distinction between semi-skilled regular employment and unskilled casual labour might well have its parallel in agriculture. The permanent labouring relationship may survive in name whilst crucially changing its nature.

The third type of employment relationship differs from the first two in that the relationship between the act of labouring and remuneration is direct, unobscured by being located in the midst of a complex of particularistic attributes. In a situation where the vast majority of households own some land and the environment does not permit staggering of operations there is a strong temporary demand for labour at the agricultural peaks.

Many villages in the terai have this characteristic. Farmers needing extra labour at such times are, in general, unable to exert extra-market coercion on poorer (but largely self-sufficient) neighbours and thus are forced to pay wages to casual labourers from outside the village system. In most areas of the terai, Indians from the adjoining districts of the provinces of Uttar Pradesh and Bihar come regularly to take on such work and in a few areas temporary migration from nearby hill villages occurs. Such labour adds about one quarter to the workforce of some villages at critical times but quickly disperses once the peak is passed. This is possible because the reverse seasonality in the construction industry allows large numbers of landless people to move between agricultural and non-agricultural labouring (for a discussion of one section of the construction industry which shows a high degree of mobility, see Chapter 7, on Highway Construction Workers). Although many labourers do return to the same area for work year after year, the existence of an effective labour market is suggested by the uniform daily wage rates paid right across the west central terai area. This can be compared with the large variations (up to 100%) in payment made to permanent labourers on an annual basis. Each casual labourer has the choice of accepting cash or kind payment. The cash arrangement can involve all meals for the labourer plus a small amount of cash, generally two Indian rupees, or a simple payment of five Nepalese rupees without meals. The arrangement for payment in kind provides the labourer with one small meal during the day plus a fixed amount of food-grain, usually paddy (expressed in kilograms this is about $2\frac{1}{2}$ kg. paddy). For a man performing hard manual labour in the fields this contains the calories needed for about three days work when supplemented with small amounts of other food-stuffs. Thus fifty days of daily paid labour in a year will barely provide the food requirements for one adult to survive even if the remainder of the year is spent 'resting'. The need for other income if the labour force is to be maintained in the long run is therefore obvious and to this extent it may be possible to describe the employers as obtaining 'super-exploited' labour since they are not required to pay labour its full reproduction cost. On the other hand the rates paid are considerably above the minimum needed to maintain the labour power required temporarily by the employer and, less abstractly, wage rates in this part of Nepal are reported to be higher than those in the Indian border districts. It is to this particular differential to which we now return to examine the processes involved in changing the casual labour relationship.

We are unable to discover the forces which had determined the daily wage rate which was invariably described as 'customary'. Certainly pressures exist to reduce the real wage into line with levels of payment in India but the only way this tendency has manifested itself so far is in the money wage (five Nepalese rupees) failing to rise in line with current inflation which has amounted to over 10 per cent per annum in the last five years. This has meant that this cash payment wage-form has virtually disappeared as an actual form except for some Indians who find money more convenient to carry and accept Indian rupees which have retained fractionally more of their real purchasing power. If payment in kind was not an alternative then inflation would have benefitted employers by reducing the value of the real wage and thus capitalised on the absence of formal organisation among labourers. But it is undoubtedly the case that the widespread distribution of labourers performing exactly comparable operations required by employers at a critical time does exert a negative influence on attempts by relatively isolated small clusters of employers to reduce the 'customary' payment in kind. Any such attempts might result in boycott or riot situations where the whole season's crop might be put at risk over a relatively short period. Very few farmers could stand the loss involved and so, in the absence of direct support to the employers by the State, the real wage is maintained and increased surplus must come from general productivity increases through 'improved' techniques or increased intensity of work not from reductions in the real wage. The limited opportunities that exist for increases in the rate of exploitation, will benefit employers due to the inability of labourers to negotiate for increased wages collectively even if they are able to resist cuts.

Various changes at present taking place suggest different directions for the total levels of casual employment. Mechanisation of irrigation and processing reduce on-farm labour required but generally these tasks were performed by permanent labourers. Growing sugar cane spreads labour peaks and thus diminishes the implicit bargaining power of casual labourers but the growing of second crops (primarily wheat) increases the general demand for labour. Like many other writers at this time we must remain agnostic on the impact of current and future changes in farming technique on the demand for labour except to say that it seems very unlikely to increase dramatically. But even in this situation of relatively static demand for agricultural labour and increasing supply we do not envisage reductions in real wage rates being achieved without a bitter struggle, neither would we expect the acceptance of such a reduction to be to the benefit of the labourers as a group since the price elasticity of demand for labourer's services is likely to be very small under present, and probable future conditions. The real wage is thus a question of class struggle not market clearing and whilst the State is willing to intervene to stop wages rising (for instance, instructing employers on construction projects to pay labourers no more than the local agricultural labourers and restricting settlement on uncultivated land), it seems less likely that it will provide the coercion necessary to enforce a wage cut.

The Origins of Agricultural Labourers

The Nepalese social formation is one with very few landless households and at no time in the past have processes acted to completely 'free' labour from land. In formal legal terms, the opposite process has been encouraged by removing the rights granted to the aristocracy over large tracts of land and confirming farmers as free-holders. Such legal attempts at land reform are often subject to abuse but, in the case of Nepal, these abuses seem to act to deprive individuals of titles or to occasionally enclose small amounts of resources which were by custom 'common' rather than to confirm any structural tendency to systematically deprive whole classes of possession of the means of agricultural production. Less than five per cent of the rural population have possession of no land and in our own rural survey we found only twenty per cent of households who obtain more than half their foodgrains from agricultural labouring for wages. Thus for the vast majority of rural households agricultural labouring for wages in cash or kind is only one of several income-generating activities. Our impression was that agricultural labouring for wages was regarded as undesirable and only to be undertaken if no other local opportunities existed. This applied even more strongly to 'permanent' labouring arrangements which were seen by outsiders, and often the labourers themselves, as a barely concealed form of slavery. Agricultural wage labourers thus tend to originate under particular conditions. The first condition is that although most households have some land, some households have very little land. The groups identified by artisan occupational caste names almost invariably have the smallest amount of land and even that land may be held under less certain 'ownership' rights then possessed by others. For instance, the land may have been a 'gift' of a powerful patron or 'sold' at a low price with uncertainty about whether the transaction was registered. Under such circumstances the household may find itself with more labour available than needed for the cultivation of its own land and under pressure to sell the surplus labour-time to another farmer. Female labour is in heavy demand at transplanting time which may mean that whilst the men may avoid the necessity of working for others, the women of these households will not. This effect is compounded as the demand for the craft-work of the men falls, due to competition with mass-manufactured substitution imported from India, thus eroding even that small area of independence which the household previously possessed. A general argument, which can be applied to many households in the terai, and in the hills wherever any, original deficiency in land owned has now been legally cemented in the context of diminishing access to common resources through legal restriction and ecological decline: such households represent the in-built agricultural labour force for a village, tied to the location by land owned, yet forced to work for others to survive.

In addition to this constantly self-reproducing local labour pool there may be special circumstances where households whose overall position is not particularly disadvantaged may seek agricultural labouring, work. A household with a number of daughters not yet married may find that *parma* arrangements cannot utilise all their labour time and pressure may exist for the girls to work for wages, if there is a neighbour with a matching deficiency of female labour. Similarly, the prospect of an expensive life-cycle ceremony may overcome any distaste for wage-work on the part of the head of the household, at least as far as his wife and children are concerned. But such temporary situations can only contribute a small, and uncertain, amount of labour-time to the pool and, in most hill villages, it is from the structural domination of disadvantaged groups described above that larger farmers derive the agricultural labour-time they need to cultivate all their land. In some parts of the hills, and in much of the terai even this mechanism is incapable of releasing sufficient labour-time in the agricultural peak periods and a more brutal 'freeing' of labour from the land is required.

In the neighbouring districts of the Indian provinces of Uttar Pradash and Bihar, the process of creating capitalist relations in agriculture appears to have proceeded much further than in Nepal. We noted in the previous section that a considerable proportion of the labour force used in Nepal in the peak season comes from India. It is not within the purview of this book to consider the origins and situation of these people but we must note that whilst we are describing the plight of the poor in Nepal and the role played in their condition by Indian manufacturing capitalist expansionism this does not mean we are unaware of the situation of the poor in the rest of the South Asian sub-continent. The Nepalese ruling class uses chauvinist arguments to divert attention from its own inadequacies but this cannot conceal the exploitation of thousands of Indian citizens which is crucial in producing the foodgrain surplus essential to the survival of Nepal as a sovereign state. Within Nepal itself the production of a fraction of the labour force which is not tied to a particular location by landholding has been much less pronounced. Ecological decline does produce local disasters, such as landslips and floods, which deprive some households of all their land thus forcing them to migrate as a household. But more typically poorer households are forced to release older sons as migrants in order for others to survive when the land cannot take further partition. Customarily these migrants have sought their fortunes in the armies and cities of other countries, gained employment in capitalist agriculture such as the tea plantations of Darjeeling and Assam or settling as farmers in ecologically similar areas all along the foothills of the Himalayas. Many of these options are now less open economically than they were twenty years ago or no longer legally exist as options for Nepalese citizens. This closing down of opportunities coincided with malaria eradication in the terai producing an unsettled frontier situation. In its efforts to restrict access to this frontier the Nepalese state is forming, as a by-product, groups of relatively mobile landless people who have already clashed several times with the police and army. It is from such groups that general demands for improvements of conditions in agricultural labouring are most likely to arise, uniting apparently local, particularistic grievances of individuals.

Evidence that individualised interpretations of position are common came from interviews with 'permanent' labourers who almost invariably discussed their descent into this condition as a chapter of personal misfortunes. Such misfortunes included ill-health of children and loss of land through deceit of relatives. Others were born into a household where the head was a tied labourer or slave and thus considered it their unfortunate lot to follow into the service of his father's master's household. This interpretation obviously has meaning for any particular individual and it is understandable that the conditions of employment militate against recognising the wider causality of subordination. The origins of most of those who depend upon agricultural labour for wages are in systems of particularistic relations which can only be broken to reveal common interests by a group sufficiently spatially mobile to grasp the general causal mechanism. The specific nature of Nepalese paddy growing with large labour peaks at critical times may produce such a group but the conditions for successful organisation require a political. aspect which the present Nepalese State is unlikely to tolerate.

The Lives of Labourers and Their Familes

So far we have discussed agricultural labouring from the viewpoint of its role in production and the dynamics which are altering the forms in which that role is played. We have seen that the labourer has been completely subordinated and separated from control of his/her activity whilst labouring, but often this is only one of several production activities undertaken by that individual. In this section we will consider briefly the wider aspects of life for labourers and their families including those other activities and consumption patterns. The information drawn on is taken from the rural survey we conducted in 1975 in the west central region of Nepal. In this survey out of an areally stratified random survey we interviewed 667 households of whom we identified 134 households as 'labouring' households, that is households whose cash equivalent income from labouring accounted for more than half the cash value of total food-grain consumed. A summary of the data for these households is shown in Table 9. We have summarised the data into four types of labouring households showing the arithmetic mean; standard deviation and median for each cell in order to indicate the shape of the distribution involved. For instance, a positive arithmetic mean with a large standard deviation and a zero median indicates that only a few households recorded a large non-zero score in that particular cell. The four types represent the various combinations of relatively large and relatively small scales of farm produce with receipts and non-receipts of income from outside agriculture. After discussing the four types we will briefly compare their situation with that of their employers (Table 10).

Row 1 shows those who can be considered most vulnerable to changes in the conditions of agricultural labouring since they have little or no income from farm sales and have not managed to gain significant access to non-agricultural income sources. The 67 households in this category whilst not selling foodgrains do in fact produce a considerable proportion of the foodgrains they consume (compare column 1 with 5 and 6) but cash earned from labouring is crucial to meet the small outgoings (well under £ 1 per household a week equivalent at 1975 exchange rates) on items such as salt and cloth. Permanent labouring involves less than 50 per cent of the households even in this most vulnerable group although for some households it is undoubtedly vital and probably the only possibility for those households other than joining the wandering destitute. In contrast a minority of this group managed to not only maintain customary payments under *jajmani* arrangements (Column 10) but, sell a little foodgrain in the year 1974 when the harvest in general was not exceptionally good. The distribution of grain consumption per caput reveals that consumption on average is not comparable with other labouring groups and the intake of high protein foods though vanishingly small does not differ greatly from other groups. Row 2 contains a much smaller number of households as we would expect if agricultural labouring is a last resort largely used when land holding is too small to even provide subsistence. However, overall, whilst these households show a higher level of activity in most measures they are still unable as a group to produce a median net cash surplus. Rows 3 and 4 reveal the vital importance of non-agricultural income to even the poorest groups of households. Not only do these households show a balanced budget but they do so without needing to reduce consumption significantly in either the areas of locally produced or imported goods.

Turning to the employers for comparative purposes we

TABLE 9

Major Characteristics of Household Budgets of Wage Labourers

Sub-groups
(1) Wage labouring, Rs. 250 farm sales, with non-agricultural income.
(2) Wage labouring, Rs. 250 farm sales, with non-agricultural income.
(3) Wage labouring, Rs. 250 farm sales, without non-agricultural income.
(4) Wage labouring, Rs. 250 farm sales, without non-agricultural income.

	% of total population	*Total grain entering household (kg)*	*Total cash earned Rs. (1)*	*Total cash earned from labouring Rs.*	*Total kind payments from labouring (2)*	*Total kind payments from labouring (3)*	*Total military remittances Rs.*	*Total civil remittances Rs.*	*Total business remittances Rs.*
	(i)	*(ii)*	*(iii)*	*(iv)*	*(v)*	*(vi)*	*(vii)*	*(viii)*	*(ix)*
Sub-group		883	1,778	359	110	360	84	105	837
(1)	6.6	613	1,720	656	321	493	326	501	1,458
		730	1,300	0	0	147	0	0	220
Sub-group		908	2,344	533	0	548	0	630	476
(2)	0.6	1,309	1,367	377	0	1,095	0	1,260	627
		331	2,077	584	0	0	0	0	272
Sub-group		1,003	855	513	237	316	0	5	40
(3)	10.2	756	1,009	647	475	428	0	37	185
		795	600	599	0	459	0	0	0
Sub-group		1,652	1,159	190	398	562	0	0	137
(4)	11.1	1,154	1,423	464	632	717	0	0	324
		1,457	472	0	0	166	0	0	0

Note : The top number in each cell is the mean; the middle number is the standard deviations; the bottom number is the median.

Source : Rural Survey, 1984/5.

Total grain paid out K.g	Total grain sold Kg.	Total cash spent Rs. (4)	Purchases of fertilizer Rs.	Per caput consumption of grain Kg.	Per caput consumption of luxury foods Rs. (5)	Expenditure on medical treatment Rs. (6)	Expenditure on consumer durables Rs.	Total cash earned minus total cash spent Rs.
(x)	(xi)	(xii)	(xiii)	(xiv)	(xv)	(xvi)	(xvii)	(xviii)
22	0	1,615	7	5.7	0.20	0.12	182	163
57	0	1,622	45	3.1	0.40	0.39	132	1,328
0	0	895	0	4.7	0	0	136	0
9	64	1,829	0	5.1	0.	0.25	153	514
9	77	1,948	0	2.5	0.04	0.50	109	2,165
8	49	987	0	3.9	0	0	138	787
27	66	854	8	5.4	0.2	0.17	115	1
85	412	623	48	3.4	0.85	0.70	75	894
0	0	667	0	4.5	0	0	100	– 107
72	114	999	1	7.2	0.06	0.30	152	160
246	268	527	4	8.2	0.20	0.77	103	1,253
20	0	948	0	4.2	0	0	135	– 17

find that the smaller employers without non-agricultural incomes appear to be little better off in many aspects than the more advantaged labourers. A much higher output of foodgrains is used to pay labourers and raise consumption levels of food and imports leaving a net cash surplus of only a few Rs. 100 per annum on average. The crucial difference not only in the cross-section comparison of consumption levels but in the vulnerability of the labouring group to fluctuations in non-agricultural incomes which are outside the control of these households whilst the employers are using their own resources. Processes of differentiation are likely to follow such cracks, tearing apart any superficial static equality in consumption levels. Similarly small employers with outside incomes, whilst tending to show higher net cash surpluses, consume slightly more and pay out higher amounts per kg. foodgrain produced. Only at this level of cash flow do more than fifty per cent of households spend positive amounts on fertiliser. But, in general, the image is of households slightly better equipped for survival than steady accumulation. Only when we reach the 33 households who employ more than a year of labour time are average cash surpluses sufficient to be considered as facilitating the active expansion of capitalist relations (N.B. Rs. 1500 purchases a year of wage labour time).

But in reviewing the life led by labourers and their families it is important to note that significant quantitative differences in consumption may mean qualitative differences in living standards. The most obvious area is that of nutrition where with a diet dominated by foodgrains the calorific values produced by eating two-thirds as much in weight as the amount chosen by the unconstrained probably marks the boundary between an adequate diet and basic malnutrition. Such dietary deficiencies are now considered to have a major impact on child development. Also the level of high protein intake, though generally low in the Nepalese diet, does increase substantially for richer groups, whose higher consumption of proteins in the form of pulses is not included here. Standards of housing also differ greatly between brick built, tile or iron roofed houses for larger employers down to sheds and out-houses used by migrant casual labourers in the monsoon. Also medical services, which might perform some function in correcting the imbalance in consumption of food and shelter, are almost totally absent in the region, less than twenty trained doctors work in three of the major towns serving an area of over two million people. Thus a pattern of living which contains a predisposition to illness is likely to be a pattern predisposing to early death. As a final note to this section it is worth adding that the labourers and their families we are discussing here were selected using a sampling frame based on residence in a village and presence on a voting roll for that village. We suspect that our sample may well be biased, therefore, towards relatively secure labourers whose position is fortunate compared with migrant Indian and Nepalese labourers.

The Future

It has been the aim throughout this chapter to use the language of processes in order to carry out analysis beyond an historical documentation of observations. This section attempts to summarise and integrate the various processes showing what they suggest for future changes including the importance of the responses of the labourers themselves going beyond a classification as passive victims. In Section 1 we saw that historical developments have resulted in relationships which idealised elements of reciprocation becoming relationships of open subordination. This subordination is expressed through three major relationships which are in a process of moving towards an explicit wage-bargaining situation no longer mediated through particularistic channels. (Section 2) At the same time potential labourers are being produced on an expanded scale as processes outside the control of particular employers, continue. (Section 3) Lastly, while at first glance rural consumption standards appear still to be relatively equal, the present situation may well span crucial borderlines especially in nutrition and the dynamics point to increasing differentiation especially with respect to a largely hidden migrant labour group but including labourers fully,

TABLE 10

Major Characteristics of Household of Employers

Sub-groups
(1) Small employers, farm sales Rs. 1,000, with non-agricultural income
(2) Small employers, farm sales Rs. 1,000, with non-agricultural income
(3) Small employers, farm slaes Rs. 1,000, without non-agricultural income
(4) Small employers, farm slaes Rs. 1,000, without non-agricultural income
(5) Large employers, farm sales Rs. 1,000, with non-agricultural income
(6) Large employers, farm sales Rs. 1,000, with non-agricultural income
(7) Large employers, farm sales Rs. 1,000, without non-agricultural income

	% of total popu-lation	*Total grain entering household (kg.)*	*Total cash earned Rs. (1)*	*Total cash earned from labouring Rs.*	*Total kind payments from labouring (2)*	*Total kind payments from labouring (3)*	*Total military remit-tances Rs.*	*Total civil remit-tances Rs.*	*Total business remit-tances Rs.*
	(i)	*(ii)*	*(iii)*	*(iv)*	*(v)*	*(vi)*	*(vii)*	*(viii)*	*(ix)*
		1,719	4,669	93	0	0	1,568	263	1,324
Sub-group (1)	2.7	794	4,408	295	0	0	4,571	933	2,040
		1,689	3,412	0	0	0	0	0	0
		2,381	6,173	60	0	1.8	723	466	790
Sub-group (2)	2.9	1,462	2,932	180	0	8.1	1,354	1,130	1,936
		1,900	5,327	0	0	0	0	0	0
		1,992	1,797	138	0	5.3	0	80	80
Sub-group (3)	0.3	1,434	1,573	225	0	14.0	0	0	212
		1,886	1,150	0	0	0	0	0	0
		3,601	3,856	9	0	9.4	0	19	63
Sub-group (4)	4.6	4,809	2,705	48	0	36.5	0	107	323
		2,670	3,300	0	0	0	0	0	0
		2,437	11,474	0	0	0	0	0	9,520
Sub-group (5)	1.0	1,792	4,444	0	0	0	0	0	6,749
		2,338	10,684	0	0	0	0	0	10,000
		5,213	9,095	0	0	0	90	0	1,509
Sub-group (6)	1.6	3,524	5,728	0	0	0	302	0	3,366
		4,690	7,500	0	0	0	0	0	0
Sub-group		2,773	9,473	0	43.6	0	0	0	495
	2.9	2,826	11,558	0	200.0	0	0	0	1,249
		2,508	4,790	0	0	0	0	0	0

Total grain paid out kg.	Total grain sold kg.	Total cash spent Rs. (4)	Purchases of fertilizer Rs.	Per caput consumption of grain kg.	Per caput consumption of luxury foods (5)	Expenditure on medical treatment Rs. (6)	Expenditure on consumer durables Rs.	Total cash earned minus total cash spent
(x)	(xi)	(xii)	(xiii)	(xiv)	(xv)	(xvi)	(xvii)	(xviii)
91	288	3,743	27	6.8	0.54	0	320	927
130	401	2,397	64	3.8	0.59	0	361	3,755
28	293	3,345	0	5.6	0.55	0	175	176
149	2,009	3,769	150	7.6	0.26	0	413	2,403
180	2,594	1,784	286	3.3	0.65	0	261	2.356
70	985	4,030	18	6.0	0.00	0	450	1,895
157	299	1,287	137	6.1	0.24	0	173	510
172	294	836	362	2.3	0.33	0	67	1,198
74	359	864	0	5.7	0	0	175	329
573	1,777	3,212	69	6.0	0.10	1.1	528	644
1,039	1,430	2,335	127	2.6	0.22	3.2	421	2,416
226	1,599	2,680	0	5.5	0	0	400	233
412	68	5,208	39	5.9	0.71	0.9	743	6,267
871	96	1,800	75	2.9	1.19	1.9	656	4,218
26	0	4,897	0	6.4	0.32	0	900	7,533
3,347	2,819	5,663	313	6.3	0.40	0	860	3,431
6,803	3,134	2,155	430	3.8	0.37	0	870	4,910
1,573	1,994	6,298	500	5.1	0.47	0	500	1,175
1,309	4,592	5,465	540	7.4	0.36	0	562	4,008
1,776	5,966	5,020	1,241	4.2	0.54	0	543	7,840
987	2,143	2,930	0	6.0	0	0	325	1,641

resident in villages (Section 4). If such a situation represents the painful process of capitalist development in Nepal, then in the interests of the future generation it might be considered necessary to accept the suffering of Nepalese to join the many others who have borne the brunt of primitive accumulation on a world scale. Certainly the characteristics of the processes described above do appear to coincide with the double-edged 'freeing' of labour which marked, for instance, the early development of capitalism in England. Thus even if we accept that we are looking at processes not a static 'traditional' society there are still three major interpretations available which centre around the interaction of the economic and political instances. In selecting one interpretation, rather than another, people identify the conditions under which they then exercise choice, in other words selecting the alternative chooses the choice of action but not the actual outcome. Our argument is that the various alternatives correspond broadly to the interests of particular classes in the Nepalese political economy.

The first interpretation can be labelled as 'politics led' and suggested that the economy is pre-capitalist. This view emphasises the progressive nature of the ruling class against the relative conservatism of other groups in society. This progressive nature is exercised through the State in its role as 'modernisation' agency. The inherent processes in much of agriculture are regarded in this view as tending to decline. Poverty is a product of such processes and the alleviation of poverty depends on stimulating market forces in agriculture towards producing commodities and provide information on manufactured inputs. In such a model the State is seen as the transmitter of lessons already learnt by the rich. This view dominates the thinking about development processes in Nepal by indigenous and many international agencies. An inevitable ecological decay has opened up the rural economy to outside influence according to this viewpoint but not all the influence offered is progressive. Full democracy and trades unions, for instance, are inappropriate at early stages of the painful development process and should not be encouraged. Thus agricultural labourers, among other groups, are expected to accept the loosening of the few remaining archaic protective ties for themselves as individuals without being able to organise to forward their interests collectively in the political and economic spheres. Some markets appear to have to be forced to be free. The cement on the virtue of this arrangement is added when it is asserted by implication that the inability of labourers to bargain for productivity increases leaves income in the hands of those most likely to invest. Any objection is attributable to the short-sightedness of other groups, unable to perceive the advantages of short-term sacrifice. Elsewhere we have put forward our argument that this model fails to locate the Nepalese State in relation to its own history and the economic interests which circumscribe its activity (Blaikie, Cameron, Seddon 1978). The outcome of pursuing the policy implications of this model in our view will not be a fundamental restructuring of production but increasing violence (in its widest sense) against the disinherited in order to preserve the appearance of stability.

> "The migrant labour force, the hill farms that support them, and the subsistence holdings in the terai, are all as much of the agricultural surplus-producing (rural capitalist?) mode of production as the free labour force and their households are a part of the industrial capital-ist mode of production". (Feldman and Fournier 1976: 453).

> "The interests of the State are diverging from those of the dominant agricultural production class. It is not a progressive force for the expansion of the means of production for Nepal, inside or outside the agricultural sector". (Feldman and Fournier 1976: 462).

In this interpretation the economic contains the progressive tendencies inhibited by an inappropriate political form. This suggests the need for a bourgeois political revolution. But to succeed such a revolution must rest on a mass base. One interpretation of the political events of the 1950's in Nepal is that they represented a bid for State power in the interests of the bourgeoisie which failed due to the absence of a mass base. The platform for such a revolution rested on an appeal to nationalism but this was fatally flawed by the complete identification of the most potent national symbol, the monarchy, with the aristocracy. But more fundamental than the 'real politik' of where to locate a broad appeal capable of overcoming the propensity of the ruling class to use coercion in 'defence of the Constitution' is the question of whether the core of an independent bourgeois class exists in Nepal today. We have mentioned above a possible division of the employer group into advantaged peasants and potential accumulators. But even the potential accumulators are unlikely to develop a collective consciousness for a number of reasons. Firstly, land-ownership ensures the weakening of the objective imperative to accumulate capital which is central to the development of capitalism and granting hegemony to bourgeois ideas. Secondly, employers do not exist in the economic instance alone but look toward the existing State structure for privileged access to sources of personal rather than class gain. Not having suffered exclusion as a group, at least since 1951, bourgeois class consciousness and cohesiveness has not developed and the populist stance of the Nepal Congress Party seems unlikely to again attract the support of any particular disillusioned section of what is now a much more homogeneous dominant class than in the 1940's. In our opinion the appearance that the State has acquired autonomy from the interests of the agricultural production fraction of the ruling class is a measure of the advance not the retreat of capitalist hegemony. This viewpoint recognises the interests of the agricultural labourer but tends to relegate them to the role of providing the basis for a bourgeois political revolution, seeing them as progressive only insofar as they serve that movement. If the basis for that revolution does not exist, as we suspect, then the energy of dissent runs the danger of being channelled into populist coups of little substance by small fractions of the ruling class seeking a larger share of State privilege.

The third interpretation rests on the basis that the historic role of capitalism has been completed in Nepal. In abstract terms we are suggesting that capitalism is the determinant form of production and capitalist interests have virtual complete hegemony over the political and ideological spheres.

But this position has involved the accommodation of relationships which were not hostile to the reproduction of capitalist relations on an extended scale. This accommodation which may be formally described as 'articulation' can be seen in its political instance as the 'historic compromise' between the feudal aristocracy and a rising bourgeoisie lacking the confidence to carry through a political revolution in its own name. The economic aspect rests on increasing access to the means of production for those few who manage to amass money capital from merchant or money-lending activity. The State's role as protector of privilege and provider of sinecures to any threatened members of the ruling class still dominates the possibility of effective intervention in production. The processes involved in this analysis suggest that the tendency is towards increasing vulnerability and misery of many Nepalese whose only hope within the Nepalese economy is casual agricultural labouring complemented by even fewer casual labouring opportunities outside agriculture (see Chapter 8). Even where new techniques are introduced there is no evidence from our own observations or reports from elsewhere in South Asia that benefits will accrue to the poor especially when collective bargaining is, in practice, regarded as a subversive activity. If this interpretation is correct then both the basis and will are created for the increasing number of marginalised households to express their collective interest directly and simultaneously in the economic and political spheres. The search for control over production by those forced to seek wage employment is taking a number of forms; demands for trades union rights, some rural development programmes organised by 'enlighted' development agencies and the underground activities of the banned political parties, especially the Nepalese Communist Party but including radical elements in the Nepalese Congress Party. The path will be long and painful but no other class in the political economy of Nepal holds the possibility of providing the overall framework for systematically developing the productive forces of the area. The production of a substantial class of agricultural labourers is assured, the possibility of applying that labour effectively in production depends upon politics not markets. Whilst such a political movement would build on the remnants of existing reciprocal labour practices and the ideology of self-sufficient rural economy in the villages the overthrow of the ruling class and capture of State power is crucial. The demands of agricultural wage-labourers can fulfil this dual role as recognisable to peasants at the village level tactically, whilst their activity in the surplus producing sector of agriculture grants them a strategic position for organising on a national scale directly against the economic basis of the ruling class. As victims of exploitation, oppression and discrimination the interests of agricultural wage labourers are an important element in the progressive movement.

CHAPTER 7

HIGHWAY CONSTRUCTION LABOURERS

The Context of Highway Constructions

Up until the mid-1950's Nepal had only a few kilometres of motorable road. Trucks could use the major bullock cart tracks in the terai in the winter months but within the hills the transport system rested upon the backs of people and pack animals. A few motor-cars had reached Kathmandu Valley by being man-handled over the hills from the Indian border. The journey from Pokhara in west central Nepal to Kathmandu took about five days even for a lightly loaded man. To go further east than Kathmandu or to the far west of Nepal from Pokhara in minimum time required the use of the Indian railway system from Nautanwa, the border rail-head, again five days journey on foot from Pokhara. But from the mid-1950's, the construction of a network of relatively high standards (in terms of width, gradient and cornering requirements and surfacing materials) has been the major production activity outside agriculture in Nepal. Pokhara was linked to the Indian border in 1968 and to Kathmandu in 1972, both roads being constructed under difficult engineering conditions using very little plant and machinery. These two roads were 350 kilometres in total length and financed through agencies of two foreign aid donors; India for the road linking Pokhara with the border and the Indian road network, China for the road linking Pokhara with Kathmandu, whence to the Chinese road network.

In the late 1960's construction of a motorable road running parallel with the Indian border began under agencies from the USSR, USA, UK and India. In west central Nepal we had the opportunity to see the efforts of agencies from India, China and the UK to come to terms with Nepalese physical and socio-economic conditions. Over twenty thousand people have worked on highway construction at one time or another in the last ten years in the West Central Planning Region (all three major highway construction projects employed over ten thousand workers at peak times) in an area in which the total number of wage workers outside agriculture, the catering section and the administration in 1974/75 was probably under five thousand (the sugar mill, by far the largest factory, employed a peak labour force of under seven hundred). Total direct labour-time input into highway construction in the area probably amounted to more than seventy-five thousand years. Even maintenance expenditure alone in the early 1970's was costing several times as much as all rural development projects, including irrigation, financed by the Nepalese State in the area.

The explosion of activity in improving the communications system appears to support the hypothesis that the Nepalese State has completely discarded its previous role as agent of a small ruling class and has become an instrument of 'modernisation' acting in the interests of the whole Nepalese people. An alternative hypothesis suggests a basic continuity in the class nature of the Nepalese State. The relevance of this question to highway labourers is clear since in the first case, the State can attempt to justify low wages, bad working conditions and repression of workers' demands on the grounds that it represents the general interest as against the narrow sectional demands of the workers. However, in the second case, the labourers become transformed into the front-line troops facing a State acting as the oppressing agent of a ruling class. This essay attempts to make the case for the second hypothesis by attempting to explain the observed qualitative change in the transportation network whilst demonstrating a fundamental continuity in the nature of the State as defender of a minority class interest.

At the time of unification in the late 18th century the transport networks were only suitable for limited movement of people within the petty principalities at times of year convenient in terms of the agricultural and climatic calendar. A few trails from Tibet to India did pass through Nepal but even these were only suitable for limited seasonal pack animal movement. The rulers of the petty states in present day west central Nepal left, as virtually their only surviving monuments, series of tiny forts (*kot* in Nepali) which suggest that their primary interest was to obstruct rather than facilitate movement. The terrain is such that invasions of small armies could be held at key passes and supply lines were very vulnerable to attacks from high defended positions. Thus at this time the precursors of the highway construction labourers were employed in projects to limit rather than encourage mobility. The consolidation of these petty states into a national Nepalese State was achieved without the construction of new transport facilities and subsequent improvements were discouraged by the threat of invasion from India by the armies of the British East India Company or from Tibet, at this time as today, virtually a province of China. The ruling class was thus faced with the contradiction of needing communications for internal control but needing to restrict movement to deter external aggression.

The resolution to this contradiction rested on the ability of the State to dispose of rights over land and to coerce labour. Land titles were given in the first decade of the 19th century with the specific stipulation to 'watch northsouth tracks and maintain only one route through the Churia Hills, whichever is the worst one' (Regmi 1971: 40). Apart from such specific requirements, more general obligations to provide transport facilities through their areas for central government officials and freight were associated with land grants of all types. Rights of a corvée-labour form ensured that movement would be relatively costless if still time-consuming for the ruling class whilst restrictions on settlement applied to peasants and merchants limited the mobility of people necessary for the creation and realisation of surplus. Open discrimination in access to mobility also brought certain other advantages to the dominant fraction of the ruling class as control of the few long-distance trade routes meant that vital military material and luxury (i.e. goods not produced locally) commodities were concentrated in few hands and could thus be used to ensure loyalty of officials. Under such circumstances there was little incentive to put the considerable potential labour force to work on improving national transport facilities and considerable reason not to encourage local initiative on such matters. The existence of such local initiative is suggested by the many minor trail improvements that were reported to have taken place in the 1950's in west central Nepal. Commemoration tablets set in porters' resting places indicate that these reports of relatively recent construction effort at a village level are reasonably accurate.

But if the ruling class in Nepal were benefitting from restrictions on internal movement, they were also finding advantage from the existence of capitalist activity on the borders of Nepal. By the end of the 19th century the British rulers in India had extended the railway network right up to the Nepalese border. The terai areas were now easily exploitable for bulk exports such as timber and foodgrains to India. However, in the 20th century, Indian capital was developing an internal mass-manufacturing potential which was hard hit by the depression of the 1930's and the disruption of the 1940's. In such a situation neither all interests in the ruling class of Nepal nor all interests of Indian capital were satisfied with the penetration of capitalism into Nepal remaining at a level of raw material extraction from the border areas. Commodities from Indian factories were moving deep into Nepal throughout the inter-war period using the rudimentary transport system available and Nepalese intermediaries. In 1951, a rebellion against the already toppling autocracy used the Indian transport system to launch a successful invasion and the stage was set for exploitation to displace direct coercion as the dominant method of appropriating surplus. The extension, not the restriction, of the transport system was necessary to ensure the success of the new method of surplus appropriation by the ruling class.

To understand why this is so it is useful to consider briefly a general theory of the form of capitalist crises and the role transportation can play in attempts at resolution. A crisis for capitalism is always a multifacetted phenomenon with an apparent coincidence of gluts in consumer industries as markets apparently fail and shortages of investment opportunities to absorb a growing surplus of capital seeking employment. When such crises precipitate a political confrontation, a partial resolution may occur through the growth of the 'arms' industry and occasionally the actual destruction of the apparently 'surplus' men and materials in war. But under other circumstances the extension of a transport network shows its property as an additional means of alleviating crisis. In this role, transport activity has a dual attractiveness since it not only facilitates the penetration of new markets, thus helping sectors with sales deficiencies or input shortages, but also the act of construction itself provides a major investment outlet for unemployed capital, thus doubly relieving the symptoms of the crisis. Perhaps it is no wonder, therefore, that as we look at the history of capitalism we find its major landmarks are often associated with the explosion of new transportation possibilities; the canal, railway, steamship, motor-car and aeroplane; which expanded markets for outputs, cheapened inputs and provided extensive investment opportunities simultaneously. But, as the crisis which is temporarily resolved is capitalist, so are the limits of that resolution essentially those of capitalism.

Capitalism is thus generally progressive as the mobility of commodities increases but in its expansion capitalism is unable by its very nature to move beyond a number of barriers. The first barrier is that no rationale exists under capitalism to provide transport facilities outside market economics, the logic of cost-benefit analysis follows this rationale, suggesting where a facility should be located giving an apparently objective criterion for the construction technique to be used.

The second barrier is the boundary of the nation-state which distorts Cartesian space into political space where costs of moving commodities across a border are increased due to either formal duties or risks and/or bribes, associated with illegal movement. A third barrier is produced by the competition of interests of various fractions of the ruling class for a share of the surplus produced in the act of construction. Landowners, merchants, financiers, construction contractors and vehicle operators compete for the benefits produced by the labourers; decisions taken are affected by this competition. The fourth barrier is associated with the fundamental class struggle of capitalism and the threat of socialist challenge which demands, for instance, the ability to swiftly bring military forces to bear upon any symptom of unrest.

The design of the Nepalese highway network has accepted all these barriers and this suggests a capitalist essential nature. The State is, in the model, the primary agent in a process of accommodation, to which the aid donor agencies have acquiesced in the case of China or actively participated in the case of India. The failure to move beyond the four barriers can be charted in a number of reports. A report commissioned through the UNDP reported in 1969 that a road network in the hills could not really be justified, even on the basis of optimistic estimates of induced activity (barrier one). When the Nepalese Government objected this report was amended to take account of 'nation-building' (barrier four) but the basic principle of production of marketable surplus as the criterion for highway construction was not questioned. (UNDP/Comtec, 1970). An internal Transport Ministry report in 1973 attempted to create a formal framework for the reform of the construction industry to place it on more open capitalist lines (barrier three) whilst accepting the existence of private contractors. The Centre for Economic and Development Administration (CEDA) produced a report in 1975 attempting to treat construction techniques as a technical problem requiring the adjustment of market prices (barrier one) by comparing the experience of the various donor agencies totally independently of the experience of the labourers involved (CEDA 1973). Lastly

CEDA produced a series of papers on the negotiating of the 1971 Trade and Transit Agreement with India (barrier two) which accepted the border as an immutable fact (CEDA 1969).

Under such circumstances we have attempted to demonstrate that both the impetus for expansion of the transport network and the directions of that expansion are based on forces outside the control of the mass of the people. The State's role in this process is not as spokesman for those masses but much more as mediator between competing fractions of the ruling class, making sure that all concerned obey the rules of capitalist reproduction. As we shall see in the next two sections these rules are very different for the contractors and the labourers. At the point of highway construction we find many parallels with the discussion of agricultural labourers, with larger landowners meeting small landowners and the landless over what is fundamentally a wage-bargain but disguised by some particularistic elements due to the specific conditions of recruitment and employment. The next two sections describe the basic conditions surrounding recent highway construction work in west central Nepal drawing heavily on information generously provided by the British engineers working on a section of the east-west highway in west central Nepal (Mahendra Rajmarga) and interviews with contractors and labourers working on that section of highway.

The Social Organisation of Major Projects: Agencies and Contractors

When embarking on a major highway construction project in Nepal a decision is made by the financing agency on whether contractors are to be used and whether such contractors should be responsible for the provision of plant and materials, as well as for labour. Superficially the choice appears to contain real policy issues, especially as we were fortunate to have Chinese, Indian and UK projects to compare. The Chinese in constructing the Privthi Rajmarga attempted to apply an organisation coming close to a "direct labour" type. Work gangs received all tools, plant and equipment from the Chinese and were allotted relatively small amounts of work for which it appears no formal contract was offered. However, this system still used work gangs of more than fifty in size and communication with the labourers went through a "leader" (Naik in Nepali) who could easily adopt the role of unofficial "contractor" and receive the rewards and the responsibilities that such a title confers. The British in the constructing of the Mahendra Rajmarga introduced a formal competitive contracting system, but the apparent inexperience of the contractors, together with the dearth of contractors of Nepalese nationality quickly convinced the British engineers that contracting as conventionally practised in the United Kingdom was not feasible. The final system arrived at as a result of this experience closely resembled that of the Chinese with "labour only" contractors obtaining all plant and materials except simple tools from the road builders on defined tasks of limited extent and a large direct labour force for specialist work. The conclusion from this experience appears to be that whilst one major Indian contractor with plant worked on the Mahendra Rajmarga, the general practical result of labour-only contractors can derive from two quite different approaches by the funding agencies. Direct labour policies on a large scale in a very pure form are difficult for a foreign agency to institute since labour recruitment outside a certain area around the road rests on a network of social contacts which penetrate throughout Nepal and into India. Even though the area of local recruitment in the case of the British road extended throughout the West Central Planning Region for the direct labour workers, the numbers were still insufficient to meet peak demands. In general terms recruitment to the labour force is a function of both distance and need, with relatively poor hill districts in the north west of the Planning Region being disproportionately heavily represented as are the relatively rich terai districts close to the road. This meant that large scale recruitment had to be an active search process rather than the passive one of waiting for applicants with minimum advertising—the process adopted by the large road building agencies. Contractors are basically men with wide networks of contracts capable of arranging movement of large numbers of labourers with minimum material incentives.

Even when construction is undertaken in areas where abundant local labour is willing and able to undertake work at the offered rates, such as seemed to have happened with the roads to Pokhara from India and Kathmandu, the absence of a skilled supervisory and managerial fraction of the working class in Nepal meant that a group of intermediaries emerged between the agency staff and the labourers. These intermediaries relieved the engineers and the surveyors of routine day-to-day tasks of management and supervision and in return obtained rights over the distribution of money to the labourers and their recruitment. In real terms these intermediaries are contractors in all but name if we understand by this term responsibility for a stated piece of work and taking the residual albeit often a very substantial residual reward, after other payments have been met. In the British project, the same effect was seen more formally when employees left supervisory positions in the direct labour force to perform exactly the same tasks as before, only as formal contractors.

The limitations of a pure contracting policy are equally evident. Contracting for most Nepalese contractors still represents a side-line from agriculture and investment is limited to an initial working capital and perhaps pledging some (about 5% of contract value), land or gold as security for 'earnest money'. Even men who have earnt more than Rs. 50 lakhs in the period of a few months (£ 10,000 at 1975 exchange rates) from contracting work possess no plant, stocks or machinery (except perhaps a truck) and hence have no need to plan a continuing work schedule. This lack of commitment to the industry makes a fully competitive policy towards contractors impossible and means that contractors are highly dependent on the funding agencies officials. It is perhaps natural that an agency with a tight schedule for completion should accept this as a limitation and "featherbed" the contractors in terms of the services they expect. However, the corollary of this is that the cost of entry (including risk) to the constructing industry is low with a small amount of finance capital needed especially if a network of contacts exists to supply labour. Thus many landowners with a few hectares but no experience are able to enter and an aggressive competitive tendering policy is not effective since lack of experience on the part of the contractor will produce tenders so low as to be unrealistic, which will either force the agency to help the contractor by raising the price after the job has started thus encouraging the tendency to underprice, or let the contractor make a loss in which case it is usually the labourers and the agency, not the contractor who suffers. To put the matter in a harsh light, the formal contractor may often turn out to be an overpaid supervisor completely dependent on the agency for technical advice, materials and plant.

Statements giving the appearance of essential independence of firms and agencies cannot conceal the strong informal relationships such as the "feather bedding" mentioned above, which are not included in the public debate. Information on such structures is always difficult to confirm due to the legal 'greyness' of the relationships involved. A rough estimate of one indication of this relationship between agency and client contractor was made from documents kept by the British engineers involved in building a part of the Mahendra Rajmarga. Nepalese interviewed said the British were exceptionally honest in their dealings but even in this case the form of records restricted us to examining a few (eight in all) tender documents for earth moving which were paid as specified, since subsequent 'variations' did not detail the further labour use allowed. That is for other cases we could find only a record of total amount paid to the contractor without any indication of inputs purchased. The calculations are based on later contracts by which time the British quantity surveyors claimed to have gained considerable experience on an acceptable rate for each type of output which implicitly (not explicitly) included a "normal" Nepalese rate of profit to the contractor. The results of these calculations are that the ratio of contractors' receipts to other payments was calculated by us to vary between 0.22 to 2.52 with a mean of 0.75 and a median of 0.50, that is a contractor received an average one-third or more of the total value of the contract. Similarly estimated contractors' profits on other roads were, Rs. 8,000 on a labour cost of Rs. 13,000 on the Chinese built road and Rs. 14 lakh on a labour cost of Rs. 36 lakh on the Indian built road. To an agency trying to meet a time-table such rates of profit may well be acceptable but the existence of a special relationship between senior agency workers and contractors does not benefit the labourers who are legally prevented in Nepal from organising to claim a share of these 'benefits' of early completion. To profits for work actually undertaken can be added additional income from over-estimation of work by agency surveyors. All contractors who have worked on highways constructed under the control of Indian agencies remarked that Nepalese terrain, requiring much earth-moving not amenable to pre-estimation, is ideal for such corrupt practices. Chinese and UK agency methods appear to have avoided flagrant abuses reported on Indian financial projects but Nepalese interviewed always talked as if these were exceptions which proved the rule.

Our interviews with five contractors revealed expenditure patterns which involved little productive investment activity with urban house construction prominent and, in those few cases where initial land-holdings were not already considerable, some land purchases. In circumstances where integration of agency officials and contractors is strongly developed and contractors have the option of disappearing into advantaged subsistence agriculture or rentier activities without the losses associated with liquidating plant and machinery, there is little chance of a fully competitive construction industry developing. It is difficult to see where the basis of a 'reformed' capitalism would arise with the aim, among others, of eliminating corruption even though intervention by the military in politics on the platform of defending the constitution and eliminating corruption is always a possibility. However, the absence of any fraction of the ruling class not benefitting from the present situation, combined with the effective exclusion of the masses which is enshrined in the constitution, suggests that the two aims are incompatible.

Labourers' Recruitment and Rewards

In contrast to the experience of contractors, whose partial integration into capitalist relations appears not only painless but positively comfortable, stands that of labourers. Whilst their employers do not face the full rigour of competition, labourers find their position actually worse than that associated with wage-paid agricultural labouring (see Chapter 6). A brief description of how the wage labour force was recruited and regarded illustrates this for the case of the Mahendra Rajmarga, drawing on some examples from other projects.

Smaller contractors (employing up to 80 people for a few weeks) use networks of contacts to obtain labourers from their own place of origin or from villages near the work site. These networks tend to link larger landowners, thus specifically harmonising the demands for wage labour in agriculture and construction although climatic consideration ensure general complementarity. Attempts to attract local labour on an open market basis by the UK agency largely failed, partially because even poorer peasants have farm tasks most days and are unable to free themselves for a full day's labouring. Contractors did pay higher daily wages than the agency and also paid bonuses at the end of successful contracts but expected their labourers to work from dawn to dusk with a few breaks. Larger contractors relied on other contractors to find them 'specialist' Indian labour. These contractors came from Orissa or Bihar, and they hired labour from these areas.

Indian labourers from Orissa had a 'four month' contract and received an advance on their future salaries from the contractor for travelling expenses to Nepal. Rewards varied according to the type of work and its organisation; for instance an Orissan labourer in a work team earnt between 70 and 100 I.C. a month with food, whilst a stone-breaker on individual piece-work arrangements from Uttar Pradesh earnt between 7 and 17 I.C. a day without food provided, the amount depending on the type of stone he or she had to break. The wages of the labourers from Orissa or Bihar were paid monthly by the contractor, mate or foreman, and sent by post to their families in India after the deduction of a sum for travelling expenses and tools. Indian labourers were, as a rule, concentrated in particular roles by place of origin but were predominantly from groups discriminated against in the caste system of north India. The stone-breakers were mostly Moslems from Uttar Pradesh, the earth movers were for the most part 'untouchables' (scheduled castes) from Orissa or Bihar, the Bihar labour being made up mostly of women who belonged to the Munda ethnic group (scheduled tribes). Nepalese labourers also tended to 'specialise' and work in the more dangerous area of side-cutting and loosening rocks. Variation in types and hours of work led to considerable variation in daily pay from as low as Rs. 2 for a Nepalese child to the equivalent of Rs. 25 for a strong, skilled Indian worker including a bonus element. However, a broad basis for comparison between agency, contractor and agricultural labour might be as below for the area around the UK agency section of the Mahendra Rajmarga. In 1974 an agricultural labourer in that area of the terai received 4 *kuruwa* ($2\frac{1}{2}$ kg approx.) of paddy plus all his other food (including salt) for about seven hours' work worth about Rs. 9 in 1974. A labourer on the Mahendra Rajmarga working for the British engineers received a basic daily wage of Rs. 5 without food, whilst for dawn to dusk work contractors paid a wage of Rs. 9 without food. Continuity of work was better in the medium term (about three years) for the direct labour force but at the completion of the particular agency project this continuity was completely broken whilst a contractor's labourer might move more easily to a new project with that same contractor, if the contractor feels disposed to take on further work.

Hiring of technicians and supervisors as wage-workers is difficult in Nepal, especially given the inadequacies of the education system. As Nepalese contractors are labour-only contractors much of the training of skilled labour in the west central region of Nepal was done by the agencies themselves.

For instance when the British established a base camp in Khasauli for the Mahendra Rajmarga in 1968, they tried to hire: qualified workers and technicians. The majority of those who applied for jobs did not have qualifications or specialised knowledge. At the time of enquiry (1974/75) only about a third of the remaining 120 monthly paid Nepalese personnel had any training prior to their engagement by the British, acquired either while serving in the Army (35), or while working with Indians in Shillong (15). These workers were the first to be paid a monthly salary. The rest were selected from the daily or weekly paid workers and trained by the British technicians, administrators and engineers. The vast majority of the latter group come from the West Central Planning Region and more than two-thirds are Magars or Gurungs, ethnic groups recruited into the British army (the two major hill tribes in the area), but only five persons belonged to the predominantly poor "occupational castes". In those cases where contractors were large enough to require intermediaries between themselves and the labourers they hired people coming from their family, local area or those who had similar experience in the past (e.g. ex-servicemen). In order to retain their technicians and skilled workers, experienced contractors will not only pay them relatively well (daily rates in excess of Rs. 20) but invite them to meals several times a week; offer them small presents; allow them to return home to work in their fields at appropriate times of the year; pay all their travelling expenses and provide them with suitable accommodation on site.

Labourers whose homes were not within easy travelling distance of work and who had to buy food and other essentials found their real wages eroded by considerable local inflation. This derived from a heavily increased demand in an inflexible monopolistic marketing situation producing large local price increases. Obviously those workers whose homes are sufficiently close to supply essentials or whose contracts include basic foods (for instance the Orissans) are less vulnerable except insofar as money wage discrimination is practised against such arrangements, or discretionary payments such as bonuses are reduced to compensate contractors for increased costs. Local price increases at camps on the Kathmandu-Pokhara highway in 1967 were reported to be about 50% for cooked rice and dal (at Damauli) and the price differential for basic food was reported as 40% between Bhairahawa and the road camp in the Muglin area. On the Mahendra Rajmarga increases in the price of rice in the years 1972 and 1973 were just over 307 in Bhairahawa, but over 80% at the relatively isolated Chormara camp in Nawalpur. This issue became the focus of labour unrest in 1972 and gave cause for concern in 1973 when further trouble was possibly averted by a light monsoon which did not disrupt transport to the expected extent. High prices encouraged the development of agriculture and marketing around the Mahendra Rajmarga in Nawalpur, but insofar as labourers are drawn from the poor whilst farmers with surplus produce and merchants are richer this was a redistributive effect towards greater inequality. The contractors were able to use discretionary payments as a buffer against any losses for themselves. Also with such prices prevailing, a labourer earning altogether about the equivalent of Rs. 7 a day in 1973 would not have had enough income to feed himself and immediate family let alone save or remit any of his earnings. It would appear that real earnings stayed at a bare subsistence minimum for a family with all adults working as labourers by a combination of contractors and food merchants working independently for their own profit. As far as the direct labour force was concerned this was reinforced by the official policy of equating money wages with those for agricultural labouring which virtually all local agricultural labourers reject in favour of conventional payments in kind.

However, remittances from single workers' incomes were sent back to villages of origin. Among the 116 Nepalese workers interviewed, just under a quarter did not own any land, the great majority of these sent part of their salaries home to their families, whether they were living in the terai or in the hills. The proportion of landless workers and the sums involved seems to imply that much of the money remitted was used immediately for current consumption. Thus the only effect on productive activity occurs in the terai with a temporarily increased local demand for paddy and rice and for consumer manufactured goods, such as metal goods, cloth and kerosene from India. The lag in response to this increased demand is such that in most cases the labourers receive little of the benefit. In summary, the overall situation is one of bare subsistence wages for long hours work brought about through a combination of agencies, contractors, merchants and landowners enforced by the State apparatus. To understand the persistence of those poor conditions we now turn to a more abstract conceptualisation of highway construction work under capitalism before considering forms of labourers' struggle for improvement.

Highway Constructions as a Specific Capitalist Labour Process

The fundamental hypothesis of this section is that highway construction labourers are involved in a continuing struggle against attempts to increase the extraction of surplus labour time, as are all other wage workers. The actual forms taken by the struggle derive from the peculiar conditions under which construction workers are recruited, the techniques of production they are employed to use, and the specific nature of the wage-form for workers who are often migrants. This struggle goes on in only slightly modified forms whether the construction is undertaken by the private, or so-called, public sector. Certainly the day-to-day experience of the labourer is little altered by whether the employer is associated nominally with national or private interest and it is from this experience, not from the labels attached by the ruling class to its various hats, that struggle derives.

Following from this general hypothesis is the analytical framework that highway construction wage-labourers are involved in a number of relationships which are structurally integrated to produce and reproduce exploitation and minimise their ability to resist that exploitation. The most noteworthy feature of this structure is the mobility expected of labourers in terms of movement, firstly, from a distant home area to the site, and secondly, within the site as work progresses. It is this mobility that has encouraged the adoption of a closed society, anthropological methodology in recording labourers' lives which represents them as 'outsiders', rejected and rejecting the local 'normal' society in which they temporarily reside. Against this it can be said that, whilst men and women forced to flee from war and famine and live a temporarily semi-nomadic existence will establish a distinctive style of life, the case that this distinguishes them totally as either a transitional group or a lumpen proletariat from the rest of the working class is unproven. The movement between sectors of agriculture and industry is sufficiently frequent in Nepal to suggest that the life of construction labourers is part of a general experience of workers and peasants not the activity of a particular group. In general, this means that the links between labourers and their source and site locations are not so weak as to be cut analytically on a priori grounds to yield an appropriate field of study. In Nepal, the complementarity between agricultural and construction wage-work for near landless people is the core of this close relationship.

The relationship between labourer and employer has in contrast to that between construction and other labourers received more emphasis in the historical literature. Links through place of origin, patronage and real or fictive kin relationships have been highlighted to explain periods of relative industrial peace in the construction sector when working conditions were harsh and dangerous. Undoubtedly, such bonds exist and have a real importance in weakening the recognition by construction labourers of their need to effectively organise to improve conditions. Mutual respect between engineer and labourer is not to be simply dismissed as romanticism. What is to be questioned is that such bonds are either typical of, or necessary to, employer/labourer relationships. The development of capitalism imposes a similar labour process on all manufacturing employers who survive which increasingly tends to mean larger production units, de-skilling of labour and machine domination work rates. The process by which calculation displaces paternalism as the dominant characteristic of production relations is associated with class divisions becoming more openly discernible. In Nepal this process is still in relatively early stages but small contractors are threatened both by legislation requiring formal registration and the economic challenge of more mechanised companies in Nepal (the National Construction Company of Nepal) and India (represented by Gannon-Dunkerley on the Mahendra Rajmarga).

This process increasingly brings to the fore the construction labourers' particular problem of the sale of labour-power for one-off projects. Once the employer has ceased to accept responsibility for the complete reproduction of a particular labour-power, other than at the time of employment, then the seasonal and 'one-off' characteristics of much construction activity become a vital consideration for the labourer. Temporary lay-offs for weather may be acceptable if associated with a busy period in agriculture but any trends in agriculture itself towards mechanisation may not allow all the labour force to gain the necessary additional means of reproduction there. Early completion is also a source of tension between employer and labourer and, although 'piece-work' payment arrangements may be acceptable locally, the tendency to increase the rate of exploitation by increasing the work-rate will meet resistance in various forms including attempts to reassert the labourer's control over his work by means of obstruction and 'sabotage'. To counter this, employers can intensify the use of machinery as a weapon in the struggle even though a considerable unemployed potential labour force exists. The struggle for control over the labour process is one largely hidden from those who see the introduction of machinery as a purely economic act irrationally resisted by 'machine-breakers'. But the recognition of such a struggle does help explain the observation of machines replacing people in production in many parts of the world. As we shall see below it is around this question that labourers' struggle in Nepal has concentrated.

The spatial, social and timing characteristics of the labour process in highway construction also have implications for the nature of the market relations in which the labourer is required to engage to purchase commodities. Large numbers of workers moving into a relatively isolated area temporarily provide an ideal opportunity for other interests, which can be identified in general as merchant capital, to exploit. The wage-goods demanded by labourers including food, material for housing and basic entertainment will almost certainly not be available in necessary quantities as commodities. As commodities, such goods can only be obtained by using either the old transportation system, probably monopolised by relatively few merchants, or by extracting produce from local previously non-commercial sources, probably controlled by relatively few land-owners. Either method offers a considerable opportunity for those with local power or information to obtain goods cheap and sell commodities dear. This process can continue until spatial and social barriers to entry are eroded; by which time the labourers may well have completed their task. and have moved to a new area.

The struggles between interests in the ruling class to control the production and distribution of surplus takes place within a framework set by the State. The State acts to moderate in the conflict within the ruling class and to repress the effectiveness of struggle by the exploited class. In its former role, the State often allocates production activity between regions and decides on highway alignments. In addition, the State will be involved in setting wage restrictions to avoid labour being drawn from agriculture, a withdrawal which would be to the detriment of larger landowners' interests; and also regulating prices in order to allow merchants to operate profitably in 'black' markets while appeasing demands for low wage-good prices by employing capitalists. Such efforts do not finally remove the anarchic tendencies of fractions of capital and, indeed, individual capitalists to attempt to destroy each other, but the rules are such that capitalism itself is under no threat from such conflict. On the other hand, the State as an instrument of class oppression can be quite open in its treatment of the exploited by banning trades unions, using the police and military to put down 'demonstrators', and the law to imprison 'ring-leaders'. Also workers may be subject to harassment if they attempt to settle in the areas their own labour has made accessible e.g. on the grounds of forestry 'protection'. The general experience of construction labourers under capitalism is one of reinforcing exploitation and repression across a wide spectrum of their relationships by the employers and State and division among themselves on the bases of place of origin and ethnicity/caste which inhibit full collective action.

Protest and Struggle

The conditions for active struggle by labourers constructing highways in Nepal are thus very inauspicious. Divided into small groups by place of origin and ethnicity, spatially mobile on a 'site' which might extend for 100 kms. facing four apparently independent sets of aggressors (the agency senior officials, contractors, merchants and landowners) in a legal framework violently opposed to effective trades unionism; the labourers found limited means of struggle which expressed their opposition to exploitation and oppression. When examining various types of resistence there are the five inter-related key arenas of struggle, daily money wage-levels, lay-offs, food prices, shelter, and control over speed and conditions of work. Expressions of dissent have to take account of the possibility of victimisation and intervention by police and/or army. In addition contractors' labourers may be subject to a form of 'lock-out' if the contractor decamps with funds which he may be able to do easily when he has no plant or machinery to lose. Four types of struggle are described below. Examples are drawn from information given by Nepalese contractors and labourers, or are interpretations of information on the files of the UK agency in charge of constructing the Mahendra Rajmarga.

Although the hierarchy of management is primarily directed to control and subordination of the workforce, by its very nature this channel of control can be used to pass up complaints which become anonymous and take on the appearance of generality. This means of struggle thus uses as a means of expression by the labourers of their common interest the very organisational structure necessary to ensure control. However, these means can only be used where such hierarchies exist and are easily diverted either by appeals to particularistic links between employer and employed or the contractor may be able to point to the agency or local merchants as the 'cause' of the problem. This 'cause' in being outside the ambit of the producing organisation is no longer amenable to using the hierarchy of control against itself. Examples were reported of labourers successfully expressing grievances on wages and bonuses to contractors through a particular worker known to be in favour with the contractor and the UK agent files had several examples of letters purporting to be from a trusted individual (e.g. a store-clerk, making points on basic food prices) which put forward a general point. Even in the absence of formal grievance procedures a type of collective negotiation by individual proxy existed.

Where 'negotiation by proxy' broke down was on the borders dividing organisations from markets as methods of communication. But in this situation a second means of struggle was available—alliances of labourers with particular interests against another. For instance, at the stage of recruitment, as we have described above, a labour contractor or local leader is often involved as an intermediary between labourer and direct employer. The labour contractor, as a seller of another's labour power has this feature in common with one part of trades union activity. He may, therefore, attempt to secure a high price for the commodity he is selling in order to be sure of retrieving the labourers in sufficiently good condition to sell their future labour-power. Similarly, the direct employer may find his interests clashing with merchants over food prices or landowners on provision of land materials for shelter. In such situations the labourers by choosing to join one side of the alliance may obtain benefits without overt struggle. How far such tactics can succeed will vary from issue to issue,but in the arenas of maintaining money wage-rates and ensuring food supplies, the Orissans can be regarded as having been successful in protecting themselves at the time of recruitment and, in general, labourers gained some temporary settlement rights by seeking agency support against land-owning interests. The two means of struggle above rely on using the nature of capitalist relations against themselves. Internally by using the channel of control essential to capitalist organisation, externally by using the anarchic competitive relations between individual capitalists.

Both these methods are limited since they accept capitalist relations rather than resist them. Non-cooperation is the simplest form of struggle which rejects the rights of the dominant class to dictate conditions. To the employer, time is capable of expression in terms of money and delay in the risk of bankruptcy. Supervision can only raise work-rates by increasing costs and, in general, highway construction in west central Nepal has not used machines to set the pace of work. Labour-only contractors, and the agencies themselves where they employ direct labour, are therefore vulnerable to labourers controlling work-rates by tacit agreement. Wide variation in work-rates for relatively similar work were reported on the Mahendra Rajmarga and concern about 'commitment and morale' led to offers of generalised improvements in working conditions on a productivity basis. However, alongside such improvements emerged the tendencies for the agency to introduce machinery to set a standardised work-rate and increased efforts to change the wage-form to piece-work. In such situations, the assaults recorded on supervisors become aspects of struggle and the sense of imminent violence expressed in reports by British supervisory staff played a role in establishing labourers' rights. Outside the immediate work situation, non-cooperation may take other forms. For instance, several restaurants were reportedly boycotted by labourers on the Kathmandu-Pokhara highway in 1970 because of alleged profiteering, and repeated demands by forestry officials for labourers to move from land on which they had settled around the Mahendra Rajmarga were disregarded even after the agency had withdrawn its support. Such acts of non-cooperation, like those at the work-place, always verge on escalation into open violence where the coercive power of the State can be called on to intervene to restore order in the interests of capital as a whole.

In a situation where strikes are treated as illegal acts, open collective struggle by the labourers is forced to take spontaneous forms. Violence against individual supervisors may be important as a check upon any tendency to increase general work-rates but in such situations the identification of the attackers allows victimisation. Similarly, threats against life and property of individuals serve only as a deterrenr to particular 'price-leaders' out of step with the general level of exploitation and oppression. However an atmosphere in which localised non-violent means of struggle by labourers can be successful may be inadvertently established if general collective destructive power is revealed. Such an act occurred on the Mahendra Rajmarga over a decision to layoff a few hundred Nepalese women labourers for the monsoon season of 1971 from the direct labour force. The women, with a number of sympathetic men, gathered at the main camp and, after not receiving any satisfactory response, a 'riot' occurred in which some of the luxury goods, such as air-conditioners and bar stocks, reserved for the British workers on the project, were damaged or destroyed. The police were called in and the demonstrators were dispersed and some alleged 'ring-leaders' arrested.

The result of this action was not immediately successful in gaining continuity of employment for the women directly involved but the effect upon the agency as an employer of thousands of workers in terms of receptivity to indications of unrest was probably significant. The riot 'encouraged' the British to raise money wage-rates above the maximum set by the Nepalese authorities for the direct labour force, improve employment continuity and make requests to Nepalese para-statal organisations that they accept responsibility for providing foodgrains at fixed prices especially during the monsoon season.

Under present conditions the highway construction labourers struggle is likely to be piecemeal and in forms which are accurately described as 'hidden' or 'violent'. Pamphlets circulated among the labourers on the Mahendra Rajmarga identifying particular grievances as part of the general experience of all labourers. But as the conclusion to this essay it is worth not only pointing to the similarities of labourers' experience across sectors within Nepal but also noting the similarity in work experience and struggle which links across space and time the millions of men and women who have laboured to construct capitalism's canals, railways and highways.

CHAPTER 8

THE URBAN LABOUR FORCE

The Urban Labour Force in Historical Perspective

All towns imply some kind of differentiation between 'urban' and 'rural', but in predominantly agrarian, pre-capitalist societies, "the town only exists ...in relation to a form of life subordinate to its own. It has to dominate an empire, however small, in order to exist" (Braudel 1973: 374). In such societies the small urban centre is essentially the location where the surplus extracted from the peasantry by the ruling class together with the revenues accruing from their control over the trade are realised. Thus the town is a manifestation in built form, not merely of a concentration of population nor even of a concentration of a specific class (or classes) within society—although it is of course both of these—but also a concentration of surplus. Often surpluses produced in the countryside are exchanged in the town for other products, and the market associated with this may give rise to a specific class of merchants and traders; on occasion, however, the surplus now accumulated in the hands of the nobility or in the state treasury is exchanged for labour, which consequently finds itself concentrated also, albeit temporarily, in the town before returning to the villages from which it is drawn (cf Marx 1964: 71).

During the first-half of the 18th century, the capitals of the petty hill states of Nepal appeared as tiny islands in a sea of peasant villages and scattered homesteads; even the settlements of the Kathmandu Valley were barely distinguishable from the villages which surrounded them and into which they merged. By the 18th century, however, the Nepalese peasantry had been subordinated for centuries, within the framework of the petty state, to a ruling nobility who pressed them into military service, appropriated surplus from their agricultural production in the form of taxes, rent and tribute, and obliged them to provide labour - often without reward - for specific projects, usually associated with construction in the capital (e.g. building temples and palaces) or with other 'public' works (e.g. maintaining trails). In 1751, for example, a royal palace was built at Jumla, capital of one of the more powerful hill states; cash was raised for the purpose through a specical levy on the rural population, and "the labourers, stone-workers, carpenters and architects employed in the construction project received wages in addition to cloth in some cases" (Regmi 1971: 21). Thus a temporary urban labour force was recruited from among the peasants and rural artisans, who also produced the surplus (appropriated in the form of a levy) from which the wages paid to the labour force were taken.

After 'unification' the expansion of the tributary state brought about an increase in the size of several existing centres (usually the former capitals of now subject petty states) and the emergence of new ones. In neither case, however, was the extent of urban growth very great. The new towns developed largely as a consequence of the institutional apparatus now required locally to enforce and administer the collection of revenue from the peasantry and to recruit troops for the state's further expansion. The growth of the state apparatus led to an increase in the number of those employed as officials, soldiers and menials in the towns. In the old towns at least, and probably in the new as well, the custom of raising both finance and labour for 'public' works from among the rural masses in the vicinity continued. Often the labourers and craftsmen were not paid but pressed to work for nothing under the *jhara* forced labour system. In 1799, for example, an order was issued to local officials in Tanahun district to impress *jhara* labour for the construction of a royal palace at Gorkha: "every Kumhale (potter) family shall supply 10 earthen pitchers each, Majhis, Darais and other castes who customarily carry loads shall come along with spades, axes, knives, etc." (Regmi 1971: 103). Frequently, they were obliged to provide not only their own implements and free Labour, but also food for themselves for the duration of the project (cf Regmi 1971: 199). Such labour was not only summoned, it was often physically compelled: in 1799, for example, troops were sent to various villages in the eastern hills to round up *jhara* labour for the building of the Jagannath temple in Kathmandu. On occasion, the inhabitants of remoter regions were 'permitted' to pay a levy in lieu of providing *jhara* labour, on grounds of distance; but it would seem that the crucial factor was not so much physical distance as the ability of the local peasantry to resist the demands of central government (or their local representatives) and the real cost to the state of forcing labour from dissident groups, particularly those who constituted the core of the imperial army. Distance was, of course, important, but the reservoir of labour available for urban projects was determined by relative political and military strength of rulers and peasants as well as by relative location. (For a discussion of 'the political economy of space' with reference to Nepal, see Blaikie, Cameron, Seddon and Fleming, 1977 Chapter 4). The ability to 'command' an urban labour force, whether temporarily from the countryside or more permanently within the town itself, was crucially determined by the 'economic strength' of the urban centre (i.e. its importance as a concentration of surplus). Only in the Kathmandu Valley—capital region of the tributary state and major recipient of state revenues from all sources—was there such a capacity, and more than a vestigial urban class structure and urban labour force; only there were there 'cities in the proper sense' (Marx 1964: 71), with a complex division of labour and forms of urban production (cf Regmi 1971: 13). Even in the Valley, however, the size of the permanent labour force must have been small and the number of those in regular employment with no other source of income (from farming or small business for example) negligible. For major 'public' works (as for private construction) the nobility was obliged to command a labour force from the rural areas.

Throughout the 19th century, and indeed during the entire period of Rana rule in Nepal, towns grew very slowly. They were never to become important centres in their own right, for during the second half of the century not only the relationship between town and country, but also the internal dynamic of both urban and rural economy and society were transformed as Nepal became progressively integrated into, and subordinated to, the political economy of British India. The underdevelopment of Nepal as a whole became manifest in the towns, as it did in the countryside. Economic activities in the urban centres remained those of artisan and petty commodity production, and of trading (see Chapter 9); indigenous capitalism failed to develop in the sphere of production and both town and country became, in Braudel's phrase, 'subordinate forms of life', dominated by an empire beyond the borders whose dynamic was provided by the development of industrial capitalism outside even the sub-continent. Those employed in the towns on a relatively permanent basis were, for the most part, state officials in sinecures or menials of various kinds working for the higher-level officials and army officers or for the members of the nobility with local town residences.

Although there is little reliable information regarding the size or composition of the urban labour force until well after the downfall of the Ranas in the early 1950's, there can be no doubt that even during the first-half of the 20th century towns outside the Valley remained small (the vast majority having less than 5,000 inhabitants) and the number of urban employees minute. Over the last twenty-five years, however, and particularly during the last decade, the rate of urban growth has dramatically increased, as has the size of the urban labour force (although it should be emphasised that it remains tiny, in comparison with the vast numbers of peasants and rural workers).

Issues in the Analysis of the Urban Labour Force

In this chapter we are concerned to examine the characteristics of the urban labour force as a whole with special reference to west central Nepal and to consider the extent to which the growth of towns in recent years has been associated with the emergence of a distinctive urban class structure, and in particular of a recognisable working class. It would of course be surprising if one could identify, in a predominantly agrarian, non-capitalist society subject for over a century to the distortions of underdevelopment, the classic features of a western-industrial urban class structure. The 'making of the working class' is a historical process of great complexity (cf Thompson 1968), which must be understood in terms of its local peculiarities if we are to appreciate its historical role within a specific underdeveloped society. The continuing importance of the peasant economy, the predominance of commercial and other speculative activities in the towns, the feeble development of industrial production, the prevalence of labour migration to India, recruitment to foreign armies and the recent massive expansion of the bureaucracy—all of these are crucial factors in the formation of the urban class structure in Nepal. It is also important to recognise that ethnic and caste differences continue to provide criteria for discrimination and division among the labour force, and to generate forms of association as well as ideological categories that cut across class lines, thus imposing their distinctive stamp upon the structure of economic and social relations in the towns —even if arguably to a lesser degree than in the countryside.

The term 'labour force' is sometimes used in a general sense to refer to all those considered economically active; here a narrower definition is applied and the urban labour force regarded as consisting essentially of those earning wages and salaries—that is, of employees. Immediately the question arises as to whether the payment of wages is an adequate criterion for the definition of urban workers, particularly in an economy where indigenous capitalism has established itself only in the weakest form. Many would argue that it obscures more important and fundamental criteria such as the distinction between 'productive' and unproductive' labour (cf Carchedi 1975 a, b; Gough 1972; Poulantzas 1973), noting that on the one hand there may be salaried employees who belong in certain respects, economically as well as socially and politically, to the petty bourgeoisie rather than to the working class proper, while on the other there may be sections of the so-called 'self employed'—such as, for example, the rickshaw pullers of Bhairahawa obliged to hire their vehicles on a daily basis from large rickshaw owners—whose class position and interests are essentially working class and not those of small businessmen (see Chapter 9 also for a consideration of a related problem).

It is not our main concern here to explore in any detail the important theoretical issues associated with the definition of the working class in underdeveloped countries (cf e.g. Allen 1972; Breman 1976; Cohen 1971; Holmstrom 1976; Jeffries 1975; Joshi and Joshi 1976), but they cannot simply be ignored. For the moment, however, we shall regard the urban labour force as a homogeneous entity consisting of those paid wages or salaries for their work in the towns. This definition also raises the question—which we shall see to be of major importance—of the precise relationship between rural and urban class structures and its implications for our understanding of urban workers and the petty bourgeoisie, their material conditions and their political role. For many of those who work for wages in the towns are also involved in farming or in other forms of economic activity; they may be urban workers at one time and peasants at another, employees in one context and 'self-employed' in another. Such a situation, arguably more characteristic of the underdeveloped than the so called 'developed' societies (cf Wright 1976: 32), where individuals and households may be involved in several different forms of economic activity and consequently have what might be termed a 'multiple class position', has important implications for the economic and political character of the working class and petty bourgeoisie, as indeed it has for that of other classes.

The Dimensions of the Urban Labour Force

While many business establishments investigated in west central Nepal during 1974 and 1975 employ wage labour (approximately 40%), only a few of these employers (about 12%) have a workforce of over ten; 887 of employers have no more than ten workers and 75% have between one and five. The vast majority of employees in the private sector, therefore, work in small enterprises whose workforce rarely exceeds five; in only a tiny minority of cases is it possible to identify the features of classic early capitalism, where significant numbers of workers are concentrated over a period of time in manufacturing establishments.

There are, however, important variations within the region in the average size of the workforce per establishment, both spatially and sectorally. The larger employers of labour in the private sector tend to be located in the terai, notably in Butwal and Bhairahawa; they also tend to be in towns on or near motorable roads. A survey of some 640 businesses in the region, carried out in 1974-75, showed clearly this overwhelming concentration of large employers in certain locations (see Table 11). But if the vast majority of all urban employees in the private sector work in small concerns, it is also the case that commercial establishments (which consititute the majority of businesses in the region) employ significantly fewer workers on average than do either manufacturers or those commodity producers conventionally referred to by economists as producing services, such as transport firms or hotels. A comparison of indutrial concerns with commercial establishments suggests that about 60% of the former employ wage labour while 17% have a workforce of ten or more, but that roughly two-thirds of the latter employ no labour at all while 97% have fewer than six employees. Given the different role of labour in the production of commodities and in commerce (discussed in Chapter 9), it is not surprising that the larger employers of labour are predomin-antly commodity producers.

In the terai towns as a whole roughly 10% of all businesses interviewed employed more than ten persons, while in the

TABLE 11

TOWN	*EMPLOYEES* 0	1	2	3	4	5	6-10	10+	*Total*
	Number of Establishments								
(Terai)									
Bhairahawa	30	8	18	10	4	7	12	13	102
Butwal	42	20	11	12	8	3	9	11	116
Kapilvastu	10	1	3		2		1	1	18
Parasi	5	2							7
Tribeni	1	1	2	1					5
Total	88	32	34	23	14	10	22	25	248

Establishments with 0 employees as % of total : 35.5%.
Establishments with 10+ employees as % of total : 10.1%

TOWN	0	1	2	3	4	5	6-10	10+	*Total*
(Hills on Siddartha Rajmarga)									
Pokhara	54	6	2	7	4		10	2	85
Tansen	35	8	13	1	1	1	1	1	61
Syangja	21		1	1				1	24
Walling	31	1		1				1	34
Armadi	12								12
Aryabhanjyang	7	1	1						9
Total	160	16	17	10	5	1	11	5	225

Establishments with 0 employees as % of total : 71.1%.
Establishments with 10+ employees as % of total : 2.2%

TOWN	0	1	2	3	4	5	6-10	10+	*Total*
(Hills: on Prithivi Rajmarga)									
Dhamauli	17	1	2	1					21
Majuwa Khaireni	19	1	1						21
Dumre	17	1	1						19
Bimalnagar	3	1		1		1			6
Total	56	4	4	2	0	1	0	0	67

Establishments with 0 employees as % of total : 83.6%
Establishments with 10+ employees as % of total :

TOWN	0	1	2	3	4	5	6-10	10+	*Total*
(Hills: off road)									
Baglung	38			1		1			40
Gorkha	18	1	1		2				22
Kusma	13	1		1					15
Bandipur	11								11

TOWN				*EMPLOYEES*					
	0	*1*	*2*	*3*	*4*	*5*	*6-10*	*10+*	*Total*
				Number of Establishments					
Karkinetta	4				1				5
Patherkot	1	2							3
Lunkhu Deurali	3								3
Total	88	4	1	2	3	1	0	0	99
Establishments with 0 employees as % of total : 88.9%									
Establishments with 10+ employees as % of total :									
Grand Total	392	56	56	37	22	13	33	30	639
	61%			29% 34%				5%	

Source : Blaikie, Cameron, Feldman, Fournier and Seddon (1976: 7.32-33).

hill centres (even those along the Siddartha Rajmarga, where 2.37 employed ten or more) the proportion was dramatically less, approaching zero in most of the towns off the roads where petty commodity production and small retailing predominate. However, when data relating to the mid-1970's are complemented by the results of enquiries into changes in employment during the first part of the decade, it becomes clear that, while the vast majority of the urban labour force in the private sector has been and remains concentrated in the terai (mainly in Butwal and Bhairahawa), the number of workers (both in aggregate and in terms of average size of workforce per establishment) has been increasing significantly in the hill towns, especially along the Siddartha Rajmarga. These last, while contributing a mere 4% of the urban labour force in 1971 accounted for 18% in 1974. This growth does not, however, indicate a fundamental and progressive transformation of the urban economy but rather a relocation and concentration of merchant activity and the proliferation of small employers of labour serving the needs of the rapidly expanding bureaucracy.

Although the survey on which the above-mentioned data were based represents only approximately one in five of the total universe of business in the region, it does provide an indication of the pattern of growth in the urban labour force as a whole in the private sector during the first-half of this decade. If we were to aggregate from the sample survey to obtain an approximate figure for the size of the total labour force within the towns of the region during this period the result would suggest a growth of about 50% from 9,300 in 1971 to 13,800 in 1974. This is still a very small number of employees in absolute terms, and it is probable that the growth rate is somewhat of an over-estimate (given that it does not take closures into consideration).

So far we have discussed only the private sector; but the massive expansion of the state sector in recent years has led to an enormous increase in the number of those employed by the state. In Pokhara, for example, (now designated administrative centre for the entire west central development region, as well as zonal headquarters for Gandaki, district headquarters for Kaski and municipal centre in its own right), bureaucratic expansion explains in considerable part its rapid growth. Where Gurung reported 17 offices in the mid-1960's (Gurung 1965), there were 75 ten years later and the number of those working in these offices (not to mention those responsible to heads of section in these offices but working in the field), had risen to around 2,000. Other major centres of administrative expansion are Baglung and Lamjung in the northern hills, Dhamauli and Syangja on the Prithivi Rajmarga and Siddartha Rajmarga respectively in the southern hills, and Parasi in the terai. Wages and salaries account for the greater part of the bureaucracy's expenditure although there is significant variation in this regard from place to place (see Table 12). In the towns mentioned the number of state employees, according to our estimates, is nearly 3,600; if one were to add the smaller number employed in other minor centres, the total for the region is probably in the vicinity of 4,000. That is roughly between a third and a quarter of the number in the private sector.

The Structure of the Urban Labour Forces: General Features

The vast majority of those employed in the towns, whether

TABLE 12

Town	*Annual wage bill (Rs.)*	*Other expenditure (Rs.)*	*Wages as % of total*
Pokhara	5,486,000	2,420,000	69%
Baglung	1,871,500	248,500	88%
Parasi	942,500	407,000	70%
Syanga	957,500	234,500	80%
Dhamauli	850,500	235,500	78%
Lamjung	658,500	91,000	88%

Source : Blaikie, Cameron, Feldman, Fournier, Seddon. (1976: 7.14).

on a temporary or a permanent basis, are male; while women are commonly employed in agriculture as wage labourers their employment as such in the urban areas is exceptional. They tend to be found in domestic forms of activity, such as domestic service and in the hotel and catering business. Some bidi (cigarette) manufacturers in the terai employ a few women on a piece-work basis and the Mahendra Sugar Mill (the only factory of any importance in the region) has a number of female employees in the bottling section and working as cleaners. Wages paid to women are generally lower than those paid to men even for comparable work, but they tend to be employed in menial and unskilled jobs in any case. In the state sector certain branches, such as the banks, the post office and the various administrative offices, employ a small minority of female clerical workers, and the health services and various sections of education have a higher proportion than most of women employees, as nurses, midwives, health-workers and teachers. The majority of these work in the rural areas and only a minority are actually employed in the towns.

The age structure of those in urban employment is highly distinctive; a survey of lower paid workers in Pokhara, Butwal and Bhairahawa carried out in 1974 suggested that around 80% of those earning less than 200 rupees a month were between the ages of 16 and 35. It is not certain to what extent the age structure derived from this survey can be regarded as the norm for all kinds of urban employment; it appears, however, from the evidence available, that better qualified (and higher paid) employees are not significantly older than those in low paid jobs—indeed, if anything, they tend to be younger on average. The elderly are not, found in any appreciable numbers in urban employment, although some old men do work as night watchmen, janitors and peons, particularly in the public sector. It is comparatively rare in this part of Nepal to find children regularly employed, although child labour is used especially in the hotel and catering business in return for board, lodging and 'pocket money'; girls are occasionally taken into domestic service at a relatively early age (say 12 or 13) on such terms. The age structure of the urban labour force is in part a reflection of the fact that most older men with families remain tied to their farms, which still provide the basis of subsistence for most households even if one or more members have other sources of income; it also reflects the relatively recent development of urban employment opportunities, particularly in the hills. It is significant, for example, that in Pokhara 90% of the jobs investigated were held by men of between 16 and 30 while in Butwal only 65% were in this age range.

If there are significant differences in terms of the age structure of the urban labour force between the towns of the terai and those of the hills, there are also differences in terms of the 'catchment area' from which the lower paid urban workers at least originate. Analysis of the place of origin of those recorded in our survey of business establishments shows that some 37% of those in Bhairahawa came originally from India, while in Butwal (somewhat further to the north but still in the terai) the proportion of workers of Indian origin was about 20%; no workers of Indian origin were recorded in Tansen, nor were there any in Pokhara. From this it would appear that the employment of significant numbers of Indian workers is a phenomenon characteristic of the terai only; furthermore, it seems that mobility is limited, for even if they cross the border the Indian workers rarely come from far away. In fact, there is some evidence that urban workers in general tend to be employed in or near their place of origin. In Bhairahawa just over 45% of those recorded as earning under Rs. 200 per month claimed to come from the town and its vicinity while 22% were from Gorakhpur or Nautanwa just the other side of the frontier; just under 10% said they were from the hill districts of the region. In Butwal roughly 46% came from the immediate vicinity of the town, if not actually from the area of Tansen and 9% from the two Indian towns across the border.

Given the generally limited 'catchment area' from which it is apparently drawn, it is not surprising that there are evident differences in the composition of the urban labour force from town to town according to caste and ethnic affiliation. The very presence of Indian workers in Bhairahawa and to a lesser extent in Butwal, for example, is associated with a number of castes not otherwise found in the region. The indigenous tribal groups of the terai, such as the Tharus, are to be found in the terai towns, but not elsewhere, while the proportion of Magars in Tansen for example, and of Gurungs in Pokhara is a reflection of their numerical importance in the surrounding area. The fact that Newars, Brahmins and Chetris are present in large numbers is explained in the case of the first by their preponderance in the towns of the region from the earliest period of urban development and in the case of the other two castes by their numerical preponderance throughout the region as a whole. 'Low caste' individuals tend to be concentrated mainly in casual employment, largely by virtue of their 'untouchable' status, which debars them from the majority of regular jobs.

Even a brief consideration of the economic and social background of urban workers shows that their origins in this regard are extremely varied. Individuals from relatively affluent families as well as those from the most impoverished are to be found in employment in the towns. Their qualifications for entry to higher or even intermediate grades of employment vary considerably, however, and a degree of stratification exists within the urban labour force which to a large extent reflects directly the inequalities of the rural economy and society from which it is largely drawn. Thus, the sons of the relatively well-off tend to enter employment at higher levels than do the sons of the poor. Also, while the majority of those in lower grades tend to be recruited locally, the higher echelons are staffed predominantly by outsiders, usually from Kathmandu, and almost always from bourgeois or aristocratic families. 'Access' to jobs is not, however, simply a matter of physical proximity nor even of class, wealth and social status; for example, the 'traditional' channels of entry to the administration tend to favour Brahmins and Chetris, although other groups, such as Newars and Gurungs, value education highly and are beginning to compete for entry to intermediate and higher level employment in the state sector. Furthermore, as in many societies, access to the more desirable jobs is determined not only by formal qualifications and proven ability, but also by social connections and personal relationships.

Whatever the mechanisms by which individuals obtain employment there is no doubt that a substantial degree of inequality exists within the urban labour force in terms of income, job security, prospects of advancement, fringe benefits etc. Such 'economic' differentiation, together with the social and even political divisions this generates, allow us to identify significant strata within the urban labour force. And although sources of income, income levels and other aspects of 'income distribution' are not themselves defining characteristics of class structure they provide crucial data for a class analysis.

For the purpose of examining income distribution within the urban labour force we identify three major categories, with the lowest paid workers (Grade 1) earning Rs. 200 a month or less, the intermediate level employees (Grade 2) receiving between Rs. 200 and 400 and the highest paid (Grade 3) being paid over Rs. 400 a month. Significant divisions exist, of course, within these major categories. At one end of the scale, for example, are the extremely low paid, earning Rs. 50 or less a month (these constituted just under 20% of lower paid workers in Bhairahawa and about the same proportion in Pokhara, with a somewhat higher percentage (30%) in Butwal); at the other end, just about 1% of employees in the public sector earned over Rs. 1,000 a month. The number of those in category 3 is always very small, but the proportion of Grade 2 to Grade 1 varies to a considerable extent from town to town. For instance, while the average proportion of the total labour force in the lowest paid category in the private sector was 56% for all towns in the region, and the highest paid a mere 3%, lower paid workers in Walling constituted only 20% of those interviewed while in Tansen they accounted for over 80% (see Table 13).

TABLE 13

Town	*No. of employees in*			*% of employees in Grade 1*
	Grade 1	*Grade 2*	*Grade 3*	
Bhairahawa	345	421	26	44%
Butwal	364	142	11	70%
Kapilvastu	20	17	-	54%
Tribeni	5	-	3	63%
Parasi	2	-	-	100%
Tansen	107	24	-	82%
Walling	3	12	-	20%
Syangja	5	4	5	36%
Aryabhanjyang	2	1	-	67%
Pokhara	73	71	2	50%
Dhamauli	2	6	-	25%
Majuwa Khaireni	3	-	-	100%
Dumre	2	1	-	67%
Bhimal Nagar	6	3	-	67%
Baglung	2	1	-	67%
Gorkha	4	7	-	36%
Kusma	3	1	-	75%
Karkinetta	-	3	1	-
Patherkot	2	-	-	100%
	950	714	48	56%

The distribution of employees between income categorics varies considerably between sectors and between branches within sectors. In the public sector, for example, the lowest paid workers constituted roughly 54% in the six towns investigated but 15% came within the highest income bracket. Within the private sector the vast majority of those paid extremely low wages (Rs. 50 a month or less) are employed in the hotel and catering business. And it is significant that, in Pokhara, the only two women in a sample of 30 lower paid workers were both earning less than Rs. 50 a month, while five out of the six in this category were in the hotel and catering business. In Butwal, although roughly 70% of all employees were in the lower paid category, in commercial establishments only 55% were paid less than Rs. 200 a month and in transport companies a mere 25%.

It is revealing to complement the data on income distribution with information relating to occupational differentiation. Some of the so-called 'middle level' trained personnel in the public sector, for instance, such as assistant nurse midwives, auxiliary health workers, primary school teachers and agricultural extension agents, fall within the category of lower paid workers, despite their 'white collar' status. Furthermore, it is possible to identify a small minority of skilled 'manual' workers earning wages in excess of Rs. 200 a month, although these tend to be concentrated in particular branches of the private sector, notably where machinery is used. Given the inclusion of a stratum of relatively, well-qualified 'white collar' workers within the category of the lower paid, and the existence of what might be suggested to constitute 'a labour aristocracy' earning relatively high wages and enjoying relative job security, it is appropriate to investigate further the extent to which class divisions, occupational strata and income categories concide, or fail to do so. In the next section we consider the characteristics of lower paid workers paying particular attention to the divisions within this category.

Lower Paid Workers

Considering lower paid workers (i.e. those paid Rs. 200 a month or less) as a whole it is possible to suggest some general characteristics of this category of urban workers. As has been observed earlier, it consists predominantly of men between the ages of 16 and 35. The majority of lower paid workers originate from areas in the immediate vicinity of their present place of work, although a minority have moved more than once from one town to another in search of work and a few were born outside the region. Most can be regarded as 'first generation' workers and the vast majority recorded their father's occupation as farming (77% of respondents in Bhairahawa identified their fathers as farmers, 78% in Butwal and 90% in Pokhara where urban employment opportunities have developed most recently); furthermore, almost all of those interviewed retained strong and in most cases permanent links with the rural areas and with the land through the members of their family who remained directly involved in farming. Virtually all claimed access to, and usually ownership or prospective inheritance of, land in the area from which they originated, although the size of plots varied considerably.

From this, it is clear that connections with the rural areas and with agriculture in particular are still extremely strong; most of the urban workers in this income category can be regarded as 'urban' only in a partial sense, for they remain also members of farming households and generally retain their links as such. This is particularly the case in towns like Pokhara where there is virtually no urban tradition and workers appear likely to remain in urban employment only for a limited period of time in most cases; many of the older interviewees expressed a concern to return 'home' and data on length of time in urban employment suggests both a rapid turnover of labour between jobs and a generally limited period in employment altogether. The phenomenon of 'multiple class position' combined with relative mobility through jobs militates against the development of a stable urban labour force and particularly against the development of a classic urban working class. Ultimately, however, as we shall argue below, the absence of a stable labour force and urban proletariat is determined by the stunted nature of commodity production in Nepal.

Although their monthly wages place all of the individuals interviewed in the survey within the single category of the lower paid, their circumstances differ considerably, depending upon the economic and social position of their family within the rural class structure as much as on their own position within the urban economy and society. There is, furthermore, a definite relationship between the social and economic background of urban workers and their present level of income, which in turn is related to their occupation and their position in the urban class structure. Among those whose fathers were not farmers and are landless, for example, there is a clear distinction to be made between those whose fathers were manual labourers, small craftsmen, personal servants or petty functionaries and those whose fathers were involved in business or were employed in good jobs. The average monthly wage of the former was Rs. 32.5 in Pokhara and Rs. 98 in Butwal; that of the latter was Rs. 167.5 and Rs. 194.3 in the two towns respectively. Among the sons of farmers and those with land the relationship is less clear, although the detailed case histories taken in the course of this investigation of lower paid workers confirm its importance. The circumstances and behaviour of urban workers cannot be understood unless the multiple class position that the vast majority of them have is taken into account. Even the common characteristic of job mobility requires a somewhat different explanation in the case of an impoverished worker with a family to support and that of a young man from an affluent family for whom his earned income is purely supplementary or even irrelevant.

In general, the length of time that those interviewed had remained in any given job tended to be relatively short. In some towns this is to be explained in large part by the recent development of employment opportunities; in Pokhara, for example, 47% of completed jobs had been held for less than a year and 87% for under three years. In Butwal roughly 35% of jobs had lasted under a year but around 86% for less than three years, while in Bhairahawa only 15% were of under a year's duration, 60% of jobs lasting less than three years. It is significant that in Bhairahawa the proportion of very short (under a year) jobs is comparatively small, while 15% had been held for over ten years and a quarter of the total for over five. In Butwal only 8% of jobs lasted for over ten years, although one-fifth of the total had been held for more than five; in Pokhara, no jobs had been of more than five years' duration.

With growing demand for employment in the urban areas and an apparently considerable turnover of labour, one would expect a 'buyer's market'; but in fact the market for wage labour appears imperfect and sticky, with considerable variation in wages for broadly similar jobs within the same sector and even the same branch, and also within the same town; there are also interesting variations in average wage levels between towns. This variation can be explained to some extent in terms of the existence of 'extra-economic' relations between employer and employee and the prevalence of such relations in a particular branch, sector and town. Especially in the small concerns that predominate in the region relations between employer and employee are often very close and their relationship frequently involves more than a simple employment of wage labour.

Firstly, a significant proportion of lower paid workers reported that they had some previous connection with their present employer. In Butwal, for example, where there is a higher than average (for the region) proportion both of lower paid workers and of the lowest paid (those earning less than Rs. 50 a month), 53% of the jobs investigated had been obtained through some previous contact or relationship; in Pokhara, by contrast, only about a quarter of jobs had been secured by such means, and in Bhairahawa an even smaller proportion. The majority of these connections were through relatives or neighbours 'back in the village', although some had been established in the town itself. In Butwal, where such personal contacts were particularly significant, roughly 25% of such jobs were obtained through kinship connections, 20% 'through a friend' and in a further 20% the employer is or used to be a neighbour or co-villager. In the case of jobs obtained through kinship connections, the data are too scanty to permit any further reliable analysis, but there is a hint that affinal relationships are important, perhaps because with agnates the job would remain a 'family affair' and not count as 'paid'. In the case of jobs obtained through a friend, the same lack of data obtained, although in one case it was mentioned specifically that the friend was 'of the same caste', and in several others the 'friendship' referred to was the specific *mit* relationship contracted with individuals of different caste or ethnic affiliation (cf Okada 1957). Only among particular groups —notably Newars, Thakalis and Gurungs—is there a tendency to employ individuals of the same ethnic group.

Secondly, when actually in employment, the majority of employees are given not just money wages but also board and in some cases lodging; in several jobs clothing of some kind was provided and occasionally other 'extras', such as cigarettes. These may be seen alternatively as supplementing the wages paid or as effectively reducing those wages to a minimum (much as can be argued in the case of 'tied cottages' in Britain); either way, the relationship between employer and employee is mediated by these forms of payment in kind more appropriate to the master-servant relationship of a wealthy landowner and his permanent workers or tenants (see Chapter 6), than to one regulated by 'market principles'. It is perhaps significant that lower paid workers themselves have an ambivalent attitude towards these 'extra' payments; for many interviewed they were included as important reasons for their 'satisfaction with the job', for others they were considered to be closely associated with the low wages that constituted the primary reason for their 'dissatisfaction with the job'. More, however, considered them as a positive factor than as a negative one, just as more declared themselves satisfied with their job than dissatisfied. As Newby (1977) has argued, paternalism give power relationships a moral quality in which employer becomes, to some extent, 'father' to the employer's 'son', with all the implied obligations of the former and deference of the latter, even if these merely qualify a fundamentally oppressive and exploitative relationship; it is not surprising, therefore, to find many of those asked why they found their job satisfactory saying that their employers 'cared for them', 'behaved well towards them' and (most pointed) 'treated them like his own children'.

Given this prevalence of patronage and paternalism in relations between employer and employee, particularly in the smaller concerns, how can we explain the relatively rapid turnover of workers between jobs? For, although there is ample evidence of the importance of personalised relations in urban employment it is also abundantly clear that this does not prevent employers from dismissing their employees, nor employees from leaving jobs with which they are dissatisfied. It is tempting to attribute the instability of the labour force primarily to the continuing connection that most of them maintain with the countryside and with farming in particular. The demands of agricultural practice limit their length of stay in urban employment and weaken their commitment to working in any given job; and many lower paid workers in particular came to the towns originally as 'target workers' with no intention of becoming part of the urban labour force on a permanent basis. But these factors, while certainly important, do not explain, for example, movement between jobs in the towns.

It is significant, in this connection, that employment in the public sector tends to be relatively more stable and the job often more 'suited' to the local Brahmin (for example) with his small farm; in the private sector the prevalence of often ephemeral and usually unreliable businesses with no long-term commitment to investment and expansion creates an environment in which a mobile and 'uncommitted' labour force is to be expected. It is important to recognise the instability of private enterprise in the region as well as the inherent seasonality of many branches of commodity production; both of these factors, themselves an aspect of the underdevelopment of indigenous commodity production, contribute to uncertainty and unreliability with regard to employment opportunities. It is significant that relatively high wages, regulated working conditions and reasonable job security, all of which tend to encourage a more stable workforce, are generally associated with the large employers of labour, who constitute a tiny minority of all employers. In addition, the very low wages paid to many of the urban workers makes their subsistence so unreliable and problematic that the search for 'better' employment continues even when actually in a regular job; this 'lack of commitment' generates its own effects. Furthermore, the existence of a considerable 'reserve army of labour' in the form of the casually employed and the unemployed makes the position of the lower paid workers examined here all the more precarious. As demand for employment in the towns grows with the deterioration of conditions in the countryside, one might expect the present 'sticky' market for wage labour in the towns to be gradually transformed and particularistic relations between employer and employee to give way increasingly to clearly market-determined relations. This cannot be forecast with any certainty, however, for particularistic relations can serve both as a means of oppression and as a protection against market forces; for employers the former, and for employees the latter, offer attractive possibilities and advantages over the 'free' play of the market. For those concerned to make the transition from casual employment to regular employment such relations often prove crucial.

In several interviews, lower paid workers remarked that prior to obtaining a regular job they had been engaged in casual work. Possibilities for casual labouring or portering exist in all the towns of the region, but such work is highly discontinuous in time and in space; consequently it involves the casual worker in considerable movement from place to place and often a considerable amount of 'waiting' for employment (see Chapter 5 for a discussion of the particular circumstances of porters). Given the inherent irregularity of such forms of employment, data is difficult to come by in other than a qualitative form, and we can say little here about the numbers involved, or about the characteristics of this very important section of the urban labour force.

Although casual labour is analytically distinct from regular employment, individuals may move from one category to another over time. Casual labour is important, not merely as a means of obtaining a daily wage but also as a means of making contact with an employer who may, at some later date, be able and willing to provide a more regular form of employment. Casual workers, therefore, try to work as regularly as possible for the same employer, in order to 'become known' and to build up a 'special relationship'. Questions asked of lower paid workers in regular employment about previous contacts with their present employer revealed that a significant number had in fact come into contact with their present employer while doing casual work, usually for him but sometimes just 'in the vicinity'. On the other hand, dismissal from a regular job or resignation through dissatisfaction or some other cause, may lead an individual to work as a casual labourer or porter while trying to obtain another regular job. Furthermore, there is a continuous movement of individuals into casual labouring in the urban areas from the rural areas as conditions there deteriorate but employment opportunities in agriculture fail to expand at a sufficient rate. At the same time many of those involved in casual labouring, or even regular employment, in the towns will eventually return to the rural areas, to work in agriculture on their own farms, or on the farms of others. Some, however, will emigrate either temporarily or permanently to work in the towns of northern India or in the tea plantations and other capitalist farming enterprises of the Indian hills.

In terms of daily wages it is often the case that casual employment is better paid than much regular employment; labourers may on occasion receive as much as ten rupees a day in the urban areas, which compares favourably at first sight with wages paid to agricultural labourers (in the region of six to eight rupees) and with the monthly wages of most lower paid workers in regular employment. But, given the unreliability of this form of employment and the often lengthy periods without any income, the 'daily' wage may in fact have to cover many days' living and waiting for employment. For many, even the low wages and often oppressive conditions of regular employment in small businesses are preferable to the uncertainty and insecurity of casual work; even agricultural labouring appeared to be more attractive to those interviewed, partly because it offered the possibility of working closer to the labourer's own home in the countryside.

Among the lower paid workers we can identify a stratum of relatively better paid employees (usually earning over 150 rupees a month) with comparatively secure jobs and a stratum of less well paid employees for whom jobs tend to last only a relatively short period before they are once again unemployed, or in casual work, or until they return to the rural areas either to their own farms or to work as agricultural labourers on the farms of others. Insecurity, low wages and generally poor working conditions characterise both the lowest stratum of the lower paid workers and the casually employed; but it is striking that, although personal dissatisfaction, resentment against employers and sheer misery tend to be greatest in these categories, it is not here that we find what few indications exist of organised attempts to improve conditions for workers.

For signs of more systematic efforts to defend and promote the interests of working people we must look to the upper stratum of lower paid workers and even to those in what we have termed the intermediate income grade 2 of employees; also to those so ambiguously termed the 'self-employed', whose circumstances often differ only marginally from those in regular employment. It has often been suggested that, in underdeveloped countries, the better paid and more secure regular employees (whether they be 'shop-floor' workers, clerical workers, teachers, minor bureaucrats or others) tend to be highly conservative, using whatever means they can, including trade unions, to defend their own position not so much against employers or the state as against the mass of unemployed or casually employed. (e.g. Arrighi 1973). This is to say the least, arguable (cf Jeffries 1975); what is certainly true, however, is that such organisations as exist in underdeveloped countries ostensibly for the advancement of the interests of working people tend to be dominated by those in relatively secure and better paid jobs whose class position is, in certain important respects, different from that of the mass of the working population. This is not surprising, given their comparatively stronger economic and political situation, their greater freedom of action and lesser pre-occupation with the daily problems of subsistence and security. Some of the so-called self-employed share these characteristics and have, in addition, a degree of economic independence which permits certain freedoms.

In the next three sections we shall discuss briefly the characteristics of the labour force in three areas—the public sector, industry and transport—where a degree of organisation on the part of employees can be identified.

Employees in the Public Sector

Within the public sector all employees are graded according to seniority, the major division being between the higher level 'gazetted' officials and the lower-level 'non-gazetted' employees. Official regulations lay down the basic wage per month for each grade and there is general correspondence between seniority of grade and salary. Gazetted officials tend to earn over Rs. 450 a. month and, according to our investigations in west central Nepal, a minority earn over Rs. 1,000 rupees a month. These tend to be individuals with relatively, high educational qualifications, generally from wealthy families belonging to the bourgeoisie or to the aristocracy; in the region, the vast majority originated from Kathmandu and were Brahmins, Chetris or Newars. This reflects the situation in Nepal as a whole. (cf Blaikie, Cameron and Seddon, 1979).

In his analysis of the structure of employment in the public sector in a small district capital in western Nepal, Caplan identified a category of 'senior technicians', whose average monthly wage was Rs. 300 but within which there existed a range from Rs. 150 up to Rs. 600 ; this category comprises "a variety of posts which carry minimal administrative responsibilities, but require special training or qualifications and so offer good salaries: high school teacher, medical officer, telegraph operator, agricultural advisor, bank accountant, etc." (Caplan 1975: 41). These 'senior' technical grades are roughly equivalent to what are more generally referred to in Nepal as 'middle level personnel'. The lower paid echelons of this category, which include non-gazetted Grades I, II and III, comprise a range of positions for which education and training are prerequisites, even if they could hardly be said to constitute 'senior' technical posts in any sense; examples of these are nurses, assistant nurse midwives, auxiliary healthworkers, rangers, foresters and agricultural extension workers. The non-gazetted Grade I personnel, which includes nurses and rangers, for example, have a basic starting salary of Rs. 250 a month, but the non-gazetted Grade II (starting at Rs. 155) and Grade III (starting at Rs. 105) fall within the range of what we have termed lower paid workers.

For personnel with high qualifications relative to the vast majority of the population,* a degree of social standing by virtue of their professional status and a family background in most cases of a relatively advantaged kind, such low wages give grounds for considerable resentment and dissatisfaction.

As early as the 1950's there was formed a Low Paid Civil Servants Union (cf Shaha 1975: 40) to attempt to improve conditions for the lower paid personnel in the public sector; but since 1961 all such organisations have been prescribed and, for the time being, dissatisfaction is expressed in other forms. A survey carried out across Nepal as a whole into the circumstances of 'middle level personnel' (New Era 1973) revealed that over 60% of those interviewed claimed that their salaries failed to meet even half of their domestic requirements; and our own survey of lower paid workers in the west central region showed that at least half of those earning Rs. 200 or less a month were unable to meet their expenditure out of such a wage. The prevalence of strong ties with the rural economy even among those in public service and the fact that nearly half of the urban households have more than one source of income serve to mitigate the difficulties that such low wages produce. But the causes of dissatisfaction among lower paid employees in the public sector are not confined to low wages;

* Generally 8th grade education is required for employment as a forester or assistant nurse midwife, and 10th grade for employment as a nurse, auxiliary healthworker, ranger or agricultural extension worker.

many complained of poor promotion prospects and of the inadequate facilities for further training, and a significant number commented unfavourably on the quantity and quality of the support, material, technical and moral, received from their superiors.

In so far as educational qualifications and personal contacts together determine the point of entry to government service, the lack of further training condemns those entering with relatively low level qualifications to remain at low grades. Educational qualifications attained tend to be strongly associated with the wealth and social class of the family from which the individual comes, and this together with low upward mobility within the public sector (except in higher reaches), ensures a clear distinction between the lower and higher grades of personnel, not just in terms of wages and prospects for advancement, but also in terms of family background and social class. Strong cleavages exist, therefore, between strata within the public sector which relate to class differences within the wider society from which its personnel are drawn (cf Poulantzas 1973 for an analysis of the relationship between class and cleavages within the bureaucracy). There is a tendency for lower-level qualified personnel within the public sector to be drawn from petty bourgeois or peasant backgrounds and thus to be distinguished from the higher-level personnel whose origins lie more usually in the commercial bourgeoisie or the land-owing class or in the professional bureaucrat category. In addition there is a tendency for such distinctions to be associated with distinctions of caste or ethnic affiliation. This ensures that, while Brahmins, Chetris and Newars do find employment in the lower echelons of public service as well as the higher, other groups are hardly represented except in the lower grades. Even within the category of 'middle level personnel' such distinctions are evident. While individuals of Brahmin, Chetri and Newar origin predominate in all grades of 'middle level personnel', there is a clear reduction in the proportion of individuals from other castes and ethnic groups as one moves from non-gazetted Grades III and II up to the relatively senior grade I, e.g. 38.4% of assistant nurse midwives (Grade II) were from 'other' groups, but only 12.7% of nurses (Grade I); 33.7% of foresters (Grade II) but only 13.3% of rangers (Grade I). Caste and ethnic affiliation are not, however, independent variables; they are strongly associated in this contact with level of education, which in turn is closely related to wealth and social class. It is therefore misleading to regard 'Brahmins', for example, as an economically and socially homogeneous category.

Given the official prescription on trades unions and all associations that might be construed as 'political' organisations, the very general dissatisfaction and resentment of lower level public servants tends to find expression in a high drop-out (or 'attrition') rate or in petty corruption which offers the means whereby to increase both personal income and influence. If attempts are made to improve conditions they generally take place through personal contacts and informal networks and on an individual basis rather than through collective action. Such a situation, of course, operates to the advantage of the already socially advantaged. State employees have been effectively prevented from active involvement in local politics outside the sphere of their own immediate circumstances by restrictions officially imposed on their participation in even the official 'class' organisations and in panchayat affairs. However, that some involvement in collective action by public sector employees is not entirely impossible is demonstrated by the membership of numbers of school teachers and other state employees in the Dalit Jana Vikash Pnrishad (see chapter 9) for a discussion of this organisation for the advancement of 'low castes'). It is significant that at present it appears to be only where caste considerations coincide with other factors that dissatisfaction and resentment is channelled into such forms of participation and action. The fact that caste discrimination, although now officially outlawed, continues to take place adds fuel to the fire of resentment.

So far, the massive expansion of the bureaucracy in particular and the state sector in general has made it possible to absorb the majority of the relatively well educated; how long this can continue, however, must be in doubt, and the increasing numbers of relatively well qualified personnel blocked in low grade employment, or even threatened with unemployment, will undoubtedly be an important factor in the development of more militant and collective action among this crucial stratum of public employees. Given the educational background of the majority of 'middle level personnel' it is probable that their growing opposition to the status quo will be closely linked to that of the students' movement in Nepal.

Among the most numerous section of public employees—the workers in menial grades—there is little indication of any systematic discontent; although some individuals in the survey of lower paid workers expressed dissatisfaction at the low wages there was a generally positive attitude towards employment in the public sector at this level, related to job security, 'extras' provided and the undemanding nature of the work.

Employees in the Private Sector: Manufacturing

In Nepal as a whole it is in the industrial towns of the eastern terai and in the Kathmandu Valley that the urban proletariat in the classic sense is concentrated; it is there too that working class action has been most visible. The development of the urban working class as a major political force is generally linked to the expansion of industrial capitalism which in the case of Nepal remains stunted and underdeveloped. It is significant that, although the earliest recorded industrial action, directed against low wages and towards the creation of a union, took place in 1947, it was not until 1961 that legislation regarding working conditions in the larger industrial establishments was implemented. The Nepal Factory Act introduced for the first time the concept of adequate working conditions and covered such subjects as hours of work, hygiene, safety, ventilation, holidays, conditions of appointment and dismissal, minimum wages, the appointment of Labour Welfare Officers and other amenities, including medical care. Under the Factory Act a joint works committee, including both workers and managements, was made obligatory for all enterprises employing over a hundred persons. The provisions of the Factory Act were essentially only a small gesture towards safeguarding the interests of workers; they applied only to those employed in the tiny minority of enterprises with more than a hundred workers and until 1974, with the amendment of the Factory Act, the right to strike was not legally recognised. Even today, certain conditions have to be satisfied as regards calling a strike, and there is no ruling in law about 'lock-outs' by employers. Since 1961 all organisations with any political objectives and even trades unions have been officially disbanded and prescribed; in their place have been established the so-called 'class organisations' supposed to articulate in restrained and controlled fashion the interests of different sections of the population. There is an official workers 'class' organisation, but its effective strength remains slight and its relevance to the majority of workers minimal.

In west central Nepal, the largest industrial employers are concentrated heavily in the two towns of the terai, Butwal and Bhairahawa, although there are a few relatively large manufacturers in Tansen and Pokhara. Industrial development in the western terai remains flight in comparison with other areas of the terai today just as it was a decade ago (Rawat 1974: 17); the total number of establishments and the average size of their workforce are both small and the urban proletariat is consequently also small and fragmented. Few enterprises apart from the exceptional Mahendra Sugar Mill have more than a hundred employees, and the vast majority fall entirely outside the provisions of the Factory Act.

The Mahendra Sugar Mill does have a joint works committee, which has representatives from all sections of the firm including management and the bottling section where virtually all of the employees are female. Industrial action on a small scale has been taken in the past and improvements in working conditions and facilities obtained. Discussions with members of the committee and with lower paid workers in the firm in 1974 showed that workers here were aware of their relatively privileged position in comparison with industrial workers in the region as a whole; they were also aware of both their strength within carefully circumscribed limits and the extent of those limits.

The 'permanent' workforce. of this factory is exceptional in a number of respects; none of those interviewed had any personal connections which helped them obtain employment in the firm and the average length of time with the firm was 7.7 years, considerably longer than in any other enterprise investigated and longer by far than the overall average; the average wage is well above that for industry as a whole in the region and a minimum wage was guaranteed to all employees with the exception of menials and peons. Even in this exceptional firm, however, certain characteristic features of industry in the region were found. As the largest employer of permanent labour in the private sector (we do not consider here the employment of large numbers of labourers in road construction, see Chapter 7) the Mill employs 608 persons in the busiest four months of the year when sugar cane is brought in for processing; but it employs only 320 workers for the rest of the year.

Seasonal variation in employment is characteristic of industry in the region: most of the larger enterprises show a very considerable difference between their maximum workforce and their minimum. Two major factors determine the period of maximum employment: the monsoon, which makes certain kinds of work difficult and when labour is often required for agriculture; and/or the harvesting of crops to be processed by the enterprise concerned, such as sugar cane. However, the variation in the duration of the maximum employment period and in its incidence during the year as between different enterprises is considerable For example, in Butwal a brick factory employs 164 workers for 4 months of the year but only two for the remaining 8 months; two bidi manufacturers employ between them 90 workers for the greater part of the year but only 12 for the remainder; a saw mill employees 31 men for 8 months and 21 for the other 4; and even a biscuit factory reduces its workforce from 13 to 8 for ten months of the year. This seasonality affects the lower paid workers more seriously than those with better paid and more secure employment. In Butwal, for example, our sample survey recorded that at maximum employment there were 11 individuals in Grade 3, 142 in Grade 2 and 364 in Grade 1 (the lowest income category); but at minimum employment, although the 11 in the highest income bracket and 126 of the grade 2 employees (89%) were employed, a mere 137 (38%) out of the Grade 1 employees remained.

Insecurity is thus at least partly related to the seasonality of the majority of industrial enterprises in the region and it is the lower paid workers who are hardest hit by seasonal redundancies. Furthermore, the very limited period of time that some industrial enterprises are at maximum employment means that for significant periods of the year industrial employment is extremely hard to come by and takes on, in certain crucial aspects, the form of casual labour, with all the associated uncertainties and difficulties for the labourer. Given this situation, the vast majority of those who might be classified as industrial workers should more properly be considered as general labourers oscillating between regular employment in industrial concerns and casual work in industry or in other branches of the economy. General uncertainties with regard to employment, widespread seasonal unemployment and the relatively small size of most industrial enterprises ensure that workers in this branch tend to be fragmented even when employed as urban workers and to have little chance of even informal collective action through continuous association in the workplace. In the enforced absence of more formal institutions, such as trades unions or political parties, systematic reinforcement of a collective 'workers consciousness' is seriously inhibited even among the tiny core of relatively 'permanent' urban industrial workers.

Within the industrial labour force, as among the labour force as a whole, there is a significant distinction to be made between these relatively low paid workers in generally insecure and unskilled employment and the more skilled workers whose pay tends to be higher and whose chances of obtaining and retaining jobs are effectively greater; although it is important to note that the average level of wages tends to be higher in industry than in all other branches of the private sector, with the exception of transport. Also it shows a generally smaller proportion of all employees in the lower paid category and a higher proportion in the highest paid category (see Table 14).

TABLE 14

Category	*Wage range in Rs.*	*Industrial*	*Commercial*	*'Service'*
1	1-200	49.2%	51.5%	67.1%
2	201-400	38.2%	46.0%	27.1%
3	400+	12.6%	2.4%	5.6%

Source : Manufacturing and Commercial Survey, 1974-75.

As we have seen above, seasonal variation in industrial activity does not affect the higher paid employees (Grades 2 and 3) to anything like the extent it does lower paid workers. In the industrial branches of the economy the Grade 2 employees are semi-skilled and skilled workers, clerical and lower-level managerial staff.

Information on this stratum of the industrial labour force is less detailed than for the lower paid workers, but it is clear that the income-defined stratum is divided into two, in terms of the nature of the work done, type of qualifications and skills, and social origins. Semi-skilled and skilled workers in this part of Nepal tend to be manual workers with a knowledge of machinery acquired through a history of casual and subsequently regular employment in workshops, small rice and oil mills, printing presses, etc., although a minority have received some more formal training in Nepal or India, or else in the British army. Clerical and lower-level managerial staff usually have higher formal (school and even college-level) qualifications and have rarely been involved in manual work, except perhaps in agriculture on their own farms. The semi-skilled and skilled workers tend to have a longer personal and family history of involvement in urban employment then do the 'white collar' workers. Like the lower paid workers the vast majority of this stratum are employed in relatively small enterprises; the semi-skilled and skilled workers are heavily concentrated in those enterprises using machinery, but the most common form of such enterprise is the oil-rice mill which rarely (except in Bhairahawa) employs more than two or three workers and, like other manufacturers, tends to be seasonal in any case.

Like the lower-paid workers, therefore, employees in this stratum tend to be fragmented and isolated by the nature and conditions of their work; unlike the majority of lower-paid workers, however, they have relative job security and a degree of distance from the struggle for subsistence that pre-occupies the lowest paid. As a result, perhaps, they are concerned about the possibility (or, generally, the difficulty) of obtaining advancement and better forms of employment; they tend to be more willing to express dissatisfaction than most of the lower paid workers. In this respect they appear to resemble the 'middle level' personnel of the public sector, with whom, clearly, they have much in common. Relatively privileged and yet often bitterly resentful of the restrictions, both economic and political, that are characteristic of the Nepalese state today, the 'white collar' workers and the skilled workers in industry represent two crucial sections of the urban labour force in terms of their potential political significance. In an important sense they represent the emergence of new economic and political forces within Nepal linked to the development, albeit feeble and stunted, of capitalist relations of production, involving not only an embryonic urban proletariat but also a specific category which has in more developed countries been referred to as 'the new petty bourgeoisie' —the technical, supervisory and managerial staff essential to the operation of machinery-using capitalist enterprises. The importance of skilled workers and the new petty bourgeoisie is seen nowhere more clearly than in the newly emergent transport 'sector'.

Employees in the Private Sector : Transport

With the construction of motorable roads in west central Nepal there has developed a new branch within the sphere of commodity production, that associated with the provision of transport facilities (cf Blaikie, Cameron, Feldman, Fournier, Seddon 1976, chapter 6; Blaikie, Cameron, Seddon 1979). Although here as elsewhere in the private sector small-scale enterprises predominate, the employment of wage labour is general even in the smallest firms such as the single-owner single-vehicle taxi operators. Apart from the industrial branch, transport employees the largest number of workers in the private sector, the majority of them at least semi-skilled.

Within transport the major employers of labour are the bus companies; each bus operating requires a driver, conductor and loader, and some supervisory and administrative. input. A study of the transport 'sector' carried out during 1974 revealed that the majority of unskilled loaders earned between Rs. 100 and 200 a month, putting them within the lower paid category; conductors, who are responsible for handling passengers' money, tended to earn between Rs. 150 and 400 a month, and drivers received generally between Rs. 200 and 500 (see Table 15). The existence of considerable variation in wages paid for similar work and levels of skill suggests an 'imperfect' market for labour, even within transport.

TABLE 15

Category	*0-99*	*100-199*	*200-299*	*300-399*	*400+*	*Total*
Drivers	—	2	19	25	15	61
Conductors	1	7	10	11	2	31
Helpers	10	26	7	1		44

In addition to these three categories of employees, bus inspectors, mechanics, accountants and managers earn relatively high salaries and have a considerable degree of responsibility, while peons and janitors earn low wages—usually below Rs. 150 a month. In terms of earnings, drivers can be ranked with the 'white collar' employees and supervisory staff, as can the mechanics; but here as in industry, a distinction can be made between the skilled workers and the clerical, and supervisory staff, in terms of qualifications and social background, as well as in terms of the kind of work done.

Wages paid to those employed by trucking companies tend to compare roughly with those in bus companies, with drivers, for example, averaging around Rs. 350 and unskilled loaders about Rs. 150 a month. The employees of the small taxi firms that operate in Pokhara and between Butwal and Bhairahawa, where often the driver is the only employee, are less well paid: drivers average around Rs. 250 and helpers (often boys), when employed at all, about Rs. 50 a month. In general, the proportion of lower paid workers among the labour force as a whole is smaller in transport than in any other sphere in private or public sectors, and the proportion of unskilled workers correspondingly lower.

It is significant therefore that it is within the transport sector above all that there are indications of a distinct 'workers' consciousness and of organisational expressions of that consciousness. The official 'class' organisation for workers has a section for transport; but its members include owners of transport companies as well as employees and like the other so-called 'class' organisations obscures rather than expresses class divisions and class interests. The formation in 1974 (in Baisakh 2031) of a Transport Workers' Welfare Fund for those employed in transport companies operating along the Siddartha Rajmarga, however, reflects the growing concern of employees in transport to defend and promote their collective as well as individual interests. Owners are not represented in this organisation among whose stated objectives was 'to look after the economic welfare of the transport workers' and 'to encourage unity among transport workers'. The organisation was granted provisional recognition by the zonal authorities in 1974 but generated considerable hostility among the powerful company owners in the official 'class' organisation. The formation of this ostensibly 'welfare' association to represent transport workers undoubtedly reflects a genuine and growing consciousness of the distinctive interests of employees as against employers within this the most 'modern' branch of the private sector. It is highly significant that such a form of collective action is associated with a generally high level of wages and skill among the labour force employed in transport for, as we have seen, much the same appears to be the case in industry and in the public sector. That is, that it is among the 'middle level' white collar workers and the skilled workers that the greatest degree of 'consciousness' is evident and here too that such few indications of organisation as do exist may be identified. The potential for collective action undoubtedly exists among the mass of lower paid workers, but it seems probable that the leadership of any large-scale working class movement will come from the relatively privileged and 'committed' strata of skilled and white collar workers.

There are, however, important divisions within the labour force in transport which must be considered. We have seen that distinctions can be made in terms of income categories and occupations; these are related to differences in educational and other qualifications (see Table 16), which are themselves related to the social class and family background of employees.

TABLE 16

Qualifications	*Clercical/ managerial*	*Drivers*	*Conductors*	*Loaders*
B.A	2	—	—	—
I.A.	2	—	—	—
S.L.C.	1	—	2	—
10th grade	1	2	—	—
9th grade	1	2	3	1
8th grade	—	—	2	—
7th grade	—	1	—	6
6th grade	—	—	4	—
5th grade	—	—	—	2
Army training	—	11	—	—
Little or no schooling	—	15	8	21

In part corresponding to these differences of social class and in part cross-cutting them are divisions along caste and ethnic lines. For example, clerical and managerial posts tend to be held exclusively by sons of relatively affluent Newar, Brahmin and Chetri families, while the sons of relatively impoverished Magar families are over-represented among the unskilled workers, from the information provided by the membership of the Transport Workers' Welfare Association (see Table 17). On the other hand, Newars, Brahmins, Chetris and Magars are all strongly represented among the semi-skilled employees, of whom the majority are drivers, and it is certainly the case that most of the Newars, Brahmins and Chetris employed as unskilled workers come from under-privileged backgrounds.

TABLE 17

Caste/ethnic group	*Clerical/ managerial*	*Skilled/ technical*	*Semi-skilled including drivers*	*Unskilled*
Newar	9	1	57	16
Brahmin	9	2	88	20
Chetri	14	2	83	15
Gurung	—	2	41	8
Sikh	—	—	29	—
'Indian'	—	1	18	1
Magar	—	—	61	22
Muslim	—	2	9	1
Other	—	—	13	7
Total	32	10	339	90

There is no reason to believe that individuals of the same caste or ethnic group necessarily have common interests, although where individuals share a common class position and a common class origin and in addition to this a common caste or ethnic affiliation the highly visible characteristic of caste or ethnic affiliation can play a significant part in increasing consciousness of major economic and social divisions. The position of the generally lower paid and unskilled Magar employees in the transport sector is a case in point; they tend to be highly self-conscious of their relatively low position and of their common ethnic affiliation. In Pokhara, taxi drivers were drawn for the most part from a limited number of caste/ethnic groups (out of fifty drivers thirteen were Chetris, eleven Newars, ten Gurungs, six Brahmins and four Magars);

approximately half of the drivers were of the same caste or ethnic group as their employer and there is no doubt that highly personalised relations between employer and employee were characteristic of these small enterprises, although only in a minority of cases could a definite kinship relationship be established.

In general, however, it can be argued that caste and ethnic divisions are of relatively minor significance when compared with those of class. This was clearly exemplified in the movement of rickshaw pullers to form an independent association to safeguard their distinctive interests. In September 1974 there were 650 rickshaws registered in Lumbini zone, the vast majority of them operating in the Bhairahawa area. The number of registered owners was 405, of whom 296 were recorded as owning a single rickshaw only; 63 owned two rickshaws, 18 owned three, 10 owned four and 18 others owned 134 rickshaws between them. While the majority of the single vehicle owners pedalled their own rickshaws most of the multiple owners hired theirs out at Rs. 6 a day and some larger rentiers received as much as Rs. 2,000 a month from this. (The price of a new rickshaw from Gorakhpur was estimated in 1974 as about 2,000 rupees). Although the rickshaw pullers who rented their vehicles had a degree of independence their position was often difficult, their income small and their relationship with the rentier rickshaw owners one of considerable antagonism. This was compounded by the fact that several of the larger multiple rickshaw owners were also co-owners of motor transport companies whose vehicles were in many cases competing directly with the rickshaws for custom. In 1974 a number of rickshaw pullers and smaller rickshaw owners attempted to break away from the official Transport Workers' Association (the 'official class' organisation dominated by owners of motor transport companies, at least one of whom was also a rickshaw rentier) to form their own association. Led by a Magar ex-soldier, the provisional organising committee included a Magar, a Chetri, a Brahmin, a Gurung and a Muslim; the range of ethnic and caste groups represented reflects a conscious effort to overcome divisions along these lines in order to stress the common interests of rickshaw pullers and small rickshaw owners. The proposed association was to take the form of a 'welfare' fund to help those in difficulties as a result of road accidents or other misfortunes, but it was also quite explicitly concerned to 'protect' its members against the larger rentier rickshaw owners and against increasing pressure on their predominantly subsistence activities from the bus and taxi firms.

It was suggested at the end of 1974 that some two hundred and fifty rickshaw pullers and small rickshaw owners contributed to the fund, but this cannot be substantiated and in any case the future of the association was already in some doubt as a result of internal divisions and the difficulties of organising those whose apparent independence as petty commodity producers tended to obscure their subordinate relationship to the rickshaw rentiers and transport company owners. The position of the rickshaw puller who rents his vehicle is somewhat similar to that of the small craftsman obliged to purchase (or rent) his means of production from a rentier capitalist or merchant; that of the small rickshaw owner essentially that of a commodity producer. It could be argued that the relatively greater degree of independence of the latter distinguishes them from the former, but in practice the significant division within the embryo association was clearly between the rickshaw pullers and owner-pullers on the one hand and those small rickshaw owners who hired out their rickshaws on the other. Throughout the struggle to form and then to maintain the association, however, it was clear that the important divisions were those of class, and not those of ethnic and caste affiliation.

Conclusion

No adequate detailed analysis of the character and dynamic of the urban labour force in contemporary Nepal has yet been undertaken; all that we have been able to do here is to present a preliminary sketch and to advance some tentative propositions on the basis of data collected in west central

Nepal. In particular, we have concentrated on the various divisions, horizontal and vertical, within the urban labour force and tired to assess their economic, social and political significance.

The growth of the urban labour force is a relatively recent phenomenon, but it is already possible to identify significant strata within the body of wage-earning and salaried employees of both the private and the public sector. The majority of the urban labour force falls into the category of lower paid workers, earning less than Rs. 200 a month and often with very little job security; but even within this category it is possible to distinguish two strata: a lower stratum of predominantly unskilled workers moving constantly between casual and regular employment, and an upper stratum of skilled and qualified white collar workers able to exert some pressure to improve conditions. Whether in the public or the private sector it is this latter section of the urban labour force that appears the most vocal and the best organised; also the most explicitly dissatisfied with their immediate condition. We would suggest that it is from this quarter, and from among the small businessmen (see Chapter 9) that is likely to develop one important base for political opposition to the status quo.

It is important to recollect, that the size of the urban labour force, both in absolute and relative terms, is very small, and that the vast majority of urban workers retain strong links with the rural economy and society. The multiple class position of very large numbers of the urban labour force will continue to inhibit their involvement in collective action (and particularly in political organisation) in the towns.

Nevertheless it is interesting that Gaige, in his recent study of the political economy of the terai has suggested that:

> "the potential for increased opposition is very real in such towns as Bhadrapur, Dharan, Biratnagar, Rajbiraj, Janakpur, Birganj, Bhairahawa and Nepalganj as lower echelon bureaucrats, small-scale businessmen, industrial labourers, teachers, students and unemployed graduates become increasingly frustrated by their political impotence in Kathmandu and even in the terai". (Gaige 1975: 189).

He clearly envisages the possibility of opposition to the government and ruling class from an alliance of the working class and petty bourgeoisie. And it is highly significant that such violent political activity as has taken place within the last decade in Nepal tends to have been located in the larger towns of the terai, particularly in the relatively industrialised eastern terai. We have not here examined in any detail, for lack of adequate data, the characteristics of the higher level bureaucrats and state employees, university teachers and 'professionals' in private enterprise; but it is highly probable that, despite their relatively privileged position, they too will, in the short and even medium term, apply increasing pressure on the government and aristocractic ruling class to adopt more radical economic and political measures, if only to prevent the collapse of the Nepalese economy and state.

CHAPTER 9

SMALL BUSINESS AND THE PETTY BOURGEOISIE

Small Manufactures and Traders in Historical Perspective

Prior to the 'unification' of Nepal in the mid-eighteenth century, small urban manufacturers or traders—concentrated at this period predominantly in the Newar towns of the Kathmandu Valley—appear to have been directly subordinate to the rulers of the petty states and the nobility (Regmi 1971: 20; Amatya 1970: 47). It is doubtful whether these then could be seen as constituting an independent petty bourgeoisie, although the large number of 'occupational castes' among the Newars is evidence of the relatively developed state of manufacturing and trade in the Valley (Regmi 1971: 23, 25). Much of the commodity production of the Kathmandu Valley directed towards export (as opposed to local consumption) went to Tibet—although some of the metalware in particular was exported to India (cf Kirkpatrick 1811: 209-210)—and during the late seventeenth and early eighteenth centuries colonies of Newar craftsmen and traders were established in Lhasa. Trade with Tibet was, however, predominantly an entrepot trade between India and Tibet, and Nepalese products were limited for the most part to metalware, ivory goods, wooden vessels and coarse varieties of cloth. Newar monopoly of the Tibet trade did not last long, for Indian merchants with better connections in India and effective networks of agents in Nepal and Tibet soon entered the field; the rôle of the Newar traders was then confined to re-exporting commodities brought by Indian merchants to Kathmandu and to retailing within Tibet itself. Outside the Valley, longdistance trade between India and Tibet was an important source of revenue to the rulers of the petty hill states who controlled it, just as it was to the kings of the Kathmandu Valley (cf Regmi 1971: 20, 25).

The 'unification' of Nepal had a significant effect on the expansion of trading and manufacturing activities outside the Valley. Under the new tributary state attempts were made to control Indian involvement in longdistance trade; it was also official policy to promote indigenous commodity production (in part as import substitution) and to encourage trade in exports while discouraging imports as far as possible (cf Regmi 1971: 155). Particularly in the last decade of the eighteenth and first decade of the nineteenth centuries state intervention in commerce and industry increased significantly, although the objective was essentially to assure control over the main sources of revenue to central government. One result of heavy taxation and interference was to drive small producers and traders out of the Valley (cf Regmi 1971: 65-67, 151-156), and during the next fifty years an increasing number of Newar artisans, craftsmen and traders escaped from the direct control of the nobility and the fiscal pressures of the central government to establish themselves throughout the hill regions. During the first part of the nineteenth century small-scale manufacturing began to develop in the hills not only in existing centres such as Pokhara and Tansen but also elsewhere. The establishment of a small Newar community, for example, at Bandipur in Tanahun around 1.830 led to the emergence thereof small-scale textile production using locally grown cotton, and the development of a small town (cf Sharma 1976). Furthermore "within years after the conquest of the Kathmandu Valley, we find Newar merchants trading even in the interior western hill regions, as physical and political obstructions in trade were eliminated" (Regmi 1971: 11).

Certain branches of petty commodity production

continued to flourish throughout the nineteenth century; Oldfield reports, for example,' in his description of the towns of western Nepal, that "the city of Pokhara is large and well-inhabited; it is famous for its copper manufactures" (Oldfield 1880: 45), and notes the importance of other towns, like Tansen, where metalworking was also important, and Baglung, where fine paper was produced. Petty commodity production in the urban areas remained directed primarily at local Nepalese custom and even in the Kathmandu Valley much of the manufacturing was for local consumption; the bulk of cotton production, for example, went to the 'poor and lower middle class people', according to Hamilton writing around 1810. Local demand remained limited throughout much of the nineteenth century, for a considerable amount of handicraft production remained in the rural areas as an integral part of the peasant domestic economy. The 'occupational castes' provided most of what was required by the peasant household that it could not produce for itself and many country folk still made their own clothes, as well as baskets, containers, wooden farm implements and other equipment; Kamis, Sarkis and Damais complemented this 'natural economy'. Some peasants and pastoralists were even involved in petty commodity production themselves (cf Oldfield 1880: 42; and Hodgson in Macfarlane 1976: 26). However, local demand for cheap imported manufactures, particularly for cotton goods, grew steadily during the second-half of the century, first among the ruling classes and then, considerably later, among the lower classes of the urban areas and among the peasantry. Consequently, rural handicrafts began the slow decline that continues to the present day as did for example the local production of cotton. At the same time, certain branches of petty commodity production in the towns, notably metalworking, appear to have enjoyed a growing local demand for their products (cf Hodgson, quoted in Macfarlane 1976: 26).

Indigenous manufacturing was never, however, to evolve beyond a primitive stage, for even as commodity production began to develop in the small towns now springing up in the hills, the foreign mass manufactures that were eventually to sweep away their local competitors were already beginning to penetrate the Nepalese market; soon the emergent petty bourgeoisie in Nepal were to be confronted by the power of developing capitalism in India and in England.

The first decade of the nineteenth saw a significant increase in trade with India. One of the reasons for this was the growing demand of the Nepalese ruling classes for foreign luxury goods and the tributary state's requirement for armaments (cf Buchanan 1928: 574); another was the flooding of the Indian market with cloth, hardware and other products of British manufacturing following the end of the Napoleonic wars (cf Hobsbawm 1975: 49, 58, 147-149). At the same time there was increasing need in India for grain and timber from Nepal's terai, and for the exotic products of the hill and mountain regions. As the century progressed, the balance of trade developed in Nepal's favour but was associated with an increasing emphasis on the export of agricultural produce and primary materials and the import of manufactured goods, thus establishing a pattern familiar throughout the under-developed world. Regmi records, for instance, how Nepalese merchants "from Palpa, Butaul and elsewhere visited Lucknow and other Indian towns for the purchase of commodities" (Regmi 1971: 171); he notes also, however, that they took cash along with them for this purpose, suggesting that Nepal had little to offer by way of exchange. The growing demand in India for primary materials did not encourage local manufacturing in Nepal on a large scale, and indeed in some cases may have contributed directly to inhibit its development; much of the copper and iron mined in Nepal, for example, was exported to India around the turn of the century (cf Buchanan 1928: 560; Kirkpatrick 1811: 176) and it is possible that this significantly reduced the amount of ore available to Nepalese metalworkers, who were certainly obliged increasingly as the century progressed to import sheet metal from India because of the lack of local raw materials.

The nineteenth century was the period par excellence of expanding trade and the rise of a merchant class. Associated with this was an increase in the number of small traders and retailers, although it was not until the twentieth century that the control of the big merchants over all branches of commerce began to be loosened and a massive expansion of the commercial petty bourgeoisie to take place. The majority of peasants continued to make the journey themselves to one of the few large market centres to purchase goods direct from the merchants (often obtaining imported commodities in direct exchange for agricultural goods such as ghee or forest products), and the longdistance trade between India and Tibet was almost exclusively in the hands of large merchants and dealers. It was during the latter part of the nineteenth century that the foundations were laid for the fortunes of many of the wealthiest members of the commercial bourgeoisie today. Newars above all participated in and enjoyed the benefits of the expansion of commerce, many of them moving out of small commodity production into trade as it became apparent that greater wealth could be acquired in this latter sphere— as did, for example, most of the Newars of Bandipur. Particularly in the old centres of Pokhara, Tansen, Butwal and Baglung, Newars dominated commerce almost to the exclusion of all other groups. But gradually others became involved. Indian merchants, for example, became increasingly prevalent in the terai and the Kathmandu Valley, their growing British interest in Nepal after the 1814-16 war and the conclusion of the Sugauli treaty, and to the progressive increase in the volume and significance of Nepalese-Indian trade throughout the nineteenth century (cf Hodgson 1874: 92).

In western Nepal, however, the most significant development was the rise of the Thakalis of the Thaksatsae area of Thak Khola in Mustang district to a position of pre-eminence in the longdistance trade of the region. The appointment in 1869 by the central government—now under the control of the Ranas since their seizure of power and subordination of the monarch (see Chapter 2)—of a Thakali of the Serchan clan as *subba* (chief official) with jurisdiction over trade, customs and local government, was the beginning of this small ethnic group's involvement in commerce on a large scale. Through their control over trade and customs the Serchans were able to dominate the longdistance trade in salt, wool, livestock and grain of western Nepal throughout the second half of the nineteenth century and the first quarter of the twentieth (cf Bista 1971; Haimendorf 1974, 1975). Their domination was threatened, however, from the 1890's onwards when the Gurungs of Ghanpokhara in northern Lamjung also became involved in the *subbaship* and competed directly with the Thakalis, particularly between 1902 and 1920 (cf Messerschmidt 1973, 1974, 1976). Not all of the Thakalis and Gurungs of the region became large merchants, of course, and only those most closely related to the *subba* were able to benefit to the full from the exceptional advantage conferred by this appointment; those outside the 'inner circle' or from other clans were, however, often involved in petty trading themselves or employed in subordinate positions by the bigger merchants and subbas. Around the turn of the century, the Thakali merchants exercised considerable economic and political power over the others in the region, largely by virtue of their exclusive control over longdistance trade. The villagers of Panchgaon, to the north of Thaksatsae, tended to engage in commerce on a smaller scale, while those of Baragaon even further north (and not regarded as Thakalis by the other two communities) were more directly subordinate to the Thakalis, often in debt to them and frequently discharging their debts as bond servants.

However, the last quarter of the nineteenth century saw the building in India of a whole network of railways along the southern border of Nepal; the exploitation of the Nepalese terai was thus much facilitated and the repercussions were felt throughout the Nepalese economy. A recent commentator has observed that:

> "There is no doubt that the opening of the Indian railways along the terai where the majority of Nepal's natural resources were concentrated, gave the whole subsequent development of the Nepalese economy a southward orientation. By 1900 the economy of Nepal had become in effect a tributary of the imperial economy of British India and the exploitation of the Nepalese

economy by the colonial system to the south established a pattern of exchange that still prevails. At that time Nepal's primary products, timber and other forest products, flowed south to supply the needs of the imperial economy, and cheap British manufactured goods flooded Nepal depressing native cottage industries and crafts" (Rana 1973: 221).

As the longdistance trade began to decline in the early years of the twentieth century, following the building of the railways in India, the diversion of trading routes to the east and the establishment of British trading posts in Tibet itself after the young husband expedition of 1904, the big Thakali and Gurung merchants turned their attentions increasingly to the profits to be made in the Nepalese-Indian border trade. There was a decrease in their direct involvement in trading operations in the far north and "while they continued to act as middlemen, the movement of goods between Thaksatsae and Tibet largely fell into the hands of the hardier people of Lo and Baragaon" (Haimendorf 1975: 183).

In 1928 the longdistance trade was freed from the control of the customs contractor (the *subba*) and all restrictions on the trade lifted; as a result, "the ordinary Thakalis... were able to profit from small-scale trade in salt, and though unable to rival the economic power of the *subba* family, many of them set up as successful merchants" (Haimendorf 1975: 146). At the same time, the domination of the Thakali merchants over the other groups of the region began to weaken and many of the people of Panchgaon and Baragaon started to move into business as small traders and transporters (particularly as muleteers), operating primarily in the northern mountains and hills. Following the abolition of the customs contract in Thak Khola, the Gurung and Thakali *subba* contended for the contract for the growing Indian border trade at Butwal and Bhairahawa, and the terai contract was successfully bid for alternately by both parties over the next two decades (cf Messerschmidt 1973: 211). The longdistance trade had begun to decline, however, and when Percival Landon travelled through western Nepal at this time he remarked, of the trail to Butwal from the north, that "the great days of this road are gone' (Landon 1928: 10). Commerce between Nepal and India, on the other hand was of steadily increasing importance and there was already clear material evidence of the direct Indian onslaught on indigenous Nepalese manufacturing in the flood of imported commodities that entered Nepal following the signing of the 1923 trade treaty which allowed for practically unrestricted import of British goods to Nepal. Naturally it had the effect of discouraging the establishment of new industries and the continued operation of ancient handicraft and cottage industries" (Lohani 1973: 205). Landon records that:

> the chief imports from India are naturally manufactured articles, of which cotton yarn and piece goods are the most important, other items being salt, petroleum, shawls, woollen cloth, rugs, oriental silk, brocade, embroideries, sugar, spice, indigo, tobacco, areca nut, vermilion, lac oils, a little fine rice, buffaloes, sheep, goats, sheet copper and sheet iron, copper and brass ornaments, beads, mirrors, precious stones, guns and ammunition, and tea..." (Landon 1928: 161).

Bhairahawa now became an increasingly important entrepot, being close to the border and to the Indian railhead. In 1928, however, it could still be observed that: "of the provincial towns of Nepal there are but three which, by any stretch of the word, can be called important centres. These are Butwal, Palpa and Pokhara" (Landon 1928: 4). In all three towns the import trade was dominated by Newar merchants, who had established themselves there gradually over the past hundred years, building up their position from their origins as petty commodity producers and small traders; but the redirection southwards of the business activities of the Thakalis presented the first threat to these powerful representatives of the Nepalese commercial bourgeoisie from within Nepal.

During the first-half of this century Indian merchants also established themselves more firmly in Butwal and Bhairahawa taking advantage of family and business connections on either side of the border to facilitate the movement of goods into and out of Nepal. The importance of the Indian 'connection' and the Indian involvement in trade within Nepal has been maintained into the second-half of the twentieth century often causing concern to the Nepalese government as well as to the commercial bourgeoisie because of the economic power, political influence and direct connections with India that Indian merchants have maintained. (cf Gaige 1975: 104-105).

By the late 1930's the small-scale production of cloth by urban manufacturers in Nepal had almost entirely disappeared and the brass and copper workers of such centres as Tansen and Pokhara were beginning to suffer from rising prices of imported raw materials and competition from Indian and other foreign manufactures. Around 1940 attempts were made to revive the once vigorous cotton weaving industry of Bandipur and skilled workers were imported from the Kathmandu Valley to operate the looms, which at one time reputedly numbered over 200; but a combination of disputes among the shareholders of the company concerned and restrictions imposed by India on the export to Nepal of the cotton thread now used extensively brought about a rapid decline (cf Sharma 1976). Heavy demand in India for grain and other agricultural produce from Nepal during the 1940's and 1950's led to more intensive exploitation of the terai, and to the growth of industrial and commercial activities there; the concentration of business in the terai was accompanied by a corresponding decline in certain hill centres. In 1954 the Rapti Valley scheme was launched and a number of Newars from Bandipur moved down to establish businesses in Narayanigarh (which was close to the Indian railhead at Bhikni Tori); the building of a road, financed by USAID, between Hetauda and Narayanigarh contributed further to the growth of this terai town as a commercial and industrial centre, and to the decline of Bandipur. Further west, the growing importance of Bhairahawa as a commercial centre (also with a rail link, through Nautanwa), had begun by the 1940's and 1950's to steal away a significant proportion of its customers from the old trading town of Butwal. In the mid-1940's the entire customs contract system was abolished, as was the office of *subba*, and although the Gurung subbas tended after that time to concentrate on local business and politics in Lamjung, the

Serchan Thakalis extended their business concerns into new branches of commerce and industry, maintaining their economic supremacy within the Thakali community but not preventing others from moving into business, albeit generally on a smaller scale. Much of the new commercial and industrial activity was centred around Bhairahawa.

During the period following the Chinese take-over in Tibet in 1959 and the Indian embargo on all goods of Chinese origin after the Indian-Chinese conflict of 1962, long distance trade was reduced to a trickle and what remained was increasingly taken over by small businessmen of predominantly non-Thakali origin. But as trade with the north declined, commerce with India continued to increase, and by 1963-64 trade with the north was reduced to 1.5% of total Nepalese trade; trade with India had grown by that year to 98% of all foreign trade. (cf Rana 1973: 221). In the period between 1956 and 1963, however, Nepal's imports rose at twice the speed of her exports, although during this period the production and export of grain and other agricultural commodities (such as mustard oilseed) continued to expand through the opening up and exploitation of the terai. The balance of trade, previously so positive, moved rapidly into heavy deficit. The volume of imported goods grew as population in the rural areas increased and indigenous forms of manufacturing declined and collapsed. Growing pressure on the agricultural economy of the hills meant, however, that there was little in the way of exports from these areas to exchange for imported commodities and cash earned from the sale of labour abroad became of even greater importance in the 'support' of the hill economy. (see Chapter 3).

As population pressure began to result in declining farm yields, dwindling per capita food production and reduced income to peasant households, so the differentiation of rural economy and society began to take place. For an increasing number of poor peasants and small artisans the complex ties of 'the domestic economy' began to prove increasingly inadequate to maintain them and their families, and many turned to other sources of income, such as labouring, and even small business as a means of supplementing declining farm income (see Chapters 3 to 8). The increasing inability of the rural areas to support their growing population resulted in substantial migration, largely from the hills to the terai and to India, but also in both the hills and the terai to the expanding urban centres. At the same time, relatively advantaged peasants (the Kulaks of Nepal) and large landowners also began to look for investment possibilities outside agriculture, both as a safeguard for their advantaged position and as a means of improving their 'portfolio' of income sources. Some of these turned to commodity production in agriculture, but a considerable number established business in the towns.

In 1952-54, when the first national census was taken, only ten towns were recorded as having populations of over 5,000, half of these in the Kathmandu Valley and most of the rest in the eastern terai; even as late as 1961 there were only sixteen towns listed as being of this size. In the last fifteen years, however, there has been a massive increase in the size of existing urban centres and an even more dramatic growth of new towns. Much of this is the result of the expansion of the bureaucracy and the development of a new wage-earning category of state employees (see Chapter 8); but probably the bulk of population growth has been associated with a massive increase in the number of small businesses resulting in large part from the transformation of rural economy and society. In western Nepal, the construction of two major roads—the Siddartha Rajmarga joining Pokhara with India via the Nepalese terai (completed in 1968-69) and the Prithvi Rajmarga linking Pokhara with Kathmandu (and finished in 1971)—also had a significant relocative effect in attracting commerce and manufacturing to the roadside, contributing to the growth of many existing towns and stimulating the emergence of new ones.

Until the 1950's the vast majority of businesses in the towns of western Nepal were either large wholesaling concerns dealing predominantly in imported goods or petty commodity producers of 'traditional' handicrafts; after that date the industrial and commercial sectors began to develop in a more complex fashion. In the terai in particular small processing industries such as rice and oil mills began to become more common, while throughout the region a variety of new branches of commodity production emerged as the towns expanded; most striking of all, however, was the growth of small retailing in the urban centres and even in the more remote villages. It still remains the case, however, that small businesses are merely a fraction of a 'business community' that itself represents 3% of the population at most.

Issues in the Analysis of Small Business

As in many underdeveloped countries, the recent history of small business in Nepal is marked by apparently contradictory tendencies of expansion and decline. Both tendencies, however, are largely explicable in terms of the gradual but uneven subjection of the Nepalese economy to the drives and demands of industrial capitalism in India and elsewhere, although other factors such as population growth have played their part (see Chapters 2 and 3).

The decline of indigenous (i.e. artisan and petty commodity) forms of production over the last fifty years or so for example is a direct result of growing competition from cheap imported manufactures and an integral part of the transformation of the agrarian-based pre-capitalist economy and society of early nineteenth century Nepal (see also Chapter 4). In the last twenty-five years, however, the decline of indigenous manufacturing has been matched by a proliferation of petty commodity producers and small capitalist enterprises largely generated by and precariously dependent on the continuing subordination of the Nepalese economy to the Indian economy (e.g. repair shops for imported manufactures); there has also been a dramatic increase in the number of small producers (e.g. transport, hotel and catering businesses) geared specifically to satisfying the needs of a rapidly expanding and relatively mobile urban population dependent largely on incomes from small business and employment in the bureaucracy. At the same time, there has been a remarkable expansion of small-scale commerce involving small retailers and petty traders dealing in imported goods; these now constitute the most numerous stratum—and the most vulnerable—in a hierarchy which extends from foreign manufacturers through Indian and Nepalese merchants to the small retailers and their customers in the towns and villages. Only in the limited sphere of small agricultural business (e.g. rice and oil mills) has there been significant growth in industrial capacity based on local resources (cf Blaikie, Cameron, Feldman, Fournier, Seddon 1976, Chapter 7).

For the majority of small businessmen in Nepal today, life is difficult; for many, particularly the poorest who constantly face the erosion of their means of livelihood and the prospect of joining the ranks of the labouring classes or the unemployed, the struggle for survival is often bitter. In our investigations of nearly 350 businesses in west central Nepal during 1974 and 1975 we found that nearly three quarters of these interviewed owned businesses that could at best be termed 'subsistence'; and most of these were clearly incapable of supporting the owner and his dependants without additional income from other sources. Such a situation is highly characteristic of underdeveloped economies, particularly among the lower strata in the urban areas. The fate of many of those whose small businesses fail can be inferred, not only from the expressed fears of those still in business but also from interviews with urban workers, a significant proportion of whom had previously owned small businesses but had been forced onto the labour market with the decline or collapse of their firm.

Although there is a distinction to be made between small businessmen and members of the working class many individuals move through these categories at least once during their lives, usually in the direction of the latter. Furthermore, the recent growth of towns and pressure on the rural economy have led to the development of a 'floating' population which maintains a precarious existence in what is often euphemistically termed 'the informal sector' in the urban areas and constitutes the lowest stratum of small business (cf Frank 1969). This stratum of predominantly transient and itinerant hawkers and pedlars provides many of the elements of the so-called lumpen proletariat as well as constituting a reservoir for casual employment. The fact that individuals at the lowest levels of the urban class structure rarely remain in a given occupation for long and that their struggle for survival usually necessitates their involvement in several different forms of economic activity at the same time seriously inhibits their ability to take collective action to improve their condition. It also poses serious problems for a class analysis. Similar analytical problems exist in the case of the minority of more successful small businesses which, as they evolve, expand and accumulate to become very different forms of enterprise. Thus, in attempting to identify and analyse the major characteristics and underlying dynamics of small business in west central Nepal we are immediately faced with questions of definition and categorisation which must themselves be informed by prior theoretical considerations (cf Rindess 1973; Lenin 1967).

A preliminary classification on the basis of stated income to the owner of the firm and its implied potential for accumulation and expansion of the business, suggests (as indicated above) that some 50% of all businesses in the region provide the owner with less than Rs. 2,000 a year (i.e. below Rs. 170 a month) and can be regarded as affording a basic livelihood at best (compare with incomes to lower paid workers, see Chapter 8); the businesses in this category might well be termed 'marginal' in so far as additional sources of income would generally be required in order to support an average family. A further 20% could be termed 'subsistence' businesses, providing owners and their dependants with at best a comfortable living from an annual income of between Rs. 2,000 and 6,000 a year. Perhaps 30% of businesses were characterised by relatively substantial owners' incomes and (by implication) by the possibility of accumulation and expansion (see Table 18). Small business in these terras (i.e. 'marginal' and 'subsistence') would account for about 71% of all business in the region.

A distinction was made earlier between small producers on the one hand and small retailers on the other, the former being involved in the production of commodities on a small

TABLE 18

Category	*Owner's income (Rs)*	*No. of observations*	*% of observations*
Marginal	0- 2,000	174	51
Subsistence	2,001- 6,000	70	20
Accumulation	6,001-25,000	51	15
Major Accumulation	25,000 plus	49	14

scale, whether as manufacturers or producers of 'services', and the latter exclusively in the circulation of commodities produced by others. Certain important aspects of small business will differ, depending into which of these two categories they fall. For example, analysis of the relationship between owners' incomes and annual turnover (based on expenditure) among businessmen in six small urban centres reveals a significant difference in this regard between those establishments involved. In commerce and those involved in commodity production; the latter tend to be smaller in terms of turnover but to generate a higher rate of return (cf Biaikie, Cameron, Feldman, Fournier and Seddon 1976, Chapter 6, Figs. 6. viii-6.x). Furthermore, as was stated in Chapter 8, there is an important difference in terms of average and maximum size of labour force employed between commercial firms and commodity producers, particularly manufacturers; for the function of labour in a productive enterprise is different from and more crucial than that of labour in a commercial establishment where it does not generate surplus value by its exploitation. The fact that accumulation in a productive enterprise depends directly on the exploitation of labour makes it different in significant respects from a commercial enterprise where levels of profits and accumulation depend not on the character and size of the labour force but on price differentials generated by the market and on the ability of the entrepreneur to control and manipulate these. While the size of the labour force may provide a direct indicator of accumulation potential in the case of commodity production, it does not do so in commercial establishments where the value of stock held may be a more accurate indicator.

Given the distinction between commodity producers and retailers it is still important, within these two categories, to determine the basis for distinguishing those businesses with accumulation potential and those without; that is, between small businesses that have a potential for growth and expansion and those that are more likely to remain 'static' or to contract and decline. In a recent discussion of small producers in urban Senegal, LeBrun and Gerry suggest a useful distinction between two fundamentally different forms of small scale production in contemporary underdeveloped societies:

> "On the one hand there are those petty producers characterised by the accumulation of wealth as the principal end-result of their productive activities. Their relations of production are capitalist ones; the employees are wage-workers and produce surplus-value. The accumulation process is manifested through the increase in the size of the production unit both in terms of labour utilised and means of production employed. On the other hand there exists petty producers, the main result of whose productive activity is simply the reproduction of their means of subsistence and their social relations of production" (LeBrun and Gerry 1975: 22-23).

The distinction made here, which follows that made by Lenin in his analysis of the development of capitalism in Russia (Lenin 1967, Chapter 5), is that between what might be termed small capitalists on the one hand—employing wage labour, producing surplus-value and able to accumulate—and petty commodity producers on the other—making use of predominantly family (or at least non-wage) labour, involved in essentially subsistence production and unable to accumulate. Accumulation potential is seen as related to the production of surplus value which depends on the scale of production, the technology involved and the quality and quantity of the labour force.

Were the employment of wage labour alone a sufficient criterion to distinguish petty commodity production and small capitalist production, then it would be possible to suggest, for example, that roughly 40% of manufacturers in west central Nepal, because they employ no wage labour at all, must be petty commodity producers, the remainder being by definition capitalists. It might also then be possible to identify as small capitalists those who employ between one and ten workers (about 45% of all manufacturers). This division between petty commodity producers and small capitalists on the one hand (85%) and medium and large capitalists (employing more than 10 workers) on the other (15%) would correspond fairly closely with the division on the basis of owner's income, in which around 70% were considered to constitute small businesses without accumulation potential. But in manufacturing, as in other branches of small-scale commodity production, employment of labour may be a poor indication of accumulation potential and thus of 'capitalist' enterprise. As with 'owner's income', the existence of a wage labour force may prove too crude an indicator, and in some cases a misleading one, if used as the sole criterion. Scott has recently drawn attention, for example, to the existence in many underdeveloped countries of some very small workshops which are able to maintain a high volume of output because of the use of advanced technology. She suggests that, in terms of accumulation potential "one could hardly refer to them as petty commodity producers" (Scott 1977: 2).

Size of owner's income or of wage labour force employed, although revealing are not adequate for it is only through an analysis of the dynamic of the business as a whole that it is possible to appreciate its accumulation potential. Other factors, such as the initial financial investment involved (the entry cost) for a given level of output and others mentioned above must also be considered. Furthermore, exclusive concentration on such 'economic' and technical elements of small business is misleading, for equally crucial may be certain features of ownership, the precise nature of the social relations of production, the relationship to the market and its mediation through suppliers and customers and, in certain contexts, the caste and ethnic affiliation of those involved.

However defined in terms of the characteristics mentioned above, the small businessman is involved in a complex set of economic, social and political relations which together constitute and generate his class position and class affiliation. Conventionally a distinction has been made between the position and affiliation of the petty commodity producer or small retailer and that of the capitalist, even if the latter could also be considered a small businessman. Poulantzas, for example, like LeBrun and Gerry, distinguishes between those petty producers and small retailers who constitute or belong to the petty bourgeoisie and the small capitalists who belong to the bourgeoisie proper. What he terms 'the traditional petty bourgeoisie' includes:

> "forms of artisanal work and small family businesses in which one and the same agent is both owner of the means of production and of labour and is the direct worker. Here there is no economic exploitation in the strict sense, inasmuch as these forms do not employ paid workers (or very rarely do so). Labour is principally provided by the real owner or the members of his family, who are not remunerated in the form of wages" (Poulantzas 1973: 37).

This is a classic description of 'the self-employed', but unless qualified would oblige us to identify as a member of the petty bourgeoisie the small producer who employed no wage labour but to categorise the small producer with one wage labourer as a small capitalist. The analytical distinction is clear, but arguably unduly restrictive. Poulantzas himself, in the passage above, recognises that "these forms do not employ paid workers (*or very rarely do so*)" thus allowing a degree of flexibility into the distinction. He argues further, that "purely economic criteria are not sufficient to determine and locate social classes", for these

> "are groups of social agents, of men defined principally but not exclusively by their place in the production process, i.e. by their place in the economic sphere. The economic place of the social agents has a principal role in determining social classes. But from that we cannot conclude that this economic place is sufficient to determine social classes. Marxism states that the

> economic does indeed have the determinate role in a mode of production or a social formation; but the political and the ideological (the super-structure) also have an important role" (Poulantzas 1973: 27).

If this is accepted, then although a clear distinction can be made between, say the small producer who employs no wage labour and the small producer with a single worker, their class position and hence their future behaviour is not so simply determined and will depend on a large number of factors—economic, social and political—that cannot be wholly determined a *priori*. The same will, of course, apply in the case of all small businessmen, and indeed the whole of 'the business community' and the urban class structure as a whole.

Given the practical and theoretical difficulties associated with the identification and isolation of small businessmen in general, it will perhaps prove helpful to concentrate on certain categories and branches of business and attempt to analyse the characteristics of each category, including the internal divisions and the relationship between those internal divisions and the wider class structure; the focus will not be exclusive, but should serve to illuminate the more general condition of certain sections of small business in west central Nepal today.

Earlier in this chapter we identified a general process of decline among certain branches of indigenous petty commodity production in the urban areas, and in Chapter 4 have discussed the causes and effects of the break-up of the *bista* system whereby increasing numbers of rural artisans are no longer able to play their former role within the domestic peasant economy but are forced to undertake new forms of activity, usually in the rural areas but sometimes in the towns. First, we examine the characteristics of those tailors and metalworkers currently practising their craft in the towns of the region and consider the wider context of these particular branches of manufacturing, and then turn to the two more prevalent forms of small business in the region today, petty commodity production in the sphere of lodging and catering and small retailing of a distinctive kind—the *kirana* shop or general stores.

Tailors

All the tailors of the region fall quite clearly within the category of small businessmen; none showed the accumulation potential nor the indications of 'size' characteristic of medium or large business. The vast majority, furthermore, can be considered as petty commodity producers, for it is extremely rare to find tailors employing wage labour; both the nature of the technology employed and the characteristics of their products tend to limit the expansion of this form of production. The spread of the sewing machine after the second World War revolutionised the productive capacity of any given individual tailor and raised, in principle at least, the possibility of a development of small factory—like establishments with several workers and several simple machines concentrated together under a single owner and manager. In fact, such a development has not taken place, largely because Indian mass manufactures already satisfy to a large extent the existing demand for the kind of product such a system creates, and tailors remain predominantly family concerns, with at most a couple of brothers or associates and an apprentice or two producing a limited range of products for a limited clientele, usually on a 'bespoke' basis.

We have used the term artisan production quite specifically in previous discussions (see Chapter 4) to refer to the form of production associated with the bista system and the domestic peasant economy, but it is of significance that tailors in the towns rarely produce for subsequent sale in an anonymous market; tailors' establishments are rarely 'shops' in the sense of retail outlets displaying finished goods to passers-by. The tailor generally produces specific items, at the request of a client or customer, and often makes use of material provided by the customer. It is relevant to note, in this connection, that many small tailors rent space next to, or even in some cases on the porch of, a cloth shop; in this way the customer purchasing cloth at the larger establishment are able to engage the tailor immediately to make it up according to their specifications. Such a 'symbiotic' relationship between cloth shops and tailors was noted quite frequently during our investigations in 1974-75. So, if tailors tend to be petty commodity producers, they also tend to have a quite specific relationship to their customers, and often to the suppliers, for the cloth shop owner may actually provide the tailor with materials (thread, cloth, etc.) and thus act as his supplier. In a few cases, particularly with the smallest tailoring businesses, the relationship between cloth shop owner and tailor is more like that between employer and employee than between two independent businessmen. Where the tailor works 'for' such a patron, it is common for him to have his premises or place of work adjacent to the cloth shop, and often to pay rent for the 'privilege'.

Even in setting up the business a tailor frequently faces the need to establish or make use of personal connections; for although 'entry costs' to tailoring in the urban areas are not high in comparison with many branches of business, acquisition of the necessary equipment is considered costly and loans are often obtained in order to purchase a sewing machine, iron, scissors and basic furniture. Investigations in Pokhara among recently established tailors suggested that the total cost of setting up shop in the mid-1970's was anything between Rs. 500 and Rs. 1,500, the major variable being the sewing machine whose cost depended upon its age and quality. In addition to the initial capital investment, premises had to be found and material purchased. Rent had to be paid as did other incidental expenses such as heating, lighting, power and a signboard.

Shirts, trousers, blouses and coats figure as the major products of the tailor's craft and these account for the vast bulk of his sales. Increasingly, readymade clothes imported from India and elsewhere are competing with local products, although the advantages of having one's clothes literally tailor-made are recognised by the urban population which provides the bulk of the urban tailors' custom. Peasants visiting the towns are more likely either to have their clothes made up in the village by a rural tailor, or to buy imported clothing. The kind of product demanded by the relatively sophisticated urban population differs significantly from that demanded by the majority of peasants and the tailor in the towns must be able to produce modish garments in order to keep his clientele. Demands on the skill and experience of the tailor impose what might also be termed 'entry costs', in that many rural tailors will not have these skills and will therefore find it difficult to set up and run a successful business in the town.

It is significant, therefore, that a relatively high proportion of tailors in the towns of the region are Newars, historically the group from which urban petty commodity producers originate. Rural tailors emigrating to find business in the urban areas tend, on the whole, not to set up in the larger towns initially, but to migrate in gradual moves from smaller roadside locations and then, if successful, to larger towns. Tailors, both in the rural areas and in the towns tend to have little in the way of security apart from their own businesses and technical skills; few own more than a little land—if that, and most depend heavily on the business for their livelihood, augmenting income from the business with wage labouring where family structure permits. Given the fact that tailors are of 'low caste' status, their possibilities are limited for the most part to their 'caste occupation' and various forms of labouring and menial work.

Annual incomes from tailoring are not high in most of the towns of the region but do generally provide a subsistence for the owner and his dependents. In Pokhara, tailors appear to earn anywhere between Rs. 150 a month and Rs. 450 a month; in Tansen incomes seemed, if anything somewhat higher. Thus, many tailors in business at the present time are 'comfortably off' and a very few have even been able to expand to become small employers of labour, using two or more machines; but the penetration of mass-manufactured clothing from India and the Far East has begun to erode the position of the local tailor generally. Nevertheless, it would seem that the period of intense competition between tailors in the towns, with many small businesses collapsing for lack of demand or through indebtedness, has passed. The unsuccessful tailors have left the business and are now wage labourers, or (in a few cases) have moved into other forms of business.

Metal Working

In the hill towns, where historically brass and copper work was done by specific sub-castes of Newar craftsmen, the small-scale production of household utensils and vessels has declined drastically over the past twenty years. The total number of such metalworking establishments was probably no more, in the mid-1970's, than around thirty households in the entire region. In Tansen, for example, once widely reputed as the major centre of indigenous metalworking in the region, barely a dozen producers remain in Taxar Tol, once the busy metalworkers' quarter. Pokhara can boast only about the same number, and other hill towns even fewer.

The exhaustion of local raw materials during the late 19th and early 20th century led to increased importation of sheet metal from India and rising prices systematically reduced the margins of these small producers until their products were no longer competitive with the cheaper Indian manufacturers. Fashion and practicality combine to account for the popularity of imported stainless steel ware among the relatively affluent and of the lighter and cheaper aluminium products among the poorer sections of the population. Many of the best-known indigenous forms (e.g. the famous Palpali jug produced in Tansen) have been copied by Indian manufacturers and are now produced in large quantities, primarily for the Nepalese market, in Indian factories.

Today, commerce in imported metal manufactures generally offer more immediately lucrative prospects to local businessmen with an interest and expertise in this sphere and it is not uncommon to find those who have moved out of small-scale metalware production, and have avoided the more common fate of being obliged to depend increasingly on wage labour, operating retail businesses, selling to local customers the very Indian goods that have been responsible for the decline of their own indigenous industry.

Those who remain in the metalworking business tend to be petty commodity producers, using predominantly family labour and apprentices (although few youngmen today are entering apprenticeship). They usually make pots to order for specific clients, although a few have a special arrangement with a retailer to display their products for sale and produce a small proportion for the market. Sometimes the client will provide the materials for production; usually old vessels or utensils in a poor state and beyond repair. Some of the smaller producers have been reduced merely to repairing old pots, for lack of raw materials and because of declining demand for new brass and copper ware. Possibilities of accumulation of any significant scale are limited and metalworking remains a predominantly subsistence activity, providing a livelihood rather than profits for reinvestment and expansion. Incomes among those who remain in the business, however, appear sufficient to allow some a comfortable living, although they are probably not on balance as considerable as those of the better-off tailors.

Metalworking in the towns used to be associated with particular Newar sub-castes, notably Tamrakar, and this remains the case today. As metalworkers leave the industry, however, their caste label no longer conforms to their present occupation; furthermore, many of those moving into retailing or into other business activities tend to change their names, usually in favour of the ubiquitous Shrestha, once signifying membership of a distinctive Newar trading sub-caste but now in effect only a very common Newar family name. We have already noted (in Chapter 4) that rural blacksmiths are probably the most securely embedded in what remains of the domestic peasant economy, by virtue of the necessary services they still provide; in the towns there is little evidence of more than a small number of Kamis and there is still opportunity for blacksmiths to ply their trade or to compete with the remaining urban Newar metalworkers. The majority of Kamis therefore find employment, usually in casual form as porters, coolies or construction workers, in much the same way as do members of other 'low castes' from the countryside.

If brass and copper work has shown a drastic decline as demand slumped in favour of imported metalware, the same cannot be said for the other, more prestigious branch of metalworking, goldsmithing. The number of goldsmiths' in the urban areas, particularly in the major towns along the Siddartha Rajmarga—the route of returning soldiers and migrants from India, the Far East and elsewhere—is striking. The major reason for the importance of goldsmiths is the continuous flow of gold into the country, and to some extent out of it, both through legal and illegal channels. Much of the business of the goldsmith today is associated simply with the purchase of gold and silver, but a certain proportion of goldsmithing and silver-smithing proper still continues, for the hoarding of precious metal in the form of female ornaments remains a common practice and there is still considerable demand for the conversion of gold and silver into such convenient modes of display and saving.

Our investigations revealed that goldsmithing is a considerably more lucrative business than either tailoring or metalworking of other kinds; the majority of goldsmiths are comfortably off while a significant proportion are able to accumulate on a modest scale. The form of production remains, however, a predominantly craft or petty commodity form in which the employment of wage labour, although it does take place, is less common than the use of family labour or apprentices. The nature of the technology (little more than a tiny furnace and a range of small hand tools) and the intricacy of much of the work (putting a premium on manual skills) together with the high value of the small quantities of gold and silver worked mean that there are few economies in larger scale production and that investment in stock beyond a certain point becomes difficult and even dangerous. The goldsmith, when operating as such rather than simply as a dealer, may use his own gold to make items for a particular client or (more commonly) be provided with gold or silver by the customer himself; it is comparatively rare for the goldsmith to manufacture commodities for sale without an order in hand. This special relationship with the client or customer does not, however, preclude the production of commodities, for there is no fixed or permanent relationship with the customer, who is obliged to pay the market price for the work done. (The same is the case for the urban tailor and the metalworker, unlike the tailor or blacksmith in the bista system).

Like other indigenous branches of petty commodity production in the towns, goldsmithing tends to be associated with a distinctive group or groups, Guvaju and Sakya are the 'traditional' Newar goldsmith sub-castes, although Bajracharya and Buddhacharya goldsmiths are found. Sunar (goldsmith) is the more general caste label found in both rural and urban areas, and it is by this term that the majority of practising goldsmiths are identified; Sunar as a caste label is also found where individuals are involved in other occupations. Like many other 'occupational castes', the Sunar is, considered 'untouchable' and therefore socially discriminated against even when relatively well off, although to a lesser extent than many other 'low caste' groups.

Commodity Production in the Hotel and Catering Business

In the rural areas, where food is usually produced and consumed at home by the members of the family (with the women and girls responsible for the production process) or else provided by an employer from his own kitchen, the demand for special establishments serving food, snacks and refreshments of various kinds is small, except on special occasions such as marriages and funerals when tiny stalls are set up on a temporary basis, or where trails provide a reasonable 'customer potential' in the form of travellers unable to provide their own food and drink while they journey. As the majority of journeys take place over short distances and even porters tend to take their provisions with them, the demand for food and drink and therefore the prospects for small business based on the production of such commodities are limited. In much the same way, there is generally little demand for over-night lodging that cannot be satisfied through personal connections and thus the number of *bhattis* (small lodging houses) in the rural areas is relatively small. The growth of towns over the last decade, however, and in particular the rapid expansion of centres along the roads (associated both with road construction and with the dramatic rise in the number of those in government service), has generated a massive increase in the number of establishments or 'enterprises' providing food, refreshment and lodging for travellers and for those employed in the towns and unable to return home. for meals or refreshment. At the same time, in certain centres, notably in Pokhara, the prospect of a certain growth in the tourist industry has generated a significant development of hotels and restaurants directed at predominantly foreign custom.

In considering this branch of commodity production we are focussing on a sphere of business that raises quite acutely the problems of definition mentioned earlier. Many of the smallest producers and pedlars of food and drink can be referred to as 'businessmen' only with considerable generosity, yet a significant proportion of even the smallest tea shops and eating houses employ wage labour, without, however, necessarily being able to rise above 'subsistence' or 'marginal' income levels by so doing. Furthermore, there would appear to be an important distinction to be made between those small businesses that might be termed lodges and eating houses, with limited entry costs, relatively low initial investment or recurrent expenditure on premises and—generally—correspondingly restricted possibilities of accumulation, and those medium and large businesses, most suitably referred to as hotels and restaurants. The latter operate on a different scale and for a different market and attract entrepreneurs of a very different kind (usually from different social backgrounds) from the owners of the smaller lodges and eating houses. Their entry costs are considerably higher as are their recurrent expenses; and their chances of both accumulation and bankruptcy considerably greater (cf Blaikie, Cameron, Feldman, Fournier and Seddon 1976, Chapter 7).

The sphere of catering is not one in which particular castes or ethnic groups hold a long historical dominance, although there is no doubt that particular groups do predominate in this branch of commodity production today. 'Northerners' (e.g. Thakalis and other groups from the district of Mustang) tend to run the majority of small lodges and eating houses throughout the region, although other ethnic groups, notably

Gurungs, are also represented. Teashops and the smallest itinerant food producers and traders are associated with a wide variety of castes and ethnic groups, only the 'low castes' being debarred from involvement by virtue of their 'untouchability'. In the category of restaurants and hotels a considerable range of castes and ethnic groups is to be found, although 'northeners' and Gurungs predominate, with Newars heavily represented in the tiny luxury hotel sector.

Entry costs at the lowest level are very small—far lower, for example, than those for tailoring or metalworking (even where the latter do not have premises of their own), and roughly on par with the smallest of those street pedlars trading in small quantities of cheap manufactured items (bangles, soap, matches, batteries, etc.) who could be regarded as the prototype of the kirana shop, or general stores (see Section 6 below). With the sellers of 'homecooked' food and sweets we are on the margin between the petty hawker who combines commodity production on a minute scale with several. other equally marginal forms of activity and the small businessmen with recognisable if often primitive premises and a more than transient existence over time. That a distinction exists in principle between street hawker and small businessman is recognised by at least one Chamber of Commerce (the institution which claims to serve the interests of 'the business community', see Section 8)—that of Bandipur, which discriminates against the former, preventing them from joining —although in practice, there is a continuum in terms of scale of operation and in the extent to which the business is able to provide a livelihood or prospects of accumulation for its owner. However, it is possible to suggest, in general terms, that the class interests of tiny street traders and commodity producers are likely to be distinct and different from those of the small businessmen and to approach more closely those of the sections of the working class in casual employment or unemployed and those of the 'lumpen proletariat'; even if for the individual such forms of 'enterprise' can appear to offer some degree of independence as an 'entrepreneur' thus affecting his perception of his own interests.

In most towns the small tea shop and eating house is (apart from the *kirana* shop) the most common form of business; indeed in a few roadside locations there is little else but small lodges, tea shops, eating houses and kirana shops. The vast majority of these businesses provide their owners with a subsistence at best; usually other sources of income are required to maintain the household concerned. Nevertheless, probably most of them employ non-family labour. Admittedly the 'wages' paid are frequently in the form of food, lodging, clothing and other 'extras' but they may be regarded as wages in the sense that they are related to the market price for labour and permit the appropriation of surplus value for the employer, even if they allow him to 'pay' less than he would were the wages paid in cash. Technically, these businesses might be identified as small capitalist enterprises, but the term would appear in these circumstances to be a misnomer in the majority of cases; it is rare that the exploitation of wage labour in these small establishments provides the basis for accumulation, more usually it is a reflection of the high opportunity cost to members of the owner's own family of working in the business (unless they are young boys or girls), and the 'surplus' generated is realised in consumption by the owner's family.

In so far as this form of production involves activities of a predominantly 'domestic' nature (cooking, cleaning, providing refreshments, etc.), it can be regarded as an extension into the market of domestic work. It is then not surprising that the proportion of women involved is high relative to any other branch of business. Whether as owner or, more usually, as manager or employee, or simply as subordinate family member working unpaid, women probably outnumber men in this branch of commodity production, particularly in the smallest and most marginal establishments where it is not uncommon to find the business operated predominantly by women. In certain localities, where the proximity of army camps or roadside location ensures an exceptional demand for such 'facilities', other aspects of 'domestic' life appear, transformed by their involvement in market into forms of commodity production: the association of prostitution, for example, with the provision of over-night lodging, food and drink is relatively common in centres like Paklihawa, Raniganj and Walling. In such places furthermore, women whose particular relationship with returning soldiers and other migrants derives from their involvement in these various forms of commodity production, sometimes also operate on a small scale as smugglers of gold, in close association with the goldsmiths who also tend to cluster around the army camps in Pokhara and Bhairahawa and at important 'bus stop' centres like Walling. Such examples not only reveal the difficulty of clearly distinguishing a petty bourgeoisie associated with small business from a lumpenproletariat usually identified with such marginal and even criminal activities, but also raise important questions about the 'class position' of women.

Kirana Business

Rather as in the 'hotel and catering sector', the range of businesses in terms of size is very great in this particular branch of commerce. At the bottom entry costs are extremely low, consisting of no more than the price of goods to be resold; but the itinerant trader can be distinguished, in principle at least, from the small kirana shop whose proprietor is obliged to pay rent but has premises in which he is able to house his stock. At the upper end are large retailers and wholesalers, more properly regarded as merchants than as small businessmen, some of whom have privileged access to the imported goods they sell through the award of a government dealership or their appointment as agents for a foreign manufacturer or trading house.

Small retailers account for a major proportion of all businesses in most underdeveloped countries; among this section of the commercial sector small multi-purpose 'general stores', stocking a wide range if not always a large volume of cheap household goods and groceries, tend to predominate. Nepal is no exception to this. It is possible, in the west central region, however, to identify a period of rapid growth in small-scale commercial activity, epitomised by the expansion of small *kirana* shops, starting around 1958. By 1965, in Pokhara, for example, just over half of all business establishments were *kirana* shops, according to the town census for that year. This surge during the 1960's reflects a combination of increasing pressure on the rural economy, growth of demand (both real and perceived) for imported goods, and exceptionally low entry costs into this particular branch of business; it is significant that a considerable proportion of existing *kirana* businesses in the rural areas were established during this period, as well as of those in the towns. There is some evidence to suggest that, even if entry costs were low and demand for the goods they carried was on the increase, the massive number of new *kirana* shops created an 'over supply', particularly in the towns, and set up very severe competition between them. In the mid-1970's *kirana* shops account for approximately a quarter of all businesses in the towns of the hills and the terai, suggesting a proportional decline over the last ten years, probably in part as a result of closures and the elimination of many of the more precarious businesses. But although closures are certainly disruptive and may be disastrous for the proprietor and his dependents, it is premature to regard closure of business as a catastrophe for the owner until other sources of income available to him are assessed and the possibilities for him of opening the business again later or elsewhere, or alternatively of moving into a different business, are investigated.

The majority of kirana shops today are 'subsistence' or 'marginal' in terms of their capacity to generate income; but the persistence of many clearly marginal businesses can be explained in a number of ways. First, many businesses generating very small incomes are maintained because the owner has other sources of income; these may enable him to continue to operate what might be a profitable business even if one unable to provide for a whole family, or even an unprofitable one in the hope of improvement through temporary 'subsidies' from a small farm or income from wages, or by obtaining a loan. In general a loan is obtained to set up a kirana shop but they can also serve as a method of delaying the eventual collapse of the business; the costs are high, however, for private loans from merchants and moneylenders are generally expensive and can lead to a situation of chronic indebtedness unless business unexpectedly improves. Secondly, many kirana shop owners attempt to reduce competition by creating and cultivating a personal and exclusive clientele as the core of their custom (i.e. by trying to domesticate the free market forces) or by reducing the real value for money obtained by their customers through adulteration or other means 'invisible' to the customer. Also there is evidence to suggest that retailers in general, whether small or not, tend to be 'price followers' and not to compete through price wars; that is to say their strategy is defensive and 'passive' rather than aggressive (see Chapter 5 for the significance of this with regard to porters' wages).

Finally, merchants, under pressure from foreign manufacturers and from competition among themselves, have also attempted to construct personal networks of clients among the retailers in order to safeguard their own interests; and while these may on occasions prove oppressive for the small retailer (in that he is thereby locked virtually inextricably together with his supplier), in general they appear to benefit, being cushioned as a result from price increases in imported goods or from other threats to their livelihood and in some cases being able to obtain loans or goods at a discount from their patron-supplier.

Given the relatively low entry costs and the fact that the expansion of this particular branch of commerce is a relatively recent phenomenon (as indeed is the growth of the commercial petty bourgeoisie as a whole), a range of castes and ethnic groups is represented among the owners of small kirana shops. As in virtually the entire 'business community', however, Newars predominate and according to our own investigations Brahmins and Chetris are very heavily represented: in one regionwide survey Newars accounted for 53% of kirana shops, Brahmins for 23% and Chetris for 15%; in another, in Pokhara, Newars constituted 54%, Brahmins 21%, Thakalis 13% and Gurungs 8%. There are differences between the hills and the terai, for obvious reasons, and the predominance of the

Brahmins and Chetris is greater in the latter. Gaige notes that the itinerant kirana traders of the terai are mainly 'high caste' Hindus, although around 307 in one district (Kapilvastu) were Muslims (Gaige 1975: 34). Even in our survey of kirana shops in Pokhara around 37 were owned by Muslims, their particular speciality being bangles and other trinkets.

In the small businesses, however, the caste or ethnic origin of the shopkeeper is less significant than the fact that the vast majority were, and in many cases still are, small peasants for whom even a marginal business is an additional support for the household, or pensioners from government or army service; only in a minority of cases are they the source of possible accumulation and to be regarded as a 'stage' in the economic, advancement of a particular individual and his family. Ownership of a small kirana shop thus generally places the household concerned in the petty bourgeoisie, unless other major sources of income are available for which the business is purely a supplement; furthermore, it generally provides a livelihood rather than a basis for growth and accumulation.

Class and Consumption

The analysis of class divisions and their significance must start from a consideration of the relations of production and exchange, for from these derive, in a complex fashion, all other economic, political and social divisions. It is important to recognise that there is a close relationship, for example, between the overall class position of a household and its style and standard of living; class differences are experienced and lived not only at work but also in the home. Patterns of consumption and style of living—which conventional sociologists tend to take as the basis of 'class' differences—in fact derive from particular forms of involvement in relations of production and exchange; but they have their own significance as a dimension of the 'condition' of any given household or class.

A brief examination of ten households located in Pokhara will serve to illustrate the importance of the relationship

TABLE 19

Household	*Main income source*	*No other sources*	*No family members*	*No servants*
1	Farm labouring	—	2	—
2	Cooking	1	6	—
3	Small tea shop	1	6	—
4	Tailoring	—	6	—
5	Kirana shop	—	4	—
6	Kirana shop	2	5	1
7	Hotel	2	7	—
8	Hotel	2	10	—
9	Cloth shop	1	15	1
10	Cloth shop	3	12	8

TABLE 20

	June 1974				*December 1974*			
House-hold	*Total Rs. or cash equivalent*	*% of rice*	*Total maize*	*Spent on millet*	*Total Rs.*	*% of rice*	*Total maize*	*Spent on millet*
1	28	—	46.4	—	26	11.6	—	46.6
2	53	18.8	36.7	—	44	27.2	—	9.1
3	86	46.4	15.1	—	102	40.7	—	—
4	86	34.8	22.6	—	128	38.2	—	—
5	81	34.2	—	—	129	21.6	—	—
6	164	31.5	—	—	286	18.5	—	—
7	176	47.0	—	—	317	30.0	—	—
8	219	44.1	—	—	278	30.4	—	—
9	263	59.3	—	—	351	52.5	—	—
10	582	59.5	—	—	707	49.0	—	—

TABLE 21

Pokhara Chamber of Commerce (February 1975)

Caste/ethnic group	*Total**	*Size of business involved*		
		Big	*Medium*	*Small*
Newar	133	56	32	31
Thakali	30	12	8	4
Chetri	20	7	4	8
Brahmin	18	2	7	5
Gurung	13	4	2	5
Tibetan	2	2	—	—
Damai	4	—	1	3
Magar	2	—	—	1
Tamang	1	—	—	1
Unknown	20	N/A	N/A	N/A
	243	83	54	58

*Includes businesses where caste/ethnic groups is known but not 'size'.

Bhairahawa Chamber of Commerce (February 1975)

caste/ethnic group	*Total*	*Big*	*Medium*	*Small*
'Indian' and Tharu	108	31	58	19
Newar	38	12	21	5
Thakali	36	17	19	—
Brahmin	35	7	18	10
Chetri	12	1	8	3
Gurung	9	2	6.	1
Muslim	4	1	3	—
Thakuri	4	1	2	1
Magar	1	—	1	—
Unknown	6	3	1	2
	253	75	137	41

Tansen Chamber of Commerce (February 1975)

caste/ethnic group	*Total*	*Big*	*Medium*	*Small*
Newar	120	20	55	45
Brahmin	8	1	6	1
'Indian'	8	1	3	4
Muslim	4	—	1	2
Chetri	3	—	1	2
Thakali	2	—	—	2
Unknown	20	3	6	11
	165	25	72	68

between class and consumption. The households were selected purposively to provide a range of circumstances and were visited regularly over a period of a year (see Tables 19 and 20).

In terms of their relations of production and exchange, the heads of households one and two are unambiguously working class, their only source of income being wage employment; household two occasionally obtains additional income from casual labouring, usually in construction. Households three and four are involved in petty commodity production, in the case of household three with supplementary income from labouring. The head of household five is a small retailer with no other source of income; but for household six, which is significantly better off than five, the retail business is complemented by income from farming and from employment in government service. Both households seven and eight receive income from farming and from British army pensions, in addition to that from their business, while household nine has income from farming as well as from the cloth shop. The head of household ten has, in addition to the business given as his main source of income, a provision store, a rice and oil mill and a large rural estate which is share-cropped in his absence. Heads of household seven, eight, nine and ten all employ non-family wage labour in their respective businesses even though some members of their household have no employment.

Identification of the overall class position of these households is not a simple matter. In terms of the relations of production and exchange we have noted that households one and two are unambiguously working class, having income only from wages. Household three includes individuals obtaining income from labouring and from petty commodity production, but a small tea shop is a fragile defence against the pressures on this household and certainly in terms of income provides no more than labouring. Household four is technically in a similar position, although the tailoring business is a little more secure and substantial than the tea shop. Household five is firmly within the petty bourgeoisie in terms of its business involvement, as is household six, although here the kirana shop is just one of three sources of income (although admittedly given as the main source). In terms both of their size and accumulation potential and also their employment of wage labour the businesses of household seven, eight, nine and ten are clearly capitalist enterprises, the first three arguably to be considered 'small' and the last clearly 'medium' or even 'large', at least within the context of Nepal's stunted indigenous capitalism. The head of household ten is clearly, by virtue of his various business enterprises, in a different league from those of households seven, eight and nine.

The combination of different economic activities, which together provide the basis for an assessment of their overall class position, generates different patterns of consumption and styles of living for the various households, which also is relevant for a class analysis. If we consider the weekly expenditure and grain consumption of these ten households we find significant differences which do correspond broadly with those discussed above. In terms of weekly expenditure households one and two are clearly the most impoverished, with three and four and five, which are marginally or firmly within the petty bourgeoisie in terms of their relations of production and exchange, spending a little more, while household ten is again, in terms of weekly expenditure, in a league of its own. In terms of grain consumption, households one, two three and four are all obliged to consume a proportion of millet or maize; households nine and ten require a considerable amount of rice to feed their large families and their servants; and while it is clearly the case the household consumption depends to some extent on the number of members, it is also true that the wealthier households are able to maintain larger numbers of co-residents than the less well-off.

If we classify the households in terms of consumption we can identify two major categories: 'the poor' and 'the relatively affluent', in which households one to five fall into the first category and the remainder into the second; we could also subdivide these to produce further categories, such as 'the very poor', and so on. Such categories are of value in that they reveal real differences in standard of living; they do not, however, constitute a basis for the analysis of class divisions (although they must be considered an important part of such an analysis), being in a sense consequences of the complex set of relationships in which the various members of the household are involved, at work and elsewhere.

Forms of Association and Small Businessmen

The set of relationships in which small businessmen are involved includes not only those directly associated with production and exchange but also those more indirectly connected to their business life, such as the various organisations or forms of association to which many small businessmen in the region belong.

In almost every town in western Nepal is a branch of the national Chamber of Commerce, an association explicitly concerned to defend and promote the interests of 'businessmen' throughout Nepal. The association does not receive official recognition as a 'class organisation' and consequently has no representation on the National Panchayat. However, despite this lack of formal recognition, "in fact the relation between the Government and the employers is very close, through the only employers' organisation, the Federation of Nepalese Chambers of Commerce and Industry, by its participation in the national as well as the regional levels" (Shrestha 1975: 69).

The ostensible purpose of the association is, in the words of the secretary of the Pokhara Chamber of Commerce, "to look after the problems of those members who request help and to represent them in discussions with the authorities"; he gave as an example the response of the Chamber of Commerce to the government decree that a sales tax should be implemented—it argued against this measure, pointing out that it would be impossible to apply given the fact that the majority of shopkeepers, particularly the smaller ones, did not keep written accounts and did not make out receipts. A more detailed statement of objectives is to be found in the preamble to the constitution of the Tansen Chamber of Commerce:

> "to bring welfare between businessmen and customers in Palpa and to encourage people to increase production throughout the country so as to help the country to progress; to establish mutual understanding by a relationship with other similar associations elsewhere in Nepal; to mediate disputes between businessmen; to maintain good relations with the authorities; to establish branches throughout the district; to promote a high level of morality in business; to participate in commercial and crafts exhibitions and other activities; and to maintain quality of goods and surveillance of weights and measures".

In so far as the chambers of commerce are explicitly formed to serve the interests of 'the business community' as a whole, membership is generally open to all businessmen irrespective of class or caste and membership fees are minimal. In fact membership of the various local associations ranges from large manufacturers and merchants, through medium sized and small capitalist enterprises, to small 'subsistence' petty commodity producers and retailers. Only in a minority of instances are certain categories of 'business' explicitly barred from membership, as in the case of the Bandipur Chamber of Commerce which explicitly does not admit petty traders and hawkers nor small lodges and tea shops (*bhattis*), although the absence of fixed premises and inherently transient nature of the smallest 'businesses' would tend to prevent their admission to most chambers of commerce.

However, in addition to this important distinction between recognised businesses and the smallest transient forms of enterprise, it is clear that potential cleavages exist within the membership of the chamber of commerce. While it is true that for certain purposes and under certain circumstances the interests of all businessmen may coincide (as in the case instanced by the secretary of Pokhara chamber cited above), in general the interests of different branches of 'the business community' and of different classes within it do diverge, and indeed may often be in direct conflict, as is often the case between merchant wholesalers and their client retailers.

Indeed, one of the stated objectives of the Tansen Chamber of Commerce is to mediate in disputes between businessmen. Small businessmen were unclear, when asked, what the direct benefits to themselves from membership of a chamber of commerce would be; those who had joined hoped that their general interests would be defended. They pointed to the fact that it was the large and powerful businessmen who dominated the associations, and suggested that these would be able to exert pressure both privately and through the association on the local authorities and other non-business interests. They did also, however, generally recognise the potential for conflict within the associations and the existence of diverging interests between the large and the small businesses.

It is relevant in this context to note that in all of the local associations, while general membership includes businesses of all sizes, the owners of large enterprises dominate the committees and have a predominant influence on policy and on the activities of the association, both with respect to its own members and with respect to external interests, such as the local authorities. Although a detailed examination of the internal structure and workings of the chambers of commerce would be required to establish precisely how they operate, it is clear that the interests of big business predominate. Discussions with small businessmen failed to elicit any strong feeling for the need for a 'small businessmen's association' to serve their specific needs and interests, but there is some indication that small businessmen have voted with their feet by not joining chambers of commerce to the same extent proportionally as do medium and large businessmen (see Table 21).

Many small businessmen, however, recognise the need to co-operate with others in 'the business community' in order to survive. One of the most striking features of the development of commodity production and commerce in the last decade has been the spread of a particular institution—the rotating credit association—which enables small businessmen to obtain credit for investment or for other purposes on relatively favourable terms without going through the official channels of government banks or undertaking the frequently disastrous commitment to a moneylender.

Several writers have noted the existence in the rural hill areas of west central Nepal of a form of rotating credit association, known locally as *dhikur* or *dhikuri* (e.g. Pignede, 1966; Messerschmidt 1972, 1973; Macfarlane 1976). The *dhikuri* is an association of shareholders who pay regular instalments at a predetermined rate and frequency and who each receive the accumulated fund once as a share to invest or to spend usually at the discretion of the individual. Instalments are the same for every shareholder in any particular turn, but increases each time by a form of simple incremental interest. Consequently, members whose turn to take the fund towards the end have a progressively greater financial advantage (receiving more than they pay in) which counterbalances any disadvantage in having to wait a relatively long time for their share; while members whose turn to take the fund falls towards the beginning have the advantage of early access to a relatively large sum for a relatively small initial contribution, but eventually pay in more than they receive. I do not intend to analyse the *dhikuri* in any detail here but merely to provide some indication of its significance for small businessmen.

The *dhikuri* is today widely used in the towns of west central Nepal as a means of raising capital for investment as well as for other purposes. The spread of the institution from its probable area of origin in the far north of the region appears to have taken place relatively recently. In 1958 the dhikuri was reportedly unknown outside the northern hills and was exclusively a rural phenomenon, according to Pignede (1966: 146) who worked in a village a few hours' walk north of Pokhara; no *dhikuri* was to be found in Pokhara itself. In 1973, Messerschmidt wrote that "until recently, *dhikurs* were found almost exclusively in Nepal's western hills. They have been documented in the districts of Mustang, Myagdi, Baglung, Kaski, Lamjung and Manang. They are most frequently found among Bhotia, Thakali, Panchgaonle, and Gurung ethnic groups" (1973: 18). He noted, however, that "by the time of my own research in 1971-72, they had spread far and wide" (1973: 27). Research carried out in west central Nepal during 1974 and 1975 identified and investigated numerous dhikuris in the towns of the region, in the terai and in the southern hills, notably in Pokhara, Gorkha, Walling, Tansen, Butwal and Bhairahawa. Messerschmidt suggests that "dhikurs found in Pokhara Bazaar, Kathmandu, Terai towns and North India can usually be traced to Thakalis or Gurungs" (1973: 18) and notes that "*dhikur*-like rotating credit associations have not been reported among other ethnic and caste groups in Nepal" (1973: 20). He does, however, himself record the presence of one Newar member in a *dhikuri* based in Pokhara and Thak Khola (1973: 33), and by the mid-1970's, although it remains the case that *dhikuris* are still predominantly associations of 'northerners' (people from Thak Khola, Panchgaon, Baragaon, Marpha, etc.) and Gurungs, particularly in the rural areas, members of other caste and ethnic groups are increasingly making use of this form of credit association in the towns, and Brahmins, Chetris, Newars, Magars, Muslims and even 'low caste' individuals and people of Indian origin were found to be involved, either in single—or in multi-ethnic dhikuris.

Given the structure of the *dhikuri*, which tends to distinguish early 'borrowers' from late 'lenders', there is no doubt that, despite the fact that it is an informal organisation of individuals engaging in a common contractual arrangement ostensibly in the interests of all with an important degree of mutual trust, it *can* serve not only as a means of providing credit but also as a means of redistributing funds from those who take their share early to those who take theirs late. The ambivalence of this institutional form of moneylending is recognised by participants, but in general it is regarded as a beneficial arrangement involving less outrageous 'interest rates' than the more normal system of bilateral moneylending and less difficulty (with questions of security and bureaucratic procedure) than the official banks. 'The community of trust' and shared interests, upon which the *dhikuri* depends for its continued existence and successful operation, has been in the past and to a large extent remains, associated predominantly with ties of common ethnicity. It has often been suggested (e.g. Bista 1971; Caplan 1970; Haimendorf 1975) that the two major trading groups of Nepal, the Thakalis and the Newars, have an exceptional degree of social cohesion and solidarity and it is clearly significant that Thakalis remain predominant in the *dhikuris* of the region while Newars more than any other ethnic or caste group have begun to make extensive use of the institution over the past few years. But consciousness of common ethnicity is itself a reflection of shared interests, and those shared interests, deriving at least as much from common economic and social position as from cultural identity, may take other forms and in some cases supersede ethnicity. Residential proximity within towns, for example, appears increasingly to provide the basis for membership of credit associations, although it is striking how it tends to coincide with other more fundamental shared characteristics, notably wealth and power.

Recognition of the different interests of small and large businessmen is growing, but the importance of 'patrons' within the institutional structure of the *dhikuri* remains important and the majority of *dhikuris* continue to have a mixed membership of small, medium and large businesses. There is some indication, however, that associations exclusively organised by and for small businessmen will become more common in future. The 'community of trust', though still predominantly based on common ethnic affiliation, is increasingly seen to be crucially associated with shared interests of a more economic and political kind. Where ethnicity coincides with these fundamental interests, as in the case of many Thakali and Newar associations, the community of trust is strong; where ethnicity alone provides the basis for membership, as in the case of several of the Gurung *dhikuris* in Pokhara, there are continual difficulties. An examination of the membership of *dhikuris* in the region reveals a number of general features of importance. Firstly, the number of multi-ethnic *dhikuris* is far greater in the terai towns (particularly in Butwal) than in the hills such as Pokhara (where the majority are exclusively or predominantly composed of 'northerners'), and the range of 'other groups' involved far larger. Secondly, many of those with multi-ethnic composition now include 'low caste' members, notably goldsmiths and tailors. Thirdly, in several instances a number of individuals clubs together to provide a single share, particularly where the premium is considered too high for a small businessman to pay reliably and regularly on his own (although both contributors still require a guarantor). Fourthly, in all of the mixed dhikuris, the larger businessmen organise the association and tend to take their turn towards the end, deriving advantages in terms of local prestige for their role in creating and maintaining the association as well as the interest on their investment (which is low relative to what might be available form bilateral moneylending). Finally, despite the prevalence of *dhikuris* with members of all 'sizes', a number of the small *dhikuris* formed recently consist entirely of small businessmen, with a significant proportion of 'low caste' members (or entirely 'low caste') in several cases. Examples of such small businessmen's *dhikuris* are those of the Marphali muleteers and small businessmen based in Pokhara but with the majority of members from the far north, the Dharma *dhikuri* at the Pokhara Indian pension camp (including a significant proportion of Sarki, Damai and Sunar members), and the *dhikuri* of 'low caste' small businessmen in Tansen.

Social discrimination on grounds of caste is officially outlawed, but continues to exist; this contradiction disturbs many of those of 'low caste', but none more than the relatively successful individuals in business or regular employment whose own position enables them to see more clearly the disadvantages under which persons of 'low caste' suffer and to act in order to improve conditions for these sections of the population, the majority of whom remain not only socially discriminated against but economically and socially deprived. Indeed, one of the most striking features of developments among small businessmen has been the increasing 'political' self-confidence of those 'low caste' individuals in the region involved in small commodity production or trade. In addition to the rather specific forms of association connected with business activities or with welfare in the immediate sense, there now exists in the region, as elsewhere in Nepal, an organisation whose objectives are more general and far-reaching: the Nepal Rastriya Dalit Jana Vikash Parishad. Investigations in Pokhara revealed that the organisation had been formed there in 1953 under the name of the Nepal Biswo Sarba Jana Sangha; in 1957 it was renamed the Nepal Pariganit Vikash Sangha and in 1964, after the promulgation of the new Constitution and the abolition of all political associations, given its present name. Membership includes representatives of many 'low caste' groups drawn from among the petty bourgeoisie and working class; the majority of those serving on local committees, however, appear to be small businessmen or state employees, notably teachers (see Table 22).

TABLE 22

	District Branches				*Zonal Branch*
Occupation	*Gorkha*	*Tanahun*	*Kaski*	*Total*	*Gandaki*
Goldsmith	—	—	9	9	6
Tailor	7	2	3	12	1
Farmer	—	8	2	10	2
Teacher	—	1	—	1	3
Other state employee	3	—	—	3	1
Shoemaker	—	1	—	1	1
Woodworker	1	—	—	1	1
Fisherman	—	—	1	1	1
Kirana shop/ tailor	—	1	—	1	1
Cloth shop/ tailor	—	—	—	—	1
Blacksmith	—	1	—	1	—
Musician	—	1	—	1	—
Student	—	—	—	—	1
	11	15	15	41	19

Although the organisation has a long history in such areas as Kaski district and in Gandaki zone in general, it has spread only fairly recently to other centres; the Tansen branch, for example, now among the most active, was started in 1968 but was still not officially recognised in 1974, while that of Syanja began in 1970 as the Acchut Uddhar Sanglia but became a branch of the Nepal Rastriya Dalit Jana Vikash Parishad in 1974.

The activists within the organisation are concentrated in the towns and are clearly drawn from a relatively privileged fraction of the general membership. The fact that the leadership and officials of the organisation are not so much working class as petty bourgeois means that there is a danger of a separation between them and the rank and file; this danger is recognised by many of the activists who think that in some instances the organisation has served the interests of personal advancement rather than the membership as a whole. The example of the president of the Gandaki branch was mentioned and it was suggested that he had used the organisation funds to establish and improve his own business; whether true or not, such rumours emphasise the potential for cleavage within the organisation as a whole. Divisions between members of different 'low' castes were also recognised to be a problem: "Up until now, Sarki, Kami, Damai, Pode and others are divided according to the old system and the Dalit has been unable to really unite the 'lower castes' argued the secretary of the Syangja branch. The secretary of the Tansen branch accepted that the organisation consisted mainly of 'untouchables' at present but emphasised that, in principle, even Brahmins could join if they were poor and recognised their interests to be those of the lower classes as a whole. One suggestion echoed by several activists was that the Dalit should be recognised like other so-called 'class organisations' and so have representation in the National Assembly.

The organisation seems likely to extend its membership in future, and this is certainly the objective of the activists, who consider recruitment and 'consciousness-raising' to be important activities. More specific programmes, however, involving education, the formation of co-operatives and so on, were also mentioned as objectives in the medium term. Despite the possible growth of divisions as a result of differences of interests between the leadership and the rank and file, the fact remains that, so far, it is from among the petty bourgeoisie within the organisation—the small businessmen and the salaried state employees—that collective action to improve the working and living conditions of major sections of the lower classes has come. It remains to be seen whether the Dalit, or other similar forms of associations, can provide the basis for a programme of action for and by the lower classes which involves wider representation from the working class, goes beyond immediate concerns of 'welfare' and contributes to the economic and social transformation so desperately required in Nepal.

BIBLIOGRAPHY

Alavi, H., "India and the Colonial Mode of Production," *Socialist Register*, pp. 160-197, 1975.

Allen, V., "The Making of the Working class in Africa," *Journal of Modern African Studies*, pp. 10-12, 1972.

Amin, S., Accumulation and Development: A Theoretical Model, *Review of African Political Economy*, No. 1, 1974.

Anderson, P., *Lineages of the Absolutist State*, New Left Books, London, 1975.

Antoniadis-Bibicou, H., "Byzantium and the Asiatic Mode of production", *Economy and Society*, Vo1. 6, No. 4, 1977.

Arrighi, G., "International Corporations, Labour Aristocracies and Economic Development in Tropical Africa," in (eds), G. Arrighi and J. Saul, *Essays on the Political Economy of Africa*, Monthly Review Press, New York, 1973.

A.R.T.E.P., *A Challenge to Nepal*, Asian Regional Team for Employment Promotions, Bangkok, 1974.

Baran, P and Hobsbawm, E., "The Stages of Economic Growth," *Kyklos*, No. 14,. 1961, pp. 234-242.

Baran, P. & Sweezy, P., *Monopoly Capital. Penguin Books*, London 1968.

Beenhakker, A., *A Kaleidoscopic Circumspection of Development Planning with Contextual Reference to Nepal*, Rotterdam University Press, Rotterdam, 1973.

Bellwinkel, Mavan, "Rajasthani Contract Labour in Delhi" (South Asia Institute of Heidelberg University, Reprint of Publication of Staff Members, 149), *Sociological Bulletin*, Vo1. 22, No. I, March 1973.

Beteille, A., *Caste, Class and Power: Changing Patterns of Stratification in a Tanjore Village*, University of California Press, Berkeley and Los Angeles. 1965.

Bista, D.B., *People of Nepal*: 1967, Ratna Pustak, Bhandar, Kathmandu.

Bista, D.B., "Political Innovations of the Upper Kali-Gandaki," *Man.* Vo1. 6 No. I. 52-60, 1971.

Blaikie, P.M., "The Theory of the Spatial Diffusion of Innovations: A Spacious Cut-de-sac," *Progress in Human Geography Forthcoming* 1978.

Blaikie, P.M., Cameron, J., Feldman, D.J.P., Fournier, A., Seddon, J.D. *The Effects of Roads in West Central Nepal*, Overseas Development Group, Norwich. 1976. 3 Vols.

Blaikie, P. M., Cameron, J., Fleming, R., Seddon, J.D., *West Central Nepal: A Statistical Guide*. Overseas Development Group, Norwich, 1976.

Blaikie, P.M., Cameron, J., Seddon, J.D., *The Effects of Roads in West Central Nepal: A Summary*, Overseas Development Group, Norwich, 1977.

Blaikie, P.M., Cameron, J., Seddon, J.D., Fleming, R., *Centre, Pperiphery and Access in West Central Nepal: Approaches to Social and Spatial Relations of Inequality*. (Report to the S.S.R.C.), Overseas Development Group, Norwich, 1977.

Blaikie, P. M., Cameron, J., Seddon, J.D., *Nepal in Crisis: Growth and Stagnation at the Periphery*, Oxford University Press, London, 1978.

Breman, J., "A Dualistic Labour System?", *Economic and Political Weekly*, 27 Nov., 4 Dec., 22 Dec., 1976.

Buchanan D.H., *The Development of Capitalist Enterprise in India*. Macmillan, 1934

Buchanan, F., *An Account of the District of Purnea in 1809-10*, Bihar and Orissa Society Patna, 1928.

Caplan, L., *Land and Social Change in East Nepal*, Routledge, Kegan and Paul, London, 1970.

Caplan, L., *Administration and Politics in the Nepalese Town: The Study of a District Capital and its Environs*, Oxford University Press, London, 1975.

Carchedi, G., "*On the Economic Identification of the New Middle Class*", Economy and Society, Vol. 4, No. 1, 1969.

Centre for Economic Development and Administration (CEDA), *Indo-Nepalese Relations*, Occasional Paper No. 1, Kathmandu, 1969.

Centre for Economic Development and Administration (CEDA) *Comparative Evaluation of Road Construction Techniques in Nepal.* Kathmandu, 1973.

Cohen, R., "Class in Africa: Analytical Problems and Perspectives" in (eds), R. Miliband and J. Saville, *The Socialist Register*, The Merlin Press, London, 1972.

Coleman, T., *The Railway Navvies. Penguin Books*, 1968.

Copans, J. and Seddon, J.D., "Marxism and Anthropology: A Preliminary Survey"In (ed), J.D., Seddon, *Relations of Production: Marxist Approaches to Economic Anthropology*, Cass, London, 1978.

Dos Santos, T., "The Crisis of Development Theory and the Problem of Dependence in Latin America," in (ed), H., Bernstein, *Underdevelopment and Development*, Penguin Books, London, 1973.

Dumont, L. *Homo hierarchicus*, Paris, 1966.

Eckholm, E.P., *Losing Ground: Environmental Stress and World Food Prospects*, W.W., Norton, New York, 1976.

Economic Intelligence Unit, Quarterly Economic Review, 1969. No. 2.

Emmanuel, A., *Unequal Exchange: A Study in the Imperialism of Change*, New Left Books, London, 1972.

Enke, S., "Projected Costs and Benefits of Population Control," in *Population and Development*, CEDA Study Series, Seminar Paper 2, Kirtipur, Kathmandu, 1971.

Epstein, Scarlett *Economic Development and Social Change in South India* Manchester University Press, 1962.

Feldman D., and Fournier A., "Social Relations and Agricultural production in Nepal's Terai, *Journal of Peasant Studies*, Vol. 3. pp. 447-464, 1976.

Foster-Carter, A., "Neo-Marxist Approaches to Development and underdevelopment," in (cd) E. de Kadt and G. Williams, *Sociology and Development*, Tavistock, London, 1974.

Frank, A.G., "Instability and Integration in urban Latin America," in A.G. Frank, Latin America: *Underdevelopment or Revolution*. Monthly Review Press, New York, 1969.

Frank, A.G., *Sociology of Development and Underdevelopment of Sociology*, Pluto Press, London, 1971.

Frank, A.G., Lumpen-bourgeoisie, *Lumpen-development*, Monthly Review Press, New York and London, 1972.

Gaige, F., *Regionalism and National Unity in Nepal*. University of California Press: Berkeley and Los Angeles, 1975.

Gallissot, R., "Pre colonial Algeria," *Economy and Society*, Vo1. 4 No. 4, 1975.

Godelier, M., "The Concept of the'Asiatic Mode of Production' and Marxist Models of Social evolution," in (ed) J.D. Seddon, *Relations of Production: Marxist Approaches to Economic Anthropology*, Cass, London. 1978.

Goil, R. M., *A Study of the General Economic Impact of Siddartha Rajmarga*, Tribhuvan University and Indian Cooperation, Kathmandu, 1971.

Goodall, M.R., "Administrative Change in Nepal," in (ed), R. Braibanti, *Bureaucratic Systems Emergent from the British Imperial Tradition*, Duke University Press, Durham, 1966.

Gough, Ian, "Marx's Theory of Productive and Unproductive Labour," *New Left Review*, Nov.-Dec. 1972, pp 47-72.

Gould, H.A., "The Hindu Jajmani System," *South Western Journal of Anthropology*, Vol. 14, pp. 428-437, 1958.

Gurung, H.B., *Pokhara Valley, Nepal Himalaya: A Field Study in Regional Geography*, Unpublished Ph.D. thesis, University of Edinburgh, 1965.

Haimendorf, C. von Furer, "Caste in the Multi-ethnic Society of Nepal, *Contributions to Indian Sociology* Vol. IV, pp 12-32, 1960.

Haimendorf, C., von Furer in (ed), Haimendorf C. von Furer, *The Anthropology of Nepal*, Aris and Phillips, Warminster, 1974.

Haimendorf, C. von Furer, *Himalayan Traders: Life in Highland Nepal*, John Murray, London, 1975.

Harnetty, P., *Imperialism and Free Trade: Lancashire and India in the Mid-nineteenth Century*. University of British Columbia Press, 1972.

Hindess, B. *The use of Official Statistics in Sociology: A Critique of Positivism and Ethnomethodology*, Macmillan, London, 1973.

Hindess, B., and Hirst, P.Q., "Letter to *Economy and Society*," Economy and Society. Vol. 4, No. 2. 1975.

Hindess, B., and Hirst, P.Q., *Pre-capitalist Modes of Production*, Routledge and Kegan, Paul. London, 1975.

Hitchcock, J.T., *The Magars of Banyan Hill*, Holt, Rinehart and Winston, New York, 1966.

Hobsbawm, E., *Industry and Empire*, Penguin Books, Harmondsworth, 1975.

Hodgson, B.H., *Essays on the Language, Literature and Religions of Nepal and Tibet*. 2 Vols, 1874.

Holmstrém, M.N., *South Indian Factory Workers: Their Life and their World*, Cambridge University Press, Cambridge, 1976.

Jeffries, R., "The Labour Aristocracy? Ghana Case Study," *Review of African Political Economy*, No. 3, 1975.

Joshi, H. and V., *Surplus Labour and the City: A Study of Bombay*, Oxford University Press, New Delhi, 1976.

Kay, G., *Development and Underdevelopment: A Marxist Analysis*, Macmillan, London. 1975.

Kemp, T., *Theories of Imperialism*, Dobson, London, 1967.

Keyder, C., "The dissolution of the Asiatic Mode of production," *Economy and Society*, Vol. 5 No. 2, 1976.

Kirkpatrick, Col., *An Account of the Kingdom of Nepal being the Substance of Observations Made During a Mission to that Country in the Year 1793*. William Miller, London, 1811.

Kumar, S., *Rana Polity in Nepal: Origin and Growth*, Asia Publishing House, Bombay, 1967.

Lacoste, Y., "General Characteristics and Fundamental Structures of Mediaeval North African Society," *Economy and Society*, Vol. 3, No. 1, 1974.

Landon, P., *Nepal* (2 Vols.), Constable, London, 1928.

Lebrun, O. and Gerry, C., "Petty Producers and Capitalism," *Review of African Political Economy* 3 May-Oct. 1975, pp. 20-32.

Lenin, V.I., *The Development of Capitalism in Russia*, Progress Publishers, Moscow, 1967-70.

Lesslie, A., *Land use Mapping by Airphoto Interpretation and Field Reconnaisance— An Aid to Development Planning in the Hill Areas of Nepal.*, Land Resource Report, No. 4, Land Resources Division, Surbiton, U.K., 1974.

Leys, C., *Underdevelopment in Kenya*: The Political Economy of Neo-colonialism, Heinemann, London. 1975.

Lohani, P.C., "Industrial Policy: the Problem Child of History and Planning in Nepal. in (eds), Rana PSJB and Malla, K.P., *Nepal in Perspective*, Centre for Economic Development and Administration, Kathmandu, 1973.

Macfarlane, A., *Resources and Population: A Study of the Gurungs of Nepal*, Cambridge Studies in Social Anthropology 12, Cambridge University Press, Cambridge, 1976.

Malla, K.P. and Rana, P.S.J.B., "Introduction" in (eds) P.S.J.B. Rana and K.P. Malla, *Nepal in Perspective* CEDA, Kathmandu, 1973.

Marx, K. (E.J. Hobsbawm intro.), *Pre-capitalist Economic Formations*. Lawrence and Wishart, London, 1964.

Marx, K. and-Engels, F., *The German Ideology*, Lawrence and Wishart, London, 1970.

Meillassoux, C., Are There Castes in India? *Economy and Society*, Vol. 2, No. 1, 1973.

Messerschmidt, D., "Rotating Credit in Gurung Society: The Dhikur Associations of Tin Gaun," *The Himalayan Review*, Vo1. 5, No. 4, 1972.

Messerschmidt, D., "*Dhikurs*: Rotating Credit Associations in Nepal," Paper presented to IXth International Congress of Anthropological and Ethnological Sciences, Chicago, Aug-Sept. 1973.

Messerschmidt, D., *The Gurungs of Nepal. Conflict and Change in a Village Society*, Aris and Phillips, Warminster. 1976.

Mojumdar, K. 1973: *Political Relations between India and Nepal*, Munishiram Mancharlal Publishers, Delhi.

Moore, B., *Social Origins of Dictatorship and Democracy: Lord and Peasant in the Making of the Modern World*, Penguin Books, Harmondsworth. 1969.

Morris, M.D., *The Emergence of an Industrial Labour force in India: A Study of the Bombay Cotton Mills*, University of California Press, Berkeley and Los Angeles. 1965.

Murray, R., *Class, State and the World Economy: A Case Study of Ethiopia*. Conference on New approaches to Trade Held at I.D.S., University of Sussex, Sept. 8-12. 1975.

National Planning Commission, *Fourth Plan (1970-1975)*, English edition, Kathmandu, 1972.

Newby, H., "Paternalism and Capitalism," in (ed), R. Scase, *Industrial*

Society: Class, Cleavage and Control, George Allen and Unwin, London, 1977.

New Era *Middle Level Manpower: Follow-up Study*, Report to the National Planning Commission, New Era, Kathmandu, 1973.

O.E.C.D., *Development Co-operation, Efforts and Policies of the Members of the Development Assistance Committee*, Organisation for Economic Co-operation and Development, Paris. 1972.

Oldfield, H.A., *Sketches from Nepal*. W.H. Allen, London, 1880.

Oxaal, I., Barnett, T. and Booth, D., (eds), *Beyond the Sociology of Development, Routledge and Kegan Paul*, London, 1975.

Pankhurst, R., "Transport and Communications in Ethiopia (1853-1935)," *Journal of Transport History*, Vol. 1, pp. 69-87, Vol. 2, pp. 233-253, 1961/2.

Poulantzas, N., "On Social Classes," *New Left Review* 78, March-April, 1973, pp. 27-54.

Pradhan, P., "Development of Political Institutions in Nepal since 1951," in (eds), P.S.J.B. Rana and K.P. Malla, *Nepal in Perspective*, C.E.D.A., Kathmandu, 1973.

Rana, P.S.J.B., "Trade" in (eds), Rana, P.S.J.B. and Malla, K.P., *Nepal in Perspective*, Centre for Economic Development and Administration, Kathmandu, 1973.

Rawat, P.C., *Indo-Nepal Economic Relations*, National Publishing House, New Delhi, 1974.

Regmi, M.C., *Land Tenure and Taxation in Nepal*, Berkeley Institute of International Studies. University of California (4 vols.) 1963-68.

Regmi, M.C., *A Study in Nepali Economic history*, 1768-1846, Manjusri Publishing House, New Delhi, 1971.

Rieger, H.C., Bieri, F., Eggers, H. and Goldschalt, W., *Himalayan ecosystems Research Mission: Nepal Report*, Heidelberg, 159 pps. Mimeo, 1976.

Rungta, R.S., *The Rise of Business Corporations in India*, 1851-1900, Cambridge University Press, 1970.

San. R., "Can Capitalism develop in Indian Agriculture?," *Economic and Political Weekly*, December, 1976.

Scott, A., "Notes on the Theoretical Status of Petty Commodity production," Mimeo, 1977.

Scott, C., "Peasants, Proletarianisation and the Articulation of Modes of Production—the Case of Sugar Cane Production in Northern Peru," *Journal of Peasant Studies*, Vo1. 3 No. 3, 1976.

Seddon, J.D., "The Physical and Social Context of Farming Strategies among Moroccan Peasants," *The Maghreb Review*, Vol. 2, No. 2. 1977.

Seddon, J. D., "Tribe and State: Approaches to Maghreb History," *The Maghreb Review*, Vol. 2, No. 3, 1977.

Shaha, R., *Nepali Politics: Retrospect and Prospect*. Oxford University Press, New Delhi, 1975.

Sharma, S., *Commercialisation, Government Intervention, Transportation and Underdevelopment in Nepal: A Case Study of Bandipur*, 1800-1975, Unpublished M.A., dissertation for the University of East Anglia, Norwich, 1976, Mimeo.

Shrestha, B.K. and Gurung, S.B., "*Equality of Access of Women to Education in Pokhara*" (a sociological survey). CEDA/Tribhuvan University, Kathmandu, 1973.

Shroeder, M.C.W. and Sisler, D.G., *Impact of the Sonauli-Pokhara Highway on the Regional Income and Agricultural Production of Pokhara Valley, Nepal*, Cornell University International Agricultural Bulletin, No. 14, Ithaca, 1971.

Terray, E., "Long Distance Exchange and the Formation of the State: The Case of the Abron Kingdom of Gyaman," *Economy and Society*, Vo1. 3, No. 3, 1974.

Treble, J.H., "The Navvies," *Scottish Labour History Society Journal*. No. 5, 1972.

UNDP/Comtec in Collaboration with Alpina and Macchi, *Nepal Road Feasibility Study*, Kathmandu, 1970.

Wright, E.O., "Class Boundaries in Advanced Capitalist Societies," *New Left Review*, 98, July-August 1976, pp. 3-41.